Addiction and Spirituality

Addiction and Spirituality

A Multidisciplinary Approach

Edited by
Oliver J. Morgan
and Merle R. Jordan

St. Louis, Missouri

Cover: Mark Edwards
Interior design: Elizabeth Wright

This book is printed on acid-free, recycled paper.

Visit Chalice Press on the World Wide Web at
www.chalicepress.com

10 9 8 7 6 5 4 3 2 1 99 00 01 02 03

Library of Congress Cataloging–in–Publication Data

Addiction and spirituality : a mutidisciplinary approach / edited by Oliver J. Morgan and Merle R. Jordan.
p. cm.
ISBN 0-8272-0023-4
1. Recovering addicts—Religious life. 2. Addicts—Religious life.
I. Morgan, Oliver J. II. Jordan, Merle R.
BL625.9.R43A44 1999 99-21210
C1P

Printed in the United States of America

Contents

About the Contributors

Robert H. Albers, Ph.D., is an ordained Lutheran pastor (ELCA) and Professor of Pastoral Theology and Ministry, Luther Seminary, St. Paul, MN. He is director of the doctoral program in pastoral care and counseling at Luther Seminary. He has served on a number of boards, advising programs, and services related to chemical dependency and is currently a member of both the Minnesota Chemical Dependency Association and the Interfaith Network for Chemical Dependency, located at Hazelden, Minn.

His most recent books include *Caring and community* (Augsburg/Fortress, 1995) and *Shame: faith perspective* (Haworth Press, 1996). He is the General Editor of the *Journal of Ministry in Addiction and Recovery.*

David Berenson, M.D., is one of the earliest pioneers in clinical research involving a family systems perspective on alcoholism and other addictions. He is currently the director of the Family Institute of San Francisco and a distinguished member of the faculty for the California Graduate School of Family Psychology. He is also a member of the Editorial Board for the *Family Dynamics of Addiction Quarterly.*

Dr. Berenson was one of the first researchers to suggest that alcoholic drinking might play an adaptive role in the family system, a perspective that is being given renewed credence today. Over the years he has contributed both thoughtful and provocative publications to the discussion of addiction, including his recent article: "Powerlessness—Liberating or Enslaving? Responding to the feminist critique of the Twelve Steps" in the *Journal of Feminist Family Therapy.*

Lyn G. Brakeman, M.Div., is an Episcopal priest serving as pastoral counselor and spiritual director as well as pastoring a congregation in Gloucester, Mass. She spent six years at Blue Ridge Health Services, a drug and alcohol treatment center. Her book, *Spiritual lemons: Biblical women, irreverent laughter and righteous rage* (Innisfree Press, 1997), is widely acclaimed.

Joseph W. Ciarrocchi, Ph.D., is director of doctoral clinical education and doctoral admissions in pastoral counseling, Loyola College (Columbia, Md). He holds a Ph.D. in clinical psychology and a master's degree in theology; he is certified by the American Psychological Association's College of

Professional Psychology for the treatment of substance abuse disorders. In addition to being a practicing clinician and clinical professor, he has served as clinical director for the Saint Luke Institute, a rehabilitation program for impaired clergy, and director of addiction services at Taylor Manor Hospital in Maryland.

Dr. Ciarrocchi's published empirical studies are in the fields of substance abuse, gambling disorders, and gender factors in images of God. His most recent publications include *The doubting disease: help for scrupulosity and religious compulsion* (Paulist, 1995) and *A minister's handbook of mental disorders* (Paulist, 1993).

Harold E. Doweiko, Ed.D., has worked for over fifteen years in the field of chemical dependency and is currently the only full-time psychologist in the substance abuse program at Gundersen-Lutheran Medical Center (La Crosse, Wis). His book, *Concepts of chemical dependency* (Brooks/Cole, 1996), is a top selection for courses in chemical dependency among counselor education programs around the country. The fourth edition of this popular text is forthcoming. He is also an avid astronomer.

Dr. Doweiko's chapter, "Substance use disorders as a symptom of a spiritual disease," is dedicated to the memory of his wife, Jan, recently deceased.

George H. Gallup, Jr., is well-known as chairman of the George H. Gallup International Institute and co-chairman of The Gallup Organization, Inc., which sponsors the Gallup Poll. Active in a variety of public service venues, he is a member of the Boards for the National Organization on Disability, the Recovery Institute, and the National Coalition for Children's Justice, as well as of the chairman's council of the National Council on Alcoholism. He is vice-president of the North Conway Institute Board of Directors, an organization that initiates interfaith action on alcohol and other drug problems.

Mr. Gallup has written numerous articles on survey research, religion, and health. His books include: *Growing up scared in america* (Morehouse, 1995, with Wendy Plump), *Varieties of prayer* (Trinity, 1991, with Margaret Poloma), *The people's religion* (Macmillan, 1989, with Jim Castelli) and *My kid on drugs?* (Standard,1981, with Art Linkletter). He is a member of All Saints' Episcopal Church in Princeton, N.J. and has had a life-long interest in soccer and Gilbert & Sullivan operettas.

Rabbi Carol Glass was ordained as a rabbi in 1984 at Hebrew Union College in New York. She has most recently served as Rabbi and University Chaplain at Boston University (Boston, Mass.). She has also served as Director of the Hillel Foundation at American University (Washington, DC). Rabbi Glass is the cofounder of the Jewish Women's Resource Center of New York City and is active in Jewish/Intergroup relations. She resides in Newton, Mass. with her husband and two children.

Her interest in addiction and spirituality began in the late 1970s when she served a synagogue community in Minneapolis, Minn. Since that time she has written and spoken on the subject in many settings and has been a friend and resource person for JACS (Jewish Alcoholics, Chemically dependent persons, and Significant others) for many years.

Howard J. Gray, S.J., is Director of the Center for Ignatian Spirituality at Boston College (Chestnut Hill, Mass.). He has served in a variety of leadership roles within the Jesuit Order (Rector, Tertian Director, Provincial Superior). He has also been a consultant to the Jesuit Conference of East Asia and to the Eastern African Province of the Jesuits.

Fr. Gray is internationally respected as an expert in the spirituality of St. Ignatius of Loyola and as a gifted retreat master and spiritual director. He has lectured and written widely on aspects of church life and ministry.

Lee Jampolsky, Ph.D., is an existential-humanistic psychotherapist who practices, supervises, and teaches. He is licensed as a psychologist in California. Active in the field of addiction treatment since the late 1970s, Dr. Jampolsky is also a core faculty member and founder of a graduate specialization in Peace Psychology at Rosebridge Graduate School, Concord, Calif.

An accomplished speaker and writer for professional and popular audiences, his most recent books include *The art of trust: healing your heart and opening your mind* (Celestial Arts, 1994) and *Healing the addictive mind: Freeing yourself from addictive patterns and relationships* (Celestial Arts, 1991). He co-authored *Listen to me: A book for men and women about father and son relationships* (Celestial Arts, 1996) with G.G. Jampolsky.

Merle R. Jordan, Th.D., is a pastoral psychotherapist and family counselor completing a long and distinguished career as professor of pastoral psychology and theology at Boston University School of Theology. He is the author of several important books in the field of pastoral care including, *Taking on the gods: The task of the pastoral counselor* (Abingdon, 1986).

Charlotte Kasl, Ph.D., is a licensed psychologist and certified addiction specialist working in private practice. She has consulted with numerous treatment programs to bring a holistic approach to healing from addiction. She brings a cultural perspective to her discussion of addiction and spirituality and has worked with numerous healing approaches that reach beyond traditional psychotherapy. She has worked on the advisory board of The Women's Recovery Network and is currently a board member for the Women's Action Alliance for Alcohol and Drug Education as well as for Save OurSelves (SOS)—The Organization for Secular Sobriety.

Dr. Kasl is the author of *Women, sex, and addiction: a search for love and power* (Ticknor and Fiels, 1989) and *Many roads, one Journey: moving beyond the twelve steps* (HarperCollins, 1992), among other titles. Her most recent publication is *A home for the heart: Creating intimacy and community with loved ones, neighbors and friends* (HarperCollins, 1997).

Earnie Larsen is a nationally known author and lecturer, and a pioneer in the field of recovery from addictive and unwanted behaviors. He has authored and produced over 40 motivational self-help books and tapes, including *Good old plastic Jesus* (1968) and *Stage II recovery* (Harper and Row, 1985). He is an advisory board member for The Recovery Network.

Raised in Omaha, Neb., Mr. Larsen holds a Master of Religious Education degree from Loyola University (Chicago) and is credentialed in chemical dependency and family counseling from the University of Minnesota. He has appeared on the Oprah Winfrey Show and the Sally Jessie Raphael Show, spreading the word about recovery.

Oliver J. Morgan, Ph.D., is Associate Professor of Counseling and Human Services at the University of Scranton (Scranton, Penn.). He is the current chair of that department and periodically teaches a course in pastoral theology for the Theology Department at that university.

Dr. Morgan is a National Certified Counselor (NCC) and a certified Diplomate in Psychotherapy (DAPA). He is also the Book Review Editor for the *Journal of Ministry in Addiction and Recovery*. He recently completed a sabbatical as Visiting Scholar at Boston University School of Theology and the Weston Jesuit School of Theology (1997). He has published a number of scholarly articles in the area of addictions with *Alcoholism Treatment Quarterly, Journal of Addictions and Offender Counseling,* and *Journal of Ministry in Addiction and Recovery.*

David E. Smith, M.D., is the founder, president, and medical director of Haight Ashbury Free Clinics, Inc., and research director of MPI Treatment Services, Summit Medical Center, and associate clinical professor of occupational health and clinical toxicology, University of California at San Francisco. A pioneer in the field of addiction medicine, Dr. Smith is current president of the American Society of Addiction Medicine (ASAM), and an alternate delegate to the American Medical Association (AMA). He has written numerous books and articles on addiction, treatment, recovery, and allied fields, including [*Drugfree: A unique, positive approach to staying off alcohol and other drugs*] (Facts on File Publications, 1987).

Richard B. Seymour, M.A., is director of information and education, Office of the President, Haight Ashbury Free Clinics (with which he has been associated for over 25 years), director of Haight Ashbury Publications, managing editor of the *Journal of Psychoactive Drugs*, and managing editor of the International Addictions Infoline. He has written 11 books and over 50 articles on drug treatment and recovery issues.

Preface

Addiction and Spirituality: A Multidisciplinary Approach is a breakthrough book, and it makes a timely appearance because while alcohol problems continue to ravage our society, one of the most effective ways to prevent and treat alcoholism and alcohol abuse has been downplayed or ignored for decades—the path of spirituality.

Yet while professionals have tended to discredit or dismiss the role of spiritual experience in the understanding and treatment of addictive illness, survey and other evidence points to spirituality as a core factor in prevention and treatment for the great mass of people.

There is no current consensus on the meaning and function of the spiritual dimension, yet this collection of essays by treatment providers (psychiatrists, psychologists, social workers, addiction specialists, pastoral counselors, and others) sheds important new light on this dimension. Spirituality is examined across a spectrum—from mind over matter, to the inner self, to a God outside, intervening directly or indirectly.

Certainly calling upon the supernatural is not an uncommon occurrence among the American people: 85 percent believe that God or a higher power performs miracles, even today; only 11 percent believe that God is not involved in their lives; and 41 percent say they have experienced something they would describe as miraculous—a physical or emotional healing, a healing in broken relationships, a shining act of forgiveness.

That serious and urgent attention should be given the relationship of spirituality and addiction is clearly seen from statistics that are found in surveys and from other sources on the impact of alcohol abuse and alcoholism in our society.

In a sense, America does not have a crime problem; America does not have a health problem; America does not have a problem of child abuse and broken marriages—America has an alcohol problem. The common thread running through virtually every major social ill in the USA today is the abuse of alcohol and other drugs: murder and lawlessness, highway deaths, suicides, accidental deaths and injustices, hospitalizations, poor school performance and dropout, job absenteeism, child and spouse abuse, low self-esteem, and depression. The list goes on and on.

The percentage of Americans who admit that drinking has been a cause of trouble in their families has reached the highest point in nearly half a century—30 percent, twice the figure recorded in 1950.

Alcohol abuse is not just a social problem, but a moral and spiritual one as well. Religious faith can play a major role not only in recovery but in prevention. Religion gives young people what they need most to combat alcohol and other drug addictions: a reason to say "no."

Particularly worrisome are the statistics on drinking and alcohol abuse among teens and pre-teens. Young people are in trouble with alcohol (and other drugs) and are crying out for help. We must not ignore their call. Young people caught up in risk behaviors such as alcohol and other drug abuse are unlikely to attain the levels of education required for survival and success in a world that is growing increasingly complex and competitive. And school failure too often leads to chronic lives of crime, unemployment, or welfare dependency.

This book, with penetrating essays by experts in many fields, will hopefully spur new ventures in the field of addiction studies. This conversation among professionals can lead to vital and life-changing approaches to addiction. And each writer stresses the need for experts to work closely with each other, across the various disciplines.

Both professionals and the general public will be receptive to this book, not only because it will strike a responsive chord with many who struggle with addictions of various kinds, but because there is clearly a surge of general interest in spiritual matters. The percentage of people who say they would like to experience spiritual growth in their lives has jumped from 58 percent in 1994 to 82 percent today. The "faith factor" and its relationship to health and other areas of life are being given new and much-needed attention.

It appears that we are entering a new era of discovery—not of the world around us, but of the world within. Given the disappointments of the external world, the headlong pursuit of hedonism and materialism, and the callous disregard of people for each other, many people have been driven to look within themselves or to God for ways to understand and deal with life. There are clear signs that people in all societies have an intense hunger for healing of mind, body, and soul.

Addiction and Spirituality: A Multidisciplinary Approach is a vitally important book that represents a courageous foray into the seriously neglected area of spirituality and its relationship to addictions. This book will, I believe, appeal on a deep level to many, not just those who are chemically addicted but those who as humans are in bondage to other addictions—pride, hedonism, materialism, and the like. Here, too, spirituality can be the path to liberation and new hope.

George H. Gallup, Jr.

Introduction

This is a book grounded in *experience*. Each of the authors—psychiatrists, psychologists, pastoral counselors, recovery counselors, pastors, spiritual directors—is a respected practitioner and scholar in her or his discipline. Each was chosen as a contributor because of relevant experience in working with addicted persons. Each had indicated an interest in exploring the role of spiritual experience in the development of addiction and the dynamics of recovery.

For some, as the reader will soon see, this interest evolved as part of the author's own growth and personal development. For others, an interest in spirituality emerged in their work with addicts and others affected by their relationship with an addict. All the authors in this volume, however, are committed to exploring and utilizing spiritual experience as an essential element in the understanding and treatment of addictive illness.

The impetus for this volume came as a result of the editors' desire to contribute to an emerging conversation that addresses spirituality and addiction. It will come as no surprise to our readers that chemical (alcohol and other drugs) and process (e.g., gambling, sex) addictions are a widespread and destructive phenomenon in modern American society. We see daily the enormous impact of addictive illness and abuse on individuals and families; we are affected by the media reports of addiction's effects in educational, work, and church settings; and we are concerned about the effects on our nation's culture and character. No one can be unconcerned, and few are unaffected.

Contemporary models for understanding and treating addictive illness are powerful tools in facing this challenge. The field of addiction studies has grown immeasurably in recent years, with insights from the biomedical, neuroscience, and cognitive science communities leading the way. An integrative biopsychosocial approach to addictive problems has brought important insights to the fore. Modern addiction specialists now have at their command a wealth of knowledge that can be brought to bear for prevention and treatment. Yet, the problem continues and is escalating.

Only in the last several years have some specialists begun to ask whether something is missing. Increasingly, a renewed interest in spirituality as an important missing variable in the models of addiction is emerging. Recent scientific concern with this spiritual element has been expressed by the

National Institute on Alcoholism and Alcohol Abuse (NIAAA) and by the National Institute on Healthcare Research (NIHR). There is growing interest in attempting to understand the (potential) role of a spiritual dimension in relation to addiction and recovery.

Alcoholics Anonymous and other Twelve Step programs, as well as persons in recovery, testify to the power of a spiritual element in their healing and ongoing sobriety. Clinicians and researchers from across the spectrum of theoretical constructs and treatment models suspect that there is something to learn from this testimony and continue to search for a way to understand. Yet, there is no current consensus on the meaning or function of this spiritual aspect. It is difficult to define and often hard to describe. While a few publications try to address the issue, they are often seen as too "soft" to engage the attention of serious addiction specialists.

We have gathered into one volume a series of reflective essays from clinical and pastoral-clinical experts with extensive experience in dealing with addicted persons. We invited a number of recognized authors to address directly their experience with and understanding of spirituality in addiction and recovery. The purpose of this volume is to present something of a "conversation" among professionals from a variety of related disciplines about this important phenomenon.

Each contributor was asked to submit a chapter in which she or he describes (a) her own basic "approach" to working with addicted persons, (b) his understanding of and/or questions about the "spiritual" dimension, as well as how it works in treatment and recovery, and (c) some suggestions for how ongoing research into this area might proceed. Contributors were asked to include a brief case vignette or other concrete examples for illustration.

Chapter 1 sets the context for the book by presenting a brief history of the field of addiction studies and, within that history, presents our current state of understanding regarding spirituality and addiction.

Section 2 contains five chapters from recognized clinical experts in addiction. Harold Doweiko (chapter 2) sees abuse and addiction as manifestations of a "disorder of the human spirit," rooted in a "divine discontent" that is part of the human condition. Lee Jampolsky (chapter 3) builds on this insight, examining the "disorder" as a search for happiness in things or experiences outside the self. In the process he describes some important insights from cognitive psychology regarding the "addictive thought system" and points the way toward effective treatment that is grounded in "awakening to love" as essential for human living.

David Berenson's chapter 4 is a reprinting of his classic article on a "systemic view of spirituality," which argues for attention to spiritual dynamics and the importance of focusing on the relational "between" as powerful resources in individual and familial healing. Chapter 5, by David Smith and Richard Seymour, colleagues in the work of the Haight Ashbury Free Clinics, speaks to the importance of understanding spirituality and recovery in cultural context and presents a model for collaboration between treatment settings and local church congregations. Their description of the team-work between their Clinic and Glide Memorial (African American) Methodist Church is a case study in cultural sensitivity in addiction treatment. Charlotte Kasl's (chapter 6) moving autobiographical essay describes her own journey to personal empowerment and her understanding of this key feminist theme as a spiritual resource in recovery. Both Twelve Step adherents and others will find this a challenging read.

Section 3 contains three essays from pastoral-clinical and recovery specialists. Chapter 7 by Rev. Robert Albers presents theological and biblical reflections on addiction, which are deeply rooted in his clinical work with addicts and others. Readers with an interest in "assessment" of addictive illness will find his thoughts an important addition to their current thinking. Earnie Larsen's essay (chapter 8) on the need to address underlying issues in recovery reminds us all of the spiritual challenges that arise in both short- and long-term recovery. Joseph Ciarrocchi's chapter 9 is an important addition to the "conversation." Addressing the issue of "process addiction" through case studies of gambling, he highlights the need for spiritual reflection and treatment in meeting the needs of recovering gamblers.

Section four brings pastors and spiritual directors into the conversation with addiction specialists. These three chapters bring the resources of biblical reflection into our thinking about addictive illness and offer some new and creative approaches for collaboration with other disciplines. Pastor Lyn Brakeman (chapter 10) presents an extended meditation on the New Testament story of the Gerasene demoniac as a fable about addictive illness, and then suggests ways in which congregations might collaborate with recovering persons. Father Howard Gray, S.J. (chapter 11) examines several biblical narratives in light of a composite case of sexual addiction and suggests the value of collaborative work between clinical counselors and spiritual directors in meeting the needs of addicted persons. In chapter 12, Rabbi Carol Glass reviews the similarities of Twelve Step "theology" with religious resources found in Judaism and describes the value of the JACS organization (Jewish Alcoholics, Chemically dependent persons, and Significant others) as complementary to recovery group involvement.

The last chapter (13) by the editors is an attempt to lay out some common themes that emerge from among the earlier chapters and presents some important points for consideration in constructing a "clinical theology" of addiction and recovery.

Several overall editorial comments should also be made here. All of the authors in this volume have experience with Alcoholics Anonymous and other Twelve Step programs. This is only natural, since the Twelve Step fellowships and programs are the oldest and most pervasive influence in the wider recovery movement. A number of authors, however, also bring experience with other recovery groups (e.g., Rational Recovery,

Secular Organizations for Sobriety) to their understanding of addictive illness. Many of the insights offered in this volume, we believe, can facilitate healing and recovery for any genuine seeker. It is our hope that readers from many different backgrounds—addiction scientists, treatment specialists, pastoral caregivers, students, recovering persons from whatever tradition, and spiritual learners—will benefit from these pages.

We have tried throughout to maintain sensitivity to diversity and women's issues. It is clearer today than ever before that addiction affects all kinds of persons including women, minorities and persons of color, persons with disabilities, gays and lesbians, the poor. This text is intended to address all of them. In particular, we have tried to be consistent—if sometimes a bit awkward—in maintaining an inclusive language focus. We hope the reader will forgive any awkwardness in view of the need to maintain an inclusive stance as a matter of justice and truth.

This book has been almost three years in the making. We would like to thank, first of all, our contributors for their willingness to share their experience and insights, and for their diligence. Their eagerness about the project and their persistence in each one's submitting several drafts of chapters to the editing process helped to make this a better book in the end. We hope that they are gratified by the final product. Thanks to George Gallup, Jr., for his generosity in writing a fine Preface. Dr. Jon L. Berquist of Chalice Press believed in this project from the outset. Our gratitude for his encouragement and patient care could go without saying...but we wanted to say it. Debbie Jones, "Rick" Barrow, Chris Steel, and Ellen Greaven—all from the University of Scranton—contributed valuable technical support at various stages of production. Thank you.

Finally, the University of Scranton, Boston University School of Theology, and the Weston Jesuit School of Theology made our collaboration possible through their support of a sabbatical year. The Danielsen Institute at Boston University sponsored a conference in May 1998 that allowed us to bring together several of the chapter contributors with a number of interested theologians for dialogue about the issues of addiction, recovery, and spirituality. To all, a hearty "thank you."

Oliver J. Morgan
Merle R. Jordan

Part One

Setting the Context

CHAPTER 1

Addiction and Spirituality in Context

Oliver J. Morgan

> Psychoactive drug use has been intertwined with spirituality throughout history. Societal views on drug use and problems often have been rooted in spiritual/religious perspectives. Indeed, few religions traditionally have been silent or neutral with regard to substance use…Given these close ties, it is surprising that spirituality has so seldom been the subject of direct scientific investigation in the alcohol/drug field…
>
> There is a need for open and honest dialogue among researchers studying spirituality and addictions. Indeed, communication…is crucial for researchers to break down suspicions and stereotypes, to stimulate collaboration on research projects, and to attract new scientists to this field. (National Institute for Healthcare Research [NIHR], 1997, pp. 69, 79).

The rise of modern addiction studies began in the 1930s, when a number of events and cultural trends coalesced to form a basic social stance toward alcoholism and other addictions (Johnson, 1973; Keller, 1975; Kurtz, 1979). This stance—barely more than 60 years old!—fueled the beginning of addiction science and has guided its research ever since. The story is a fascinating one.

The relatively young field of addiction studies combines a science of understanding with the art of treatment and healing. The field has its own pioneering figures, its own areas of specialization, its phases of development and emerging issues, among which is the nature and role of spirituality in addiction and recovery.

This chapter cannot offer a complete and comprehensive history of the field or a complete review of its vast literature. It will, however, trace the developmental outlines of addiction studies and the continuing need for study of the "spiritual" component in addiction and recovery.[1] In this way the chapter will provide a context for exploring addiction and spirituality. The notes and references will also provide a foundation of scholarly, mutual-help and popular sources for the interested reader.

A Brief Overview of Addiction Studies

Prior to World War I, chronic drunkenness and drug addiction were largely viewed through the moralistic lenses of sin, moral weakness, or personal defect and were met with condemnation, guilt, shame, and ostracism (Stevens-Smith and Smith, 1998). The alcoholic and addict were social pariahs, the objects of both scorn and snide humor. Such predominant attitudes in American culture fueled much of the religious moralism and temperance attitudes which led to Prohibition (Johnson, 1973; Kurtz, 1979; Mercadante, 1996).

Bruce Johnson documents a gradual change in this attitude in the period following World War I. Driven by enormous shifts in the number of abstainers and drinkers in American society (Heath, 1989a; Jellinek, 1947; Johnson, 1973), there evolved a kind of cultural "readiness" to reassess the traditional moralistic concepts of drunkenness and addiction in American culture. Increasingly the culture became receptive to an alternative point of view, one more accepting of the notion of a physiological or psychological aberration as part of the addict's inner makeup (Johnson, 1973).

The emergence of this "amoral" perspective regarding addiction was influenced by a number of factors, including (a) the growing ascendency of psychoanalysis and psychological theories of motivation, (b) the influence of pioneering researchers and new discoveries in medicine and physiology, (c) the apparent success of the newly-founded Alcoholics Anonymous, and (d) the support and cooperation of a number of the leading religious figures of the time, their denominations, and a variety of unconventional religious and healing movements (Kurtz, 1979; Johnson, 1973; Mercadante, 1996; Morgan, *in press a*). This new view became part of the national dialogue through magazines, films, books, periodicals, and scholarly conversation. All this added plausibility to the idea that habitual drunkenness and drug addiction could be caused by physiological or other factors over which the individual had little control (Johnson, 1973). With these shifts, the stage was set for the 1930s, 1940s, and 1950s in which chronic drinking and drug

[1] The focus in this chapter will be on developments in the United States, although addiction studies have had a similar history in Europe and elsewhere.

addiction could be viewed as other than moral depravity or a tragic flaw in character.

Following the repeal of Prohibition in 1934, hospitals began to open their doors, although slowly at first, to the care of "inebriates." While most psychiatrists and other physicians were still reluctant to treat "inebriates," several specialized in this practice. Changes in treatment led to interest in research, as several prominent physicians and physiologists began studies on different aspects of chemical use and consequences. A series of events between 1935 and 1940 led to (a) the publication of a comprehensive review on alcohol and its effects from a medical-scientific rather than moralistic point of view, (b) the collaboration of a number of researchers including E. M. Jellinek and Mark Keller, (c) the founding of the *Quarterly Journal of Studies on Alcohol*, and (d) the beginnings of the Yale Center of Alcohol Studies. Many of the researchers at that time, despite differing views of etiology, treatment, and policy, shared a common conviction that "inebriety" must be studied and recognized as a medical problem more than a moral one (Johnson, 1973; Keller, 1975).

In January 1940 the Research Council on Problems of Alcohol and its Scientific Committee adopted a statement defining the "alcoholic" as "a person who cannot or will not control his drinking, and needs thorough and systematic treatment"; the members went on to define "alcoholism" as a "disease" (Johnson, 1973, 242–243). The use of the term "disease" had a profound effect on subsequent attitudes, public and professional, toward alcohol and other drug research. Over time, the "disease model" became the primary paradigm in addiction research, and received scientific support through the World Health Organization in 1951, the American Medical Association in 1956, the American Psychiatric Association in 1965, and the American College of Physicians in 1969 (Gitlow, 1973; Nace, 1987).[2]

With this change in definition and attitude, the way was opened for development of research and understanding vis-à-vis addiction. Below is a brief sketch of the historical phases and development of issues in addiction studies.

Phase 1: Short-lived collaboration and scientific developments

At the third annual meeting of the Research Council in October 1940, along with the assembled scientists and physicians, Dr. Harry Tiebout, M.D. was in attendance as a new Council member; William Wilson and Marty

---

[2] Levine (1978) argues that the 1930s were a time of "re-discovery" of the disease model of addiction. He makes a coherent case for the influence of this model in some Temperance circles. Nevertheless, the American experience and disillusionment with Prohibition set the stage for a new paradigm and the beginning of addiction studies.

There are a number of historical and theoretical discussions about various "models" of addiction. The interested reader may wish to consult the following select bibliography of sources as a way to begin exploring this area of study: Drew (1986); Keller (1990); Seigler, Osmond & Newell (1968).

The adoption of the "disease model" of addiction by the major U.S. religious denominations is extensively discussed in Johnson (1973) and Morgan (*in press a*).

Mann, among the founders of Alcoholics Anonymous, participated from the audience. These three figures were to be increasingly important in broadening the cultural acceptance of alcoholism as, at least in part, a disease. At the same time the Center of Alcohol Studies was becoming a primary site for research, treatment, public education, and publication in the science of alcoholism and addiction (Johnson, 1973; Keller, 1975).

Another influential effort in this new field of addiction studies began in 1943 with the first Yale Summer School of Alcohol Studies (Johnson, 1973). Conceived as an interdisciplinary and interfaith effort, the first session of the Summer School was attended by 80 professionals (physicians, social workers, school teachers, lawyers, ministers) and was covered by both *Newsweek* and *Collier's* magazines. It was to exert a profound impact on the basic professional and public stance toward addiction.

From the earliest days of addiction studies, the pioneers saw themselves as engaged in a collaborative, interdisciplinary, interprofessional, even "ecumenical" enterprise of research and understanding that could lead to effective treatment, education, and prevention (Keller, 1975). The active role played by clergy and churches in this early collaboration was significant (see Johnson, 1973; Kurtz, 1979; Morgan, *in press a*).

The first phase of development in addiction studies began with the Research Council, the Yale Center, and the growing recognition of alcoholism and drug addiction as medically-related illnesses. This period lasted from the 1930s into the 1950s and beyond. It gave birth to a number of advances in understanding that continue to be important today.

In biology and physiology, for example, the development of research into the genetics of alcoholism and addiction, using intergenerational studies (Schuckit, 1983, 1989), as well as adoption and "twin" studies (Anthenelli and Schuckit, 1992; Goodwin, 1985; Goodwin et al., 1973), and research into "typing" of addicts by drinking patterns (Jellinek, 1960) or by genetic vulnerability (Cloninger, 1987; Goodwin, 1988) is by now well documented. Advances in understanding the brain pathways and neurochemicals related to addiction (Blum, 1991; Sunderwirth, 1985), as in the "dopamine hypothesis" and its further revisions (DiChiara, G. and Imperato, A., 1988), have given much needed solidity to the science of addiction. Research by Milkman and Sunderwirth (1987) with the chemistry of addiction and the "drug of choice" phenomenon (Milkman and Frosch, 1977) demonstrates the importance of this scientific research.

In psychology, research into various "vulnerabilities" of the self that potentially predispose to addiction (Khantzian, 1986; Khantzian et al., 1990; Khantzian & Mack, 1989; Mack, 1981), the "stages of change" that can lead to successful recovery (Prochaska, DiClemente, and Norcross, 1992, 1994), and the development of "relapse prevention" strategies for maintenance of recovery change (Gorski, 1986; Marlatt and Gordon, 1980) are also making significant contributions.

The fields of epidemiology, cognitive science, and sociocultural studies, represented by George Vaillant (1983, 1995), Arnold Ludwig (1988, 1985), and Dwight Heath (1990, 1989a & b, 1986) respectively, have also improved the knowledge base of addiction studies. The formulation and acceptance of a broadly biopsychosocial theory of addiction that encompasses many of the elements reviewed above into a coherent research paradigm has been an important step forward (Morgan, 1992; Zinberg and Bean, 1981).

In the field of treatment, the development of the Minnesota Model, a comprehensive and multidisciplinary program geared toward holistic care, personal dignity, and spiritual growth, allowed for the application of growing scientific and clinical knowledge to the process of helping alcoholics and addicts. Begun in the 1940s, this approach emphasizes collaborative effort involving physicians, counselors, concerned members of Alcoholics Anonymous, and others toward the healing of addictive illness. Many addiction treatment centers today have their roots in this model (Cook, 1988a & b; Spicer, 1993).

These fields of endeavor all began with the earlier, interdisciplinary move toward interest in addiction as a "disease" or "behavioral disorder" needing scientific attention. Each of these developments has had important benefits for patients in the field of treatment and recovery.

However, what began with such promise as a collaborative and interdisciplinary field of exploration quickly devolved into separate and sometimes competing areas of inquiry. The "science" of addiction and treatment (medical, physiological, psychological) became the primary way of thinking about addiction; other ways of thinking became less prominent.[3] Mirroring developments in other areas of medicine and psychology, the field focused on research that could be scientifically demonstrable, controlled, and manipulated. Neurochemical pathways, genetic patterns, measurable psychological traits, and concrete, observable patterns of interaction assumed pride of place in addiction studies. While science has contributed much to the understanding and treatment of addiction, other more holistic ways of thinking and working had to wait for a more auspicious time to grow and develop.

Phase 2: Family systems theory

The second phase of development in addiction studies coincided with the beginnings and development of family systems theory and exploration of a variety of familial dynamics that co-occur with addiction. Early studies

[3] Even the religious denominations found an interdisciplinary focus hard to maintain. Often the denominations simply adopted the "medical disease" model of addiction uncritically and, at the same time, muted their own spiritually-based voice. This left the realms of understanding and treatment in the hands of disciplines that were not particularly open or sensitive to the influence of spirituality (Morgan, *in press a*). The task of a proper role for religious faith and theology in a renewed dialogue about addiction and spirituality is under some discussion today (Mercadante, 1996; Morgan, *in press a & b*).

in this area focused on intergenerational patterns, adaptive mechanisms, and consequences for family interactions that seemed to cause or maintain addictive behaviors (Berenson, 1976; Davis, Berenson, Steinglass, and Davis, 1974; Jackson, 1954). Alcohol and other drugs came to be seen as a "central organizing principle" in the lives of addicts and their families (Steinglass et al., 1987). Scholarly treatments of these topics gave rise to more popular presentations of the interactions of alcohol and other drug abuse and addiction with family life (Beattie, 1987; Black, 1982; Bradshaw, 1990; Wegscheider-Cruse, 1989) and serious debate about some applications of these principles (see, for example, Collins, 1993).

Family therapists working specifically with treatment of addicts have developed sophisticated models for working with individuals, couples, and families, which are used in a variety of treatment settings, inpatient and outpatient (Berenson and Schreier, 1994; Liepman, Silvia, and Nirenberg, 1989; O'Farrell, 1993; Silvia and Liepman, 1991; Stanton et al., 1982; Treadway, 1989).

These developments from systems thinking have become welcome additions to the knowledge base and clinical skills of addictions specialists. It is interesting to note that the ideas of several systemic writers helped lead to the next phase of addiction studies development (Bateson, 1972; Berenson, 1990; see Morgan, 1998).

Phase 3: A focus on recovery

The third and most recent phase of addiction studies is identified with renewed interest in the dynamics of recovery (Brown, 1985; Larsen, 1985). It is from this interest in the recovery process that science is taking a new look at the role of mutual-help groups like Alcoholics Anonymous and the importance of a "spiritual" component to addiction and recovery.

Several national research efforts have recently shown renewed appreciation of the potential for learning that can come through study of these two phenomena (American Psychiatric Association Task Force, 1989; NIHR, 1997).[4] Renewed exploration of AA and of the "spiritual" component in addiction and recovery may well be the current "growing edge" in this young field.

The Perspective of Alcoholics Anonymous

From the earliest days of addiction studies, the presence and perspective of Alcoholics Anonymous and similar support groups, have been a powerful, and sometimes controversial, force. Twelve Step experience continues to influence the field of addiction and its treatment (American Psychiatric Association Task Force, 1989), and current researchers attribute significant positive healing of addictive illness to Twelve Step programs

[4] A 1999 scientific conference entitled, "Studying Spirituality in Alcoholism and Recovery," is being prepared by the National Institute on Alcohol Abuse and Alcoholism.

(Chappel, 1992, 1993; Khantzian and Mack, 1989; Tasman, Hales, and Frances, 1989; Vaillant, 1983, 1995).

Beginning in the mid-1930s, AA was founded on the experience of a small group of persons who found a path to recovery and pursued it. Interestingly, the discovery and pursuit of this path is now described by a noted psychiatrist as "a form of field research...[that has been] validated in prospective scientific studies" (Chappel, 1993, 181). A number of historical and research publications have been written about the successes (and failures) of AA with various hypotheses for how and why AA "works" (Alibrandi, 1978; Clinebell, 1963, 1985; Gellman, 1964; Kurtz, 1982; Leach and Norris, 1977; Maxwell, 1984; Robertson, 1988; Rudy, 1986).

A series of simultaneous (some might say "providential") events led to the founding and development of AA. Bill Wilson's religious dabblings, a chance conversation with an alcoholic friend and subsequent "hot flash" or **spiritual experience** while in detoxification at Towns Hospital, as well as his increasing frustration in trying to help other alcoholics, led to a fateful meeting between Wilson and Dr. Bob Smith, a chronically relapsing alcoholic physician. Their **conversation of shared pain and hope** eventually led to a strategy for approaching other alcoholics and to providing hospital stays for them with a dose of AA philosophy (Darrah, 1992; Kurtz, 1979).

Over several years this **outreach and mutual support** gave birth to a small band of early members of the fledgling Alcoholics Anonymous. As they reflected on their experience and with the leadership of Wilson, Smith, and others, this group formulated the *Twelve Steps* and authored *Alcoholics Anonymous*, the "Big Book" that codified their approach to recovery (1937\1976). These writings, the experience of these early recoverers, and the influence of several unconventional religious movements like the Oxford Group, solidified the element of **fellowship** and the **program principles** that guide and support recovering persons today (Kurtz, 1979).[5]

Subsequent years saw the development of AA into an **ongoing path of growth and recovery** as well as the publication of two other sourcebooks of AA wisdom, *Twelve Steps and Twelve Traditions* (1953\1981) and *A.A. Comes of Age* (1957).

These elements of spiritual experience, conversation and sharing of stories, outreach and mutual support, fellowship, program, and principles of recovery became hallmarks of the AA approach. However, the notion of a "spiritual" component was, and continues to be, "the most controversial and most misunderstood" element in AA's understanding of illness and recovery (Chappel, 1992, 414). Virtually ignored by some in the field of addiction science, the role of a "spiritual" component has been treated with

[5] The roles played by a number of more conventional religious leaders in the formation and development of the AA approach and beliefs is still an active area of exploration. The interested reader may consult the work of Mary Darrah (1992), Bruce Johnson (1973), Ernie Kurtz (1979), Linda Mercadante (1996), and Ollie Morgan (*in press, a & b*).

disdain by others (Christopher, 1989; Ellis, 1985; Ellis and Schoenfeld, 1990). A number of addiction researchers have "translated" spiritual experience into seemingly more acceptable secular and humanistic terms, as one of a number of important "natural healing factors" (Edwards, 1984; Shaffer and Jones, 1989; Vaillant, 1988; Vaillant & Milofsky, 1982) or "extratreatment" components of recovery (Billings and Moos, 1983; Moos, 1994).

Nevertheless, central to the AA approach to recovery, based on the experience of recovering persons, is the notion of spirituality (Kurtz, 1986). It is important to notice the roots of this conviction. Ernest Kurtz, the noted historian of AA, describes it this way:

> From their own experience, the earliest AA members worked out a way of life that involved a way of thinking that became incorporated in a "language of recovery"—a way of seeing, and of thinking about, and of feeling, and of responding to, and especially of *expressing* their reality that emerged in the practice of their telling their own stories of "what we used to be like, what happened, and what we are like now." It is in this "language of recovery" that I find the cornerstones of the enduring reality that deserves to be called an "A.A." or "Twelve Step" *spirituality*. (Kurtz, 1986, p. 36)

As a preview of later developments, the reader should note that Kurtz speaks of the roots of AA spirituality as "a way of life" and "a way of thinking" that leads to new language, feelings, and responses. A number of the studies to be referenced later will utilize these same categories.

A disease with a difference

Bill Wilson, Dr. Bob Smith, and the early members of AA believed that addiction is an illness, related to notions of "disease" in the medical model, but that it is a disease with a difference. They believed that alcoholism and other addictions were a triple sickness of the body, mind, and soul. This perspective became an integral part of the addictions field early on, espoused at the Yale Summer School and in the *Quarterly Journal*.[6] Even though the early founders of AA and researchers in the addictions field clearly hoped for discovery of a biological cause of addiction, they were also adamant (if a bit unclear) about the psychological and spiritual nature of addictive illness (Morgan, *in press b*).

This is still the view of AA today. As new and prospective members of AA are told, addiction is a "physical, psychological and spiritual disease" (Bean, 1975a & b). A number of addiction specialists believe that this

[6] For example, the Rev. John C. Ford, S.J., became an early collaborator and lecturer at the Yale Summer School, often offering a course entitled, "Alcohol Addiction In the Light of Moral Philosophy." He maintained a set of relationships with AA's founders, with the scientific community, and with a variety of denominational leaders. Within this collaborative network, Ford consistently maintained the value of an interdisciplinary, bio-psycho-socio-spiritual perspective of addiction (Morgan, *in press b*).

description accounts, in part, for AA's success (Brown, Peterson and Cunningham, 1988a; Buxton, Smith, and Seymour, 1987; Chappel, 1992, 1993; Siegler, Osmond, and Newell, 1968). In addition, one of the major agencies responsible for accrediting treatment and health care settings has suggested that assessment of each patient's "spiritual orientation," as well as "biopsychosocial needs," be included as part of a comprehensive treatment package (Joint Commission on Accreditation of Healthcare Organizations [JCAHO], 1989).

One difficulty that confronts this conceptualization today is the increasing "medicalization" of the notion of disease. The search for biological and genetic explanations for compulsive and other troublesome behaviors has obscured the classic, more holistic, interdisciplinary point of view (Morgan, *in press a & b*). In part, the difficulty is due to a one-sided, medicalized notion of addictive illness as well as to the influence of narrowly quantitative versions of scientific research (Morgan, 1992). In part, however, the problem is also due to the loss of a fully interdisciplinary model for understanding and treating addiction as well as the absence of religious and theological experts as full participants in addiction studies (Mercadante, 1996; Morgan, *in press a & b*; Svendsen and Griffin, 1991).

With the emergence of the recovery process as a focus for addiction studies, there is renewed interest in factors that begin and maintain a return to health from addiction. This interest has once again opened the door to study of spirituality as one such potential factor (Miller, 1997, 1998). In the process, the way has been cleared for a return to a more holistic, collaborative and multi-dimensional path in addiction studies.

Movement Toward Spirituality

The notion that some "spiritual" element is involved in both addiction and recovery has been the consistent witness of AA and other Twelve Step programs. It also runs like a golden thread through the clinical observations and writings of a number of addiction researchers over the years. Significantly, many of these researchers have kept alive their connections to Twelve Step programs and have stayed close to the recovering community and the experience of their patients.

Harry Tiebout, M.D. was one of the earliest and most prominent of the early addiction specialists. His interest began simply; he noticed that his difficult patients were recovering from alcoholism by using the new Alcoholics Anonymous, and he was impressed with evidence of real character change as well. His investigations led him to listen to the story of recovery as told by his patients. This produced some unexpected insights.

> I found myself facing the question: What had happened? My answer is that the patient had had a religious or spiritual experience. The answer, however, did not prove particularly enlightening and it was not until much later that I began to appreciate the real meaning of the answer. (Tiebout, 1944, pp. 468–469)

Tiebout's explorations into this uncharted territory are documented in a variety of publications that validate the importance of spiritual elements in addiction and recovery experience (1946, 1949, 1953, 1954). In 1961, Tiebout published "Alcoholics Anonymous—An experiment in nature," which serves as a summary and concise statement of his discoveries over the course of his explorations. In Tiebout's view, the "change which A.A. induces" is a spiritual process of conversion and surrender with clear psychoemotional, cognitive, and behavioral dynamics.

> A conversion occurs when the individual hits bottom, surrenders, and thereby has his [*sic*] ego reduced. His salvation lies in keeping that ego reduced, in staying humble. These insights, gained from long study of Alcoholics Anonymous and the process it initiates, appear to give meaning and order to the change which A.A. induces. Conversion is no longer an event "out of the blue" but a logical outgrowth of human responses, [namely] hitting bottom and surrender. (Tiebout, 1961, p. 65)

Others have undertaken the task of exploring and understanding these dynamics since Tiebout's work, and they have done so by remaining close to recovering persons and listening to their testimony.

A new focus

Beginning in the late 1970s, factors began to coalesce that gave serious attention to spirituality as a factor in addiction and recovery. Much literature and research had been devoted to the pathology of addiction over the years; relatively little attention had been devoted to understanding the process of recovery and the resources that lead to successful recovery (Morgan, 1995). With the introduction of research into the "natural history" and recovery "careers" of addicted persons (Edwards, 1984; Raistrick, 1991; Vaillant and Milofsky, 1982), the imbalance in addiction studies began to change.

As recovery research began to grow, addiction specialists began to appreciate and attend to the lived experience, narrative descriptions, and stories of recovering persons. This newer focus, similar in many ways to the research style of Tiebout and the AA way of proceeding, seemed to be productive in providing a more holistic understanding of addiction and recovery. This focus also allowed for understanding about the experience of women, as well as of ethnically diverse people and cultures, which were areas of interest that had been largely excluded from investigation prior to this time (Kasl, 1992; Tucker, 1985; Westermeyer, 1997).

This narrative approach validated a long-held contention of AA and some researchers, namely that some "spiritual" element was at play in the experience of recovering persons. Kurtz has suggested that spirituality is so deeply ingrained in the realm of personal experience that attention to narrative and story may be the only way that spiritual dynamics will reveal themselves (Kurtz, 1986, 1991).[7]

Many who have experienced recovery through the Twelve Steps, or who have worked closely with recovering persons (for example, pastors, counselors, therapists) reach for language about a "spiritual" dimension or "spirituality" as the *sine qua non* for the lifesaving change in addicts' lives (Berenson, 1990; Buxton, Smith, and Seymour, 1987; Clinebell, 1985; Larsen, 1985; May, 1988; Royce, 1985, 1987; Whitfield, 1985). Yet, there has been little sustained attention to it as a factor worthy of scientific study (Morgan, 1995; NIHR, 1997).

Spirituality, however, is difficult to study, and there are ingrained biases within several disciplines that inhibit discussion about its potential role in the recovery process. Much of the standard addiction science of today focuses on physiological and psychological factors that are clearly of great importance. The *science* of addiction and recovery utilizes methodological assumptions and a quantitative research paradigm that offer much value for addiction and recovery scholarship. These areas of exploration must continue (NIHR, 1997). Yet, the very paradigm of scientific study, as currently understood and utilized, may obscure or exclude from view important information that can be just as valuable. A more *holistic* and yet fully *empirical* model of investigation in addiction studies as a human science may be called for (Morgan, 1992).

Elements of Spirituality

As we saw in the work of Harry Tiebout, initial attention to the role of a spiritual component in recovery yields some understanding of phenomena like "surrender" and "conversion" as they pertain to addiction. These are terms more traditionally familiar to religion than to science. Yet they point to something critical in studying addiction and recovery.

"Something" happens to an addict's ways of thinking, feeling, and acting in the world when she or he turns to recovery. The addict experiences a profound change. The change that occurs gives rise to new ways of thinking, feeling, and seeing the world as well as to alterations of life stance and lifestyle, that is, to cognitive, affective, and behavioral consequences (Brown, 1985; King and Castelli, 1995).

The recovering addict feels more comfortable with self, more connected and at home in the world, and more open to others. The recovering addict relates to others differently, becomes more honest, more engaged, more

[7] The interested reader will benefit from some examples of narrative approaches to understanding addiction and recovery. The rest of this chapter will document various studies that attempt to understand via this approach. The chapters that follow in this book will also convey some insight through the "narrative" ways in which the authors approached their task. However, other sources of learning about these dynamics are also available in films, fictional accounts, and autobiographical descriptions. A list of some contemporary source materials in these areas is included in a section on Narrative Sources.

patient, humbler, and grateful. The recovering addict is more mature, psychologically and emotionally, and is able to relate with others with humor, altruism, and hope (Chappel, 1992; Khantzian and Mack, 1989). Many addicts attribute these changes to the protection and intervention of a Higher Power. They have a sense of being cared for and caring.

All these elements contribute to a series of lifestyle changes that help to ground and maintain recovery over the long-term (Morgan, 1992). It is these elements of change and discovery, taken together, that AA and addiction researchers highlight as essential "spiritual" components in the recovery process.

Gregory Bateson (1972), anthropologist and a major figure in the development of family systems theory, suggested that an important cognitive and affective shift occurred in recovery, a revisioning of self-in-relation-with-others and self-in-world that affects the recovering person's attitudes and entire frame of reference for living. The addict's change at depth ("surrender") leads to a stance of "complementarity" or "shared humanity" which entails a shift of one's center of control, sense of self, and view of the world and others. The occasion for this change is "hitting bottom" ("defeat by the bottle"), a "spiritual" experience that, when aided by the program and "theology of AA," leads to a lifetime of recovery (Bateson, 1972, pp. 331, 336). His view of the "spiritual" in these matters has influenced a number of other researchers.

Arnold Ludwig (1985, 1988) developed a cognitive model that similarly addresses issues of "craving," "hitting bottom," and "surrender" in addiction. He addresses the role of cognition and attributions in the evolution of recovery and development of a spiritual view of addiction and recovery. Recovering persons, he believes, attribute spiritual causality to their turn-to-recovery ("My Higher Power was watching out for me…"). This leads to a "conversion" and the development of a "spiritual lifestyle" (Ludwig, 1988).

Stephanie Brown's research (1977, 1985) into alcoholism and addiction is firmly rooted in the insights of Tiebout and Bateson. She has laid out a "developmental model of recovery" that has been used by several recent researchers. It was Brown's intent to elaborate a more detailed study of the process of recovery than had been attempted previously; her study became a pivotal moment in the trend toward recovery research. Brown's research began with an interest in studying abstinent alcoholics in order to understand the issues and events with which they contend in the process of recovery.

Brown's key insight came in exploring the difference between being "dry" and being "sober." While remaining dry focuses on continued abstinence from alcohol and other drugs as well as a fundamental movement away from dependency, "sobriety" entails achieving a kind of life-balance and expanded awareness, involving psychological, interpersonal, and spiritual exploration and change. This insight allowed her to develop a "continuum" model of recovery, maintaining a focus on abstinence while allowing her to chart changes in feeling, thinking, sense of self, relationships, and world view over time.

In this model, the **addictive process** is essentially a downward decline of progressive losses, failures, and increasing isolation. If and when the addict is fortunate enough to encounter a "turning point," it comes as the result of "the multiple impact of many experiences and interventions," which, when coupled with internal feelings of desperation and self-disgust, combine to form a kind of "readiness" that frames the decision to change. The **recovery process**, then, begins with the attempt to remain "dry" and moves into the maintenance of "sobriety." This results in "the emergence of new attitudes, values, and beliefs" which, in turn, create new experiences and change the meaning of others.

From this reshaping and building in recovery, a new self emerges and a journey of discovery begins. This is the stage of development Brown describes as Ongoing Recovery, which results in a "new identity" as well as radical changes in attitudes, feelings, beliefs, values, and in personal frames of reference.

A critical event in this process, Brown believes, is the emergence of spirituality. This involves a shift from self as the center of the universe toward a different center or authority. She notes that AA calls this the belief in a "Higher Power."

> Through altering their identities, working the twelve steps, and developing a personal concept of a higher power, individuals dramatically alter their attitudes, beliefs, values and thus their interpretation of themselves and others...This shift attacks egotism and omnipotence and alters the individual's sense of him or herself in relation to others...Members suddenly experience a feeling of shared humanity and hostile defensiveness disappears. Members of AA refer to such a happening as a "spiritual awakening." (Brown, 1985, p. 210)

Recent additions to the literature

Brown's research was a catalyst for new ways of conceptualizing recovery dynamics and the nature of a spiritual component in the lives of recovering addicts. Within a broadly biopsychosocial perspective, her "continuum" confirmed the experience of AA in spotlighting some development over time in the recovery process. People get better as time goes on; recovery looks different at different times.

Her work also highlighted different avenues of approach to recovery research. Attending to narrative data about recovery sensitizes researchers to resources that initiate and maintain recovery, that is, to different cognitive, affective, and behavioral elements in the recovery process. The value of a spiritual component in the lives of recovering persons becomes more apparent.

Earlier research studies and doctoral dissertations had spoken about the spiritual element from a more theoretical and theological point of view. Clinebell (1954, 1963) described alcoholism as a "pseudo-religious solution" and suggested that "surrender" was the key to understanding the psychodynamics of recovery. He elaborated on these ideas in his classic book on pastoral counseling with alcoholics (1985). Woodruff spoke about "spiritual transformation" as "the most reliable cause of permanent recovery from alcoholism" (1968, p. 10). Hall (1984), in studying alcoholism counselors, also spoke about spiritual transformation, describing the dynamics of surrender, powerlessness, and the reordering of one's affairs through recognition of a Higher Power. Both Albers (1982) and Roessler (1982) spoke about the need for conversion and transformation. It is easy to see that many of these studies relied on the previous work of Bateson and Tiebout (see Albers, 1994).

Each of these studies offered valuable insights. However, Brown's work began a series of studies that utilized more narrative and qualitative information from recovering persons themselves. These studies added more empirical and clinical rigor to research into recovery spirituality than had been previously available.

Brown (1977) had examined the experience of 80 abstinent alcoholics in AA with varying lengths of time in recovery. Her information came from surveys and in-depth interviews. With this information, she was able to describe different stages of recovery along her continuum. Turner (1993) interviewed recovering persons who were sober two years or more; Sommer (1992) did the same with those having between four and seven years of recovery. Each noted the importance of changes in self-perception and worldview, as well as changes in behavior, as significant elements in recovery spirituality. Sommer was able to describe recovery dynamics that were essential for persons in mid-recovery (4–7 years) and make recommendations for treatment. Morgan (1992) documented changes in life stance and lifestyle in interviews of persons with ten or more years in abstinent recovery. He described a process of spiritual and psychological transformation in the recovery process that built on changes in thinking and feeling, and resulted in a variety of recovery tools being used (for example, personal inventory, confession, making amends, prayer) to maintain behavioral change (Morgan, 1995). Hennessey-Heine (1995) studied persons with an average of 19.5 years in recovery. She noted dynamics such as (a) a "gradual perceptual shift" from an isolated self to a self-in-relation, (b) a shift from self-destructive behaviors to life-enhancing ones, and (c) the beginnings of a "new life." The recovering women she interviewed spoke about spirituality as being more "connected" to others and to a presence or source of power that fueled continued growth (1995, p. 137).

Next steps

Each of the studies listed above utilized recovery stories and groups of recovering persons who had some experience in AA or other mutual-help groups. This approach has both strengths and weaknesses. On the one hand, AA members often tell their stories easily and are able to be quite articulate about their perceptions of the "spiritual"; on the other hand, it is difficult to know whether these persons are able to speak for all recovering persons. Does their experience with AA language and culture somehow skew their perceptions of the recovery process?

A recent study may help to overcome this limitation and may signal a new approach to qualitative studies of recovery. Kubicek (1998) studied persons with six or more years in continuous recovery, half of whom were somehow involved in AA and half of whom were in "spontaneous remission," that is, recovery without any group support. He was searching for attributes or elements of successful recovery. Overall, Kubicek discovered thirteen elements that recovering persons described as important in their recovery. Importantly, five of these were overwhelmingly identified as essential for recovery success by *both* AA members and spontaneous remitters. In addition to social support, remembering negative consequences, renewed honesty in living, and having a desire for health, these persons described a spiritual component and "accepting help from a higher power" as essential to their recovery.

The work of Brown, Peterson, and Cunningham (1990, 1989, 1988a, b, and c) is important to note as this review of the literature and history of addiction studies comes to an end. These researchers have also taken a "next step" in recovery research, codifying notions about spirituality learned in qualitative interviews into a "psychospiritual checklist" and treatment format suitable for use with a wider population.

> The Twelve Steps of recovery include both behavioral and cognitive components...Such activities as taking a written personal inventory, making direct amends to others, and prayer and meditation are specific behaviors. Such activities as admitting powerlessness, "coming to believe in a power greater than ourselves," and making decisions are cognitive in nature. Thus, our model is behavioral/cognitive and includes psychological techniques from both therapeutic perspectives.
>
> We postulate that specific psychotherapeutic interventions must be included in any spiritual program for relapse prevention. (Brown, Peterson, and Cunningham, 1988a)

In their behavioral/cognitive approach to spirituality, Brown and his associates attempt to formulate ways in which recovering persons may better relate to self, to others, and to a Higher Power. They do so by combining an approach that is comfortable for psychotherapists with practices and changes in attitude that have been familiar to spiritual seekers for centuries. The goal is "whole recovery," through a multidimensional approach to spirituality (Brown et al., 1988b).

In order to develop a format for general use, Brown et al. defined "spiritual behaviors" as "any behavior, either cognitive or overt, that facilitates, improves, deepens, or enhances our ability to 'relate positively' to ourselves, others or a higher power." By examining the Twelve Steps, interviewing a number of recovering persons, utilizing psychological instruments on values and self-concept, and consulting the literature of recovery, they developed the BASIC-IS model of treatment (Brown and Peterson, 1990).[8] "We believe that the key to continued sobriety lies in facilitating daily spiritual behaviors in the life of the recovering individual" (Brown, et al., 1988c).

An ongoing agenda

The checklist and treatment approach developed by Brown and his colleagues have been added to a number of other potential research instruments that are available in the field of addiction studies and that have particular applicability to recovery dynamics and spirituality. These have arisen from qualitative studies and the clinical experience of counselors and treatment centers.[9] Much more experience and testing with these instruments is necessary. However, the development of such instruments offers real potential for greater understanding of a "spiritual" component in recovery, particularly when used in conjunction with sensitivity to more narrative and qualitative methods of study.

The National Institute of Healthcare Research report, quoted at the beginning of this chapter, calls for sustained, scientific research into recovery spirituality. The combination of quantitative and qualitative methods of inquiry will provide a sound basis for this research effort, and will reestablish the original collaboration and multidisciplinary approach that was the hallmark of early addiction studies. The investigation of recovery dynamics and the role of spirituality will continue to be important in this collaboration (Miller, 1997, 1998). This research will also make a significant contribution to a related field of endeavor.

Spirituality as a New Field of Study

A modern interest in spirituality is developing across a number of disciplines and in popular consciousness. The shelves of any bookstore bear

---

[8] The letters in the acronym BASIC-IS stand for: behaviors, affective processes, sensations, images, cognitions, interpersonal relationships, and spiritual behaviors. The format is based on the "multimodal therapy" work of Lazarus (1981, 1976).

[9] See, for example, Joachim (1988). Other instruments and complementary ways of thinking may be helpful and available from the "spiritual well-being" movement (Moberg, 1986, 1971; Moberg and Brusek, 1978).

witness to this interest. In academic circles, the discipline of spirituality is flourishing as scholars turn their attention to understanding "spiritual experience." The emergence of this new academic field has important connections to the investigation of spirituality in addiction studies.

Sandra Schneiders (1986, 1990) is an important voice in this newly emerging discipline. It is remarkable, she suggests, that a term ["spirituality"] which connoted mindless piety in some circles and "subjectivism" in scientific circles not so long ago is now used so freely within many religious, secular and even scientific circles. Importantly, it is used with some sense of enthusiasm for its potential contribution to deeper knowledge of human life and activity (Schneiders, 1990, pp. 30–31).

Schneiders (1990) describes the lived experience of spirituality broadly as "the experience of consciously striving to integrate one's life in terms... of self-transcendence toward the ultimate value one perceives" (p. 23). The experience of integrating many elements of the person in view of some ultimate value is an experience open to engagement with the Absolute; it is an activity of human living as such and is available to the genuine seeker (pp. 21–22). Her description of the lived experience of spirituality comes close to many elements elaborated in our review of the spiritual components of recovery.

Spirituality is also a discipline, or field of investigation, within the academic and scientific worlds. Schneiders describes some of the characteristics of this young discipline in ways that are similar to our suggestions regarding study of the dynamics of recovery (Schneiders 1986, 1990). As a discipline, spirituality needs to be *descriptive, interdisciplinary, and holistic.* The discipline seeks to understand deeply human phenomena with the aid of many disciplines working together. It must be committed to an *ecumenical and cross-cultural* approach, while focusing on the *experience of individuals*. It is necessarily a *participant discipline* with researchers who are themselves familiar with spiritual dynamics working to recognize analogous experiences in others. It will be characterized by a *triple objective* of trying to understand the variety of spiritual experiences under study, while fostering one's own experience and the spirituality of others (1986, pp. 267–269).

> For Schneiders and others involved in this emerging discipline, interest in spirituality represents a profound and authentic desire of 20th Century humanity for wholeness in the midst of fragmentation, for community in the face of isolation and loneliness, for liberating transcendence, for meaning in life, for values that endure. Human beings are spirit in the world, and spirituality is the effort to understand and realize the potential of that extraordinary and paradoxical condition. (Schneiders, 1990, p. 36).

Many recovering addicts, and the addiction specialists who study them, could echo the same sentiment. They could also agree with Philip Sheldrake, another important author in the contemporary discipline of spirituality:

"The roots of contemporary (postmodern?) spirituality are to be found in an emphasis on human experience, in all its variety and pain, as the immediate context for God's self-disclosure" (Sheldrake, 1996, p. 7).

Conclusion

This book seeks to restore some of the collaboration and interdisciplinary cooperation that marked early addiction studies. By inviting researchers and addiction specialists from various disciplines to explore their notions of "spirituality," the book describes recovery spirituality from a multidisciplinary perspective.

Some of the writers in this volume are well known experts in the field; some are new voices. Each was invited to contribute his or her view of recovery spirituality to a text that would be multidisciplinary, and to seek the renewal of a collaborative effort.

It is the belief of the editors that a return to collaborative and interdisciplinary work can shed light on this important and fascinating dimension of addiction studies.

Narrative Sources

Films

Arthur
Long Day's Journey into Night
Basketball Diaries
Lost Weekend
The Boost
Man with the Golden Arm
Bright Lights, Big City
My Name Is Bill W.
The Champ
Trainspotting
Clean and Sober
Voice in The Mirror
Cocaine: The Anatomy of One Man's Seduction
Where the Day Takes You
Come Back, Little Sheba
When a Man Loves a Woman
Days of Wine and Roses
Who's Afraid of Virginia Woolf?
Drugstore Cowboy
Ironweed

Fiction

John Berryman, *Recovery: A Novel* (Farrar, Strauss, & Giroux, 1973).
Ivan Gold, *Sam's in a Dry Season* (Houghton Mifflin, 1990)
Miriam Dow and Jennifer Regan, *The Invisible Enemy: Alcoholism and the Modern Short Story* (Graywolf, 1989).

Autobiographies

Sylvia Cary, *The Alcoholic Man: What You Can Learn from the Heroic Journeys of Recovering Alcoholics* (Lowell House, 1990)

Christina Grof, *The Thirst for Wholeness: Attachment, Addiction and the Spiritual Path* (Harper San Francisco, 1993)

Pete Hamill, *A Drinking Life: A Memoir* (Little, Brown and Co, 1994)

Katy Hendricks, *The Party's Over: Diary of a Recovering Cocaine Addict* (American University Press, 1992)

Mark Gauvreau Judge, *Wasted: Tales of a GenX Drunk* (Hazelden, 1997)

Caroline Knapp, *Drinking: A Love Story* (Dial, 1996)

Jack London , *John Barleycorn*

Carl Adam Richmond, *Twisted: Inside the Mind of a Drug Addict* (Jason Aronson, 1992)

Nan Robertson, *Getting Better: Inside Alcoholics Anonymous* (William Morrow, 1988)

Dan Wakefield, *Returning: A Spiritual Journey* (Penguin Books, 1989)

References

As a chapter that sets the context and background for the rest of this book, references will be made to important scientific and historical publications as well as to more popular and accessible publications for a general readership.

Albers, R. H. (1994). Spirituality and surrender: A theological analysis of Tiebout's theory for ministry to the alcoholic. *Journal of Ministry in Addiction and Recovery*, *1*(2), 47–68.

Albers, R. H. (1982). The theological and psychological dynamics of transformation in recovery from the disease of alcoholism. *Dissertation Abstracts International*, *43*, 1198A. [University Microfilms No. 82–21501].

Alcoholics Anonymous World Services. (1937/1976). *Alcoholics Anonymous: The story of how many thousands of men and women have recovered from alcoholism, third edition*. New York: Author.

Alcoholics Anonymous World Services. (1957). *Alcoholics Anonymous comes of age*. New York: Harper.

Alcoholics Anonymous World Services. (1953/1981). *Twelve steps and twelve traditions*. New York: Author.

Alibrandi, L. A. (1978). The folk psychotherapy of Alcoholics Anonymous. In S. Zimberg, J. Wallace and S. Blume(Eds.), *Practical approaches to alcoholism psychotherapy* (pp. 163–180). New York: Plenum Press.

American Psychiatric Association Task Force (1989). *Treatments of psychiatric disorders*. Washington, DC: American Psychiatric Association.

Anthenelli, R. M. and Schuckit, M. A. (1992). Genetics. In J. H. Lowinson, P. Ruiz, R. B. Millman, (Eds.), and J. G. Langrod (Assoc Ed.), *Substance abuse: A comprehensive text, second edition* (pp. 39–50). Baltimore: Williams & Wilkins.

Bateson, G. (1972). The cybernetics of "self": A theory of alcoholism. In *Steps to an ecology of mind*. New York: Ballantine. [Original work published in 1971. *Psychiatry*, *34*(1), 1–18].

Bean, M. (1975a). Alcoholics Anonymous. *Psychiatric Annals*, 5(2), 45–72.

Bean, M. (1975b). Alcoholics Anonymous II. *Psychiatric Annals*, 5(3), 83–109.

Beattie, M. (1987). *Codependent no more*. San Francisco: Harper/Hazelden.

Berenson, D. (1990). A systemic view of spirituality: God and Twelve Step programs as resources in family therapy. *Journal of Strategic and Systemic Therapies*, 9 (1), 59–70.

Berenson, D. (1976). Alcohol and the family system. In P. Guerin (Ed.), *Family therapy: Theory and practice* (pp. 284–297). New York: Gardner Press.

Berenson, D. and Schrier, E. W. (1994). Current family treatment approaches. In N. S. Miller (Ed.), *Principles of addiction medicine* (Section 15: The Family in Addiction, Chapter 3). Chevy Chase, Md: American Society of Addiction Medicine, Inc.

Billings, A. G. and Moos, R. H. (1983). Psychosocial processes of recovery among alcoholics and their families: Implications for clinicians and program evaluators. *Addictive Behaviors*, 8, 205–218.

Black, C. (1982). *It will never happen to me*. Denver: MAC Publishing.

Blum, K. (1991). *Alcohol and the addictive brain*. New York: Free Press.

Bradshaw, J. (1990). *Homecoming: Reclaiming and championing your inner child*. New York: Bantam Books.

Brown, S. (1985). *Treating the alcoholic: A developmental model of recovery*. New York: John Wiley.

Brown, S. (1977). Defining a continuum of recovery in alcoholism. *Dissertation Abstracts International*, 38, 1393. [University Microfilms No.77–18285].

Brown, H. P., Jr., and Peterson, J. H., Jr. (1990). Rationale and procedural suggestions for defining and actualizing spiritual values in the treatment of dependency. *Alcoholism Treatment Quarterly*, 7(3), 17–46.

Brown, H. P., Jr., and Peterson, J. H., Jr. (1989). Refining the BASIC-ISs: A psychospiritual approach to the comprehensive outpatient treatment of drug dependency. *Alcoholism Treatment Quarterly*, 6(3/4), 27–61.

Brown, H. P., Jr., Peterson, J. H., Jr. and Cunningham, O. (1988a). Rationale and theoretical basis for a behavioral/cognitive aproach to spirituality. *Alcoholism Treatment Quarterly*, 5(1/2), 47–59.

Brown, H. P., Jr., Peterson, J. H., Jr. and Cunningham, O. (1988b). A behavioral/cognitive spiritual model for a chemical dependency aftercare program. *Alcoholism Treatment Quarterly*, 5(1/2), 153–175.

Brown, H. P., Jr., Peterson, J. H., Jr. and Cunningham, O. (1988c). An individualized behavioral approach to spiritual development for the recovering alcoholic/addict. *Alcoholism Treatment Quarterly*, 5(1/2), 177–196.

Buxton, M. E., Smith, D. E., & Seymour, R. B. (1987). Spirituality and other points of resistance to the 12-step recovery process. *Journal of Psychoactive Drugs*, 19(3), 275–286.

Chappel, J. N. (1993). Long-term recovery from alcoholism. *Psychiatric Clinics of North America*, 16(1), 177–187.

Chappel, J. N. (1992). Effective use of Alcoholics Anonymous and Narcotics Anonymous in treating patients. *Psychiatric Annals*, *22*(6), 409–418.

Christopher, J. (1989). *How to stay sober: Recovery without religion*. Buffalo, N.Y.: Prometheus.

Clinebell, H. J., Jr. (1985). *Understanding and counseling the alcoholic: Through religion and psychology* (revised edition). Nashville: Abingdon.

Clinebell, H. J., Jr. (1963). Philosophical-religious factors in the etiology and treatment of alcoholism. *Quarterly Journal of Studies on Alcohol*, 24, 473–488.

Clinebell, H.J., Jr. (1954). Some religious approaches to the problem of alcoholism. *Dissertation Abstracts International*, 14/08, 1266. [University Microfilms No. 00–08634].

Cloninger, C.R. (1987). Neurogenetic adaptive mechanisms in alcoholism. *Science*, 236, 410–416.

Collins, B.G. (1993). Reconstruing codependency using self-in-relation theory: A feminist perspective. *Social Work*, 38(4), 470–476.

Cook, C. C. H. (1988a, June). The Minnesota Model in the management of drug and alcohol dependency: Miracle, method or myth? Part I. The Philosophy and the programme. *British Journal of Addiction*, 83, 625–634.

Darrah, M. (1992). *Sister Ignatia: Angel of Alcoholics Anonymous*. Chicago, Ill: Loyola University.

Davis, D. I., Berenson, D., Steinglass, P. and Davis, S. (1974). The adaptive consequences of drinking. *Psychiatry*, 37, 209–215.

DiChiara, G. and Imperato, A. (1988). Drugs abused by humans preferentially increase synaptic dopamine concentrations in the mesolimbic system of freely moving rats. *Proceedings of the National Academy of Science, USA*, 85 (14), 5274–5278.

Drew, L. R. H. (1986). Beyond the disease concept of addiction: Drug use as a way of life leading to predicaments. *Journal of Drug Issues*, 16(2), 263–274.

Edwards, G. (1984). Drinking in longitudinal perspective: Career and natural history. *British Journal of Addiction*, 79, 175–183.

Ellis, A. (1985). Why Alcoholics Anonymous is probably doing itself and alcoholics more harm than good by its insistence on a higher power [Review of *Alcoholics Anonymous, 3rd ed.*]. *Employee Assistance Quarterly*, 1(1), 95–97.

Ellis, A. and Schoenfeld, E. (1990). Divine intervention and the treatment of chemical dependency. *Journal of Substance Abuse Treatment*, 2, 459–468.

Gellman, I. P. (1964). *The sober alcoholic: An organizational analysis of Alcoholics Anonymous*. New Haven: College University Press Services, Inc.

Gitlow, S. E. (1973). Alcoholism: A disease. In P. B. Bourne and R. Fox (Eds.), *Alcoholism: Progress in Research and Treatment*. New York: Academic Press.

Goodwin, D. W. (1988). *Is alcoholism hereditary?* (revised edition). New York: Ballantine.

Goodwin, D. W. (1985). Genetic determinants of alcoholism. In J. H. Mendelson and N. K. Mello (Eds.), *The diagnosis and treatment of alcoholism, Second edition* (pp.65–87). New York: McGraw Hill.

Goodwin, D.W., Schulsinger, F., Hermansen, L., Guze, S. B. and Winokur, G. (1973). Alcohol problems in adoptees raised apart from alcoholic biological parents. *Archives of General Psychiatry*, 28, 238–243.

Gorski, T. (1986). Relapse prevention planning: A new recovery tool. *Alcohol Health and Research World*, 11(1), 6–11.

Hall, H. A. (1984). The role of faith in the process of recovering from alcoholism. *Dissertation Abstracts International*, 45, 3369A. [University Microfilms No. 85–00721].

Heath, D.B. (1990). Cultural factors in the choice of drugs. In M. Galanter (Ed.), *Recent developments in alcoholism*, volume 8 (pp.245-254). New York: Plenum.

Heath, D. B. (1989a). The new temperance movement: Through the looking glass. In E.S.L. Gomberg (Ed.), *Current issues in alcohol/drug studies* (pp.143–168). New York: Haworth.

Heath, D. B. (1989b). Environmental factors in alcohol use and its outcomes. In H. W. Goedde and D. P. Agarwal (Eds.), *Alcoholism: Biomedical and genetic aspects* (pp. 312–324). New York: Pergamon.

Heath, D. B. (1986). Drinking and drunkenness in transcultural perspective: An overview. *Transcultural Psychiatric Research Review*, 21, 7–42, 103–126.

Hennessey-Heine, B. (1995). The sober alcoholic woman: A portrait. *Dissertation Abstracts International*. [University Microfilms No. 9536781].

Hewitt, T. F. (1980). *A biblical perspective on the use and abuse of alcohol and other drugs*. Pastoral Care Council on Alcohol and Drug Abuse, North Carolina Department of Human Resources. Available from: North Carolina Council on Alcoholism, P.O. Bos 6007, Greenville, N.C. 27834.

Jackson, J.K. (1954). The adjustment of the family to the crisis of alcoholism. *Quarterly Journal of Studies on Alcohol*, 15, 562–586.

Jellinek, E. M. (1960). *The disease concept of alcoholism*. Highland Park, NJ: Hillhouse Press.

Jellinek, E. M. (1947). Recent trends in alcoholism and in alcohol consumption. *Quarterly Journal of Studies on Alcohol*, 8(1), 1–42.

Joachim, K. (1988). *Spirituality and chemical dependency: Guidelines for treatment*. Oxford, Mich. The Oxford Institute.

Johnson, B.H. (1973). The alcoholism movement in America: A study in cultural innovation. *Dissertation Abstracts International*, 34(9a). [University Microfilms No.74–05603].

Joint Commission on Accreditation of Healthcare Organizations. (1989). *Consolidated standards manual*. Chicago, Ill.: Joint Commission.

Kasl, C. (1992). *Women, sex and addiction: A search for love and power*. New York: HarperCollins.

Keller, M. (1990). *Models of alcoholism: From days of old to nowadays*. [Pamphlet Series]. New Brunswick, N.J.: Center of Alcohol Studies, Rutgers University.

Keller, M. (1975). Multidisciplinary perspectives on alcoholism and the need for integration: An historical and prospective note. *Journal of Studies on Alcohol*, 36(1), 133–147.

Khantzian, E. J. (1986). A contemporary psychodynamic approach to drug abuse treatment. *American Journal of Drug and Alcohol Abuse*, 12(3), 213–222.

Khantzian, E .J. and Mack, J. E. (1989). Alcoholics Anonymous and contemporary psychodynamic theory. In M. Galanter (Ed.), *Recent Developments in Alcoholism,* volume 7 (pp. 67–89). Plenum Press.

Khantzian, E. J., Halliday, K. S. and McAuliffe, W. E. (1990). *Addiction and the vulnerable self: Modified dynamic group therapy for substance abusers*. New York: Guilford.

King, E. and Castelli, J. (1995). *Culture of recovery, culture of denial: Alcoholism among men and women religious*. Washington, D.C.: Center for Applied Research in the Apostolate at Georgetown University [CARA].

Kubicek, K. (1998). Self-defined attributes of success: A phenomenological study of long-term recovering alcoholics. *Dissertation Abstracts International.* [University Microfilms No.].

Kurtz, E. (1991). The twelve-step approach to spirituality. *The Addiction Letter,* 7(8), 1–2.

Kurtz, E. (1986, June). Origins of A.A. spirituality. *Blue Book*, 38, 35–42.

Kurtz, E. (1982). Why A.A. works—The intellectual significance of Alcoholics Anonymous. *Journal of Studies on Alcohol*, 43, 38–80.

Kurtz, E. (1979). *Not-god: A history of Alcoholics Anonymous*. Center City, Minn. Hazelden Educational Materials.

Larsen, E. (1985). *Stage II recovery: Life beyond addiction*. San Francisco: Harper & Row.

Lazarus, A. A. (1981). *The practice of multimodal therapy*. New York: McGraw-Hill.

Lazarus, A. A. (1976). *Multimodal behavior therapy*. New York: Springer.

Leach, B. and Norris, J. L. (1977). Factors in the development of Alcoholics Anonymous. In B. Kissin and H. Begleiter (Eds.), *The biology of alcoholism,* volume 5: *Treatment and rehabilitation of the chronic alcoholic* (pp. 441–543). New York: Plenum Press.

Levine, H. G. (1978). The discovery of addiction: Changing conceptions of habitual drunkenness in America. *Journal of Studies on Alcohol*, 39(1), 143–174.

Liepman, M. R., Silvia, L. Y. and Nirenberg, T. D. (1989). The use of family behavior loop mapping for substance abuse. *Family Relations*, 38, 282–287.

Ludwig, A. M. (1988). *Understanding the alcoholic's mind: The nature of craving and how to control it*. New York: Oxford University Press.

Ludwig, A. M. (1985). Cognitive processes associated with "spontaneous" recovery from alcoholism. *Journal of Studies on Alcohol*, 46(1), 53–58.

Mack, J. E. (1981). Alcoholism, AA and the governance of the self. In M. H. Bean and N. E. Zinberg (Eds.), *Dynamic approaches to the understanding and treatment of alcoholism* (pp. 128–162). New York: Free Press.

Marlatt, G. A. and Gordon, J. R. (1980). Determinants of relapse: Implications for the maintenance of behavior change. In P. Davidson (Ed.), *Behavioral medicine: Changing health lifestyles* (pp.410–452). New York: Brunner/Mazel.

Maxwell, M. A. (1984). *The Alcoholics Anonymous experience*. New York: McGraw-Hill.

May, G.A. (1988). *Addiction and grace: Love and spirituality in the healing of addictions*. San Francisco: Harper Collins.

Mercadante, L. (1996). *Victims and sinners: Spiritual roots of addiction and recovery*. Louisville, Ky: Westminster John Knox.

Milkman, H. and Frosch, W. (1977). The user's drug of choice. *Journal of Psychedelic Drugs*, 9(1), 11–24.

Milkman, H. and Sunderwirth, S. (1987). *Craving for ecstasy: The consciousness and chemistry of escape*. Lexington, Mass.: D.C. Heath.

Miller, W. R. (1998). Researching the spiritual dimensions of alcohol and other drug problems. *Addiction*, 93(7), 971–982.

Miller, W. R. (1997). Spiritual aspects of addictions treatment and research. *Mind/Body Medicine*, 2(1), 37-43.

Moberg, D. O. (1986). Spirituality and science: The progress, problems, and promise of scientific research on spiritual well-being. *Journal of the American Scientific Affiliation*, 38(3), 186–194.

Moberg, D. O. (1971). *Spiritual well-being: Background and issues*. Washington, D.C.: White House Conference on Aging.

Moberg, D. O. and Brusek, P. M. (1978). Spiritual well-being: A neglected subject in quality of life research. *Social Indicators Research*, 5, 303–323.

Moos, R. H. (1994). What I would most like to know: Why do some people recover from alcohol dependence, whereas others continue to drink and become worse over time? *Addiction*, 89, 31–34.

Morgan, O. J. (*in press, a*). Practical theology, alcohol abuse and alcoholism: Methodological and biblical considerations. *Journal of Ministry in Addiction and Recovery*.

Morgan, O. J. (*in press, b*). "Chemical comforting" and the theology of John C. Ford, S.J.: Classic answers to a contemporary problem. *Journal of Ministry in Addiction and Recovery*.

Morgan, O. J. (1995). Extended length of sobriety: The missing variable. *Alcoholism Treatment Quarterly*, 12(1), 59–71.

Morgan, O. J. (1992). In a sober voice: A psychological study of long-term alcoholic recovery with attention to spiritual dimensions. *Dissertation Abstracts International*, 52 (11), 6069–B. [University Microfilms No. 92–10480].

Musto, D. F. (1987). *The American disease: Origins of narcotic control.* (revised edition). New York: Oxford University Press.

Nace, E. P. (1987). *The treatment of alcoholism.* New York: Brunner/Mazel.

National Institute for Healthcare Research (1997). *Scientific Research on spirituality and health: A consensus report.* Washington, D.C.: NIHR.

O'Farrell, T. J. (1993). *Treating alcohol problems: Marital and family interventions.* New York: Guilford.

Prochaska, J. O., Norcross, J. C. and DiClemente, C. C. (1994). *Changing for good.* New York: Williams Morrow.

Prochaska, J.O., DiClemente, C.C. and Norcross, J.C. (1992, September). In search of how people change: Applications to addictive behaviors. *American Psychologist*, pp.1102–1114.

Raistrick, D. (1991). Career and natural history. In I. B. Glass (Ed.), *The international handbook of addiction behaviour,* (pp. 34–40.

Robertson, N. (1988). *Getting better: Inside Alcoholics Anonymous.* New York: William Morrow and Company.

Roessler, S. J. (1982). The role of spiritual values in the recovery of alcoholics. *American Doctoral Dissertations*(1981–1982), 406.

Royce, J. E. (1981). *Alcohol problems and alcoholism: A comprehensive survey.* New York: Free Press.

Royce, J. E. and Scratchley, D. (1996). *Alcoholism and other problems.* New York: Free Press.

Rudy, D. R. (1986). *Becoming alcoholic: Alcoholics Anonymous and the reality of alcoholism.* Carbondale and Edwardsville, Ill.: Southern Illinois University Press.

Schneiders, S. M. (1986). Theology and spirituality: Strangers, rivals, or partners? *Horizons*, 13(2), 253–274.

Schneiders, S. M. (1990). Spirituality in the academy. In B.C. Hanson (Ed.), *Modern Christian spirituality: Methodolgical and historical essays* (pp.15–37). Atlanta: Scholars Press.

Schuckit, M. A. (1989). *Drug and alcohol abuse: A clinical guide to diagnosis and treatment, third edition.* New York: Plenum.

Schuckit, M. A. (1983). Alcoholic men with no alcoholic first-degree relative. *American Journal of Psychiatry*, 140, 439–443.

Shaffer, H. J. and Jones, S. B. (1989). *Quitting cocaine: The struggle against impulse.* Lexington, Mass.: Lexington.

Sheldrake, P. F. (1996, Summer). The crisis of postmodernity. *Christian Spirituality Bulletin*, 4(1), 6–10.

Siegler, M., Osmond, H., & Newell, S. (1968). Models of alcoholism. *Quarterly Journal of Studies on Alcohol, 29*, 571–591.

Silvia, L. Y. and Liepman, M. R. (1991). Family behavior loop mapping enhances treatment of alcoholism. *Family and Community Health, 13*(4), 72–83.

Sommer, S. M. (1992). A way of life: Long-term recovery in Alcoholics Anonymous. *Dissertation Abstracts International, 53*(7), 3795B. [University Microfilms No.9236722].

Spicer, J. (1993). *The Minnesota Model: Evolution of the multidisciplinary approach to addiction recovery*. Center City, Minn.: Hazelden Educational Materials.

Stanton, M. D., Todd, T. C., Heard, D. B., Kirschner, S., Kleiman, J. I., Mowatt, D. T., Riley, P., Scott, S. M. and Van Deusen, M. M. (1982). A conceptual model. In M. D. Stanton, T. C. Todd and Associates. *The family therapy of drug abuse and addiction* (pp.7–30). New York: Guilford Press.

Steinglass, P., Bennett, L. A., Wolin, S. J. and Reiss, D. (1987). *The alcoholic family*. New York: Basic Books.

Stevens-Smith, P. and Smith, R. L. (1998). *Substance abuse counseling: Theory and practice*. Upper Saddle River, N.J.: Prentice Hall.

Sunderwirth, S. (1985). Biological mechanisms: Neurotransmission and addiction. In H. Milkman and H. Shaffer (Eds.), *Addictions: Multidisciplinary perspectives and treatments* (pp. 11–19). Lexington, Mass: Lexington Books.

Svendsen, R. and Griffin, T. (1991). *Alcohol and other drugs: A planning guide for congregations*. St. Paul, Minn: Health Promotion Resources.

Tasman, A., Hales, R. E. and Frances, A.J. (Eds.) (1989). *Review of psychiatry, vol. 8*. Washington, D.C.: American Psychiatric Press.

Tiebout, H. M. (1961). Alcoholics Anonymous—An experiment in nature. *Quarterly Journal of Studies on Alcohol*, 22, 52–68.

Tiebout, H. M. (1954). The ego factors in surrender in alcoholism. Center City, Minn: Hazelden Educational Materials. [Reprinted from *Quarterly Journal of Studies on Alcohol*, 15, 610–621.

Tiebout, H. M. (1953). Surrender versus compliance in therapy with special reference to alcoholism. Center City, Minn.: Hazelden Educational Materials. [Reprinted from *Quarterly Journal of Studies on Alcohol, 14*, 58–68].

Tiebout, H. M. (1949). The act of surrender in the therapeutic process with special reference to alcoholism. *Quarterly Journal of Studies on Alcohol*, 10, 48–58.

Tiebout, H. M. (1946). Psychology and treatment of alcoholism. *Quarterly Journal of Studies on Alcohol, 7*, 214–227.

Tiebout, H. M. (1944). Therapeutic mechanisms of Alcoholics Anonymous. *American Journal of Psychiatry, 100*, 468–473.

Treadway, D. C. (1989). *Before it's too late: Working with substance abuse in the family*. New York: W. W. Norton.

Tucker, M. B. (1985). U.S. ethnic minorities and drug abuse: An assessment of the science and practice. *International Journal of Addiction, 20*, 1021–47.

Turner, C. (1993). Spiritual experiences of recovering alcoholics. *Dissertation Abstracts International, 56*(3), 1128A. [University Microfilms No.9521866].

Vaillant, G. E. (1996). A long-term follow-up of male alcohol abuse. *Archives of General Psychiatry*, 53, 243–49.

Vaillant, G. E. (1995). *The natural history of alcoholism revisited*. Cambridge, Mass.: Harvard University Press.

Vaillant, G.E. (1988). What can long-term follow-up teach us about relapse and prevention of relapse in addiction? *British Journal of Addiction, 83*, 1147–57.

Vaillant, G. E. (1983). *The natural history of alcoholism*. Cambridge, MA: Harvard University Press.

Vaillant, G.E. (1980). The doctor's dilemma. In G. Edwards & M. Grant (Eds.), *Alcoholism treatment in transition* (pp. 13–31). Baltimore: University Park Press.

Vaillant, G. E. & Milofsky, E. S. (1982). Natural history of male alcoholism: Four paths to recovery. *Archives of General Psychiatry, 39*, 127–133.

Wegscheider-Cruse, S. (1989). *Another chance: Hope and health for the alcoholic family, second edition*. Palo Alto: Science and Behavior Books.

Westermeyer, J. (1997). Native Americans, Asians and New Immigrants. In J.H. Lowinson, P. Ruiz, R. B. Millman, J. G. Langrod (Eds.), *Substance abuse: A comprehensive textbook*, 3rd edition, (pp.712–16). Baltimore: Williams and Wilkins.

Whitfield, C. L. (1985). *Alcoholism, attachments and spirituality: A transpersonal approach.* East Rutherford, N.J.: Thomas Perrin.

Woodruff, C. R. (1968). *Alcoholism and Christian experience*. Philadelphia: Westminster.

Zinberg, N. E. and Bean, M. H. (1981). Introduction: Alcohol use, alcoholism, and the problems of treatment. In M. H.Bean & N. E. Zinberg (Eds.), *Dynamic approaches to the understanding and treatment of alcoholism* (pp.1–35). New York: Free Press.

Part Two

Clinical Views

CHAPTER 2

Substance Use Disorders as a Symptom of a Spiritual Disease[1]

Harold E. Doweiko

> In truth, wantonness itself has many names, as it has many branches or forms, and when one of these forms is conspicuously present in a man it makes that man bear its name, a name that it is no credit or distinction to possess...if desire has achieved domination in the matter of drink, it is plain what term we shall apply to its subject who is led down that path, and no less plain what are the appropriate names in the case of other such persons and of other such desires. *Phaedrus*, Plato *(translated by Hackforth, 1989, p. 493)*

As Plato suggests, the excessive use of a substance is hardly a problem unique to the United States on the brink of the twenty-first century. However, chemical abuse is a social problem that extracts a terrible toll on both the afflicted individual and upon society. For example, it is estimated that alcohol use/abuse alone costs every man, woman, and child in the United States $600 each year (Kaplan, Sadock, and Grebb,1994).

Further, in terms of direct mortality, the abuse of illegal recreational drugs is thought to result in between 25,000 (Office of National Drug Control Policy, 1996) to 30,000 (Samet, Rollnick, and Barnes, 1996) premature deaths in the United States each year. These deaths are in addition to the estimated 100,000 (Lieber, 1995) to 200,000 (Hyman and Cassem, 1995)

[1] This chapter is dedicated, with love, to the memory of Jeanette M. ("Jan") Doweiko.

premature deaths caused in the United States each year by alcohol abuse.[2] Yet these figures, as frightening as they are, still do not reflect the *indirect* suffering in terms of broken families, children who suffer emotional and/or physical abuse, spousal abuse, or the number of direct and indirect substance-related suicides.

Society's response has been to declare "war" on the problem of chemical abuse/addiction. A part of the response to this call to arms has been the search by medical science to understand the causes of substance use problems. Further, society has invested billions of dollars in efforts to interdict sources of illicit chemicals, and to punish those who might traffic in these materials. Finally, there have been significant efforts to treat those who are abusing or addicted to chemicals with the latest weapons that medicine can offer. Unfortunately, in waging this battle, the one school of thought that offers the most insight into the evolution of and treatment for the problem of recreational substance abuse is virtually ignored by society. This is the view that alcohol and other drug use problems are a disease of the human spirit, or soul.

That society would ignore this perspective is not surprising, since issues surrounding the concept of spiritual growth, or spirituality, are to a large degree ignored in the Western world (Moore, 1996). But, in ignoring the spiritual component to the addictive disorders, medical practitioners overlook the fact that the addictive disorders have physical, emotional, *and* spiritual components (Doweiko, 1996; Martin, 1990).

Collectively, the substance use disorders might be viewed not as a traditional "disease," but as a form of spiritual insanity. Proponents argue loudly, and at length, that the various forms of chemical abuse are disease states, and point to similarities to such disorders as cardiovascular or genetic diseases. Yet proponents of the "disease model" overlook one glaring fact: Unlike any other disorder other than suicide, alcohol and other drug addiction is a "disease" that requires the active participation by the "victim" of the disorder (Doweiko, 1996). Thus, to understand and treat the problem of alcohol or other drug misuse, it is necessary to understand how substance use disorders can be manifestations of a disorder of the human spirit.

How the Soul Was Lost

There once was a time when the exploration of the "self," questions surrounding the meaning of life, or the role of experience in the growth of the individual spirit, occupied the best minds of the age. But as society stands on the brink of the twenty-first century, where many seek spiritual insights (Jacobson, 1995), issues pertaining to the study of the human spirit, or soul, have come to be all but ignored by large segments of society. There

[2] Although adults might legally purchase tobacco products in this country, they are thought to be the cause of 450,000 additional premature deaths each year in the United States alone (Hilts, 1994).

are many reasons for this drift away from the spiritual. Many who follow the quest for instant gratification view the need to make an individual commitment to the lifelong development of any aspect of the "self" as unnecessary, unrewarding, or perhaps most ruinous of all, pointless. Others have found that the spiritual world has become so elusive that it can be understood not as a way of life, but only as an intellectual abstraction (Moore, 1997). Many, drawing upon the insights and resources of modern science, demand not the theoretical possibilities of spiritual growth, but the concrete strength of scientific certainty (Kaiser, 1996). For far too many, the mandates of day-to-day survival preclude the possibility of making a personal commitment to spiritual growth.

Further, the quest for the modern, the trendy, or the sophisticated has resulted in earlier generations being viewed as less intelligent and naive. This misperception contributes to the tendency to dismiss lessons learned by our forefathers as being simplistic or unrealistic. The truth of the matter, however, is that earlier generations were not less *intelligent* than we are today. They only lacked the information and technology that surround us in the present world (Freedman, 1992). If earlier generations invested so much time and energy into an investigation of spirituality, perhaps it was because this matter was of vital importance to them. It is suggested here that, in dismissing the lessons of the past, those who place so much emphasis on the Modern are doomed to have to rediscover the importance of the human spirit.

Ancient philosophers concluded that the human animal is, somehow, unique on the face of the Earth. Each individual seemed to possess a special gift from the gods, a divine spark of life which could neither be measured nor replicated, but which seemed to define the individual's existence. Once this spark is extinguished, life ceases. In Latin, this divine gift was called *Spiritus,* from which the English words "spirit" and "spiritual" have evolved.

One aspect of *Spiritus* is that the individual becomes aware of his or her existence, of "self-hood." Unfortunately, the intangible element that allows the individual "self" to be aware of personal existence, what might be termed the individual's "soul," is as mysterious as the experience of life itself (Moore, 1996; Jacobson, 1995). Because this soul cannot be measured or quantified, verification of its existence by modern science is impossible. The emphasis by science on external verification results in a fundamental dilemma when it comes to exploring personal truth(s). Matters of the spirit or soul must be *experienced,* but they cannot be adequately expressed in words alone (Jacobson, 1995; Martin, 1990).

The Modern has lost touch with the basic mysteries of life. For example, it has long been recognized that while an artist could produce a statue of stone that is exceptionally lifelike, she or he can:

> put into it neither entrails nor bowels, nor can he [*sic*] endow it with a soul; yet the Holy One creates not only the human body but

> also its internal organs, and puts into it also breath and spirit. (quoted in Feinsilver, 1980, p. 19)

In this ancient text of the Talmud, one encounters not only the admission of the existence of *Spiritus,* but also the acceptance of a Higher Being, who bestows upon the individual the spark of life that makes him or her alive. Indeed, it can be argued that the human spirit/soul is the central manifestation of individual existence (Jacobson, 1995; Kurtz and Ketcham, 1992; Martin, 1990). By implication, spirituality might be viewed as the living expression of the relationship between the individual and the Higher Power (Jacobson, 1995).

The importance of a Higher Power will be discussed in a later section of this chapter. The point being made here is that those who have examined the problem of recreational chemical abuse as a disease of the spirit have gained a perspective on substance abuse that science has failed to recognize. In a very real sense, the "scientific" method of addressing the problem of recreational substance use/abuse has focused on the identification of the causal agent(s) that result in the individual's coming to misuse alcohol and other drugs. In other words, the scientific explanation has focused on the physical and the emotional components of recreational drug abuse. This is a *prospective* point of view, in the sense that scientists are attempting to establish an equation that would predict that

> if such-and-such a condition exists, then this individual will have 'Y' percentage risk of becoming addicted to alcohol or other drugs.

To this end, scientists have conducted extensive probes into the genetics of alcohol and other drug abuse, the dynamics of those families where there is a substance abusing member, and so on. The utility of this approach is open to question, especially in light of the fact that modern medicine has yet to prove unequivocally that the alcohol and other drug use disorders are really "diseases" (Kaiser, 1996).

Of Self-awareness and Discontent

Ancient scholars suggested that humankind acquired *Spiritus* within the Garden of Eden. Many modern philosophers believe that the story of the Garden of Eden, as related in the Bible, might refer not to the physical act of Adam's taking a bite from the fruit of the Tree of Knowledge, but to the development of self-awareness (Fromm, 1956). However, few people seem to appreciate the value of self-awareness. Rather than accept the gift of "selfhood," many humans grumble about their lot in life. They are, in a word, *discontent* with their awareness of "self."

Within the definition of humanness is the painful, often crippling sense that the individual is *incomplete* in some manner (Jacobson, 1995). This is unavoidable, for one consequence of the awareness of "self" is the knowledge that the individual is also separate from Nature. In becoming a self-aware individual, each person loses the mindless anonymity of being just a part of the animal kingdom, and gains the great and terrible knowledge that s/he is separate from his or her fellows (Fromm, 1965; 1956).

It is not entirely clear whether this was a side-effect of the Fruit, or, the intended effect. In either case, in contrast to the other members of the animal kingdom, the human animal

> is the only discontented creation of God, and no doubt God intended to make him so. In the human breast there has been implanted what has rightly been called a 'divine discontent.' (Lefkowitz, 1966, p. 199)

One might argue that the divine discontent implanted within each individual is the force that drives the human animal to become more than just a member of the animal kingdom. To be human is to be aware of isolation, of separation from one's fellows. To combat this sense of isolation, the individual seeks a sense of *belonging* or *connectedness* (Kurtz and Ketcham, 1992). The individual seeks to connect to some thing greater than the self, be it to nature as a whole, a family, a social group, or a specific religion (Fromm, 1965). This sense of belonging brings with it an advantage, for through this connectedness the individual gains

> security. He [*sic*] belongs to, he is rooted in, a structuralized whole in which he has an unquestionable place. He may suffer from hunger or suppression, but he does not suffer from the worst of all pains—complete aloneness and doubt. (Fromm, 1965, p. 51)

Thus, part of the human experience is that of a sense of being less than whole, a feeling of isolation that is so strong that it prompts the individual to seek a remedy. For many, the solution to this problem is to belong to something greater than the "self." However, as will be discussed later in this chapter, others turn to a chemical solution to this problem.

The Pain of Being Human

In addition to this basic sense of isolation and incompleteness that each individual must struggle with simply because s/he is human, the daily experiences of living conspire to shatter the individual's spirit in a thousand-and-one different ways. The ultimate outcome of this sustained assault is that the individual learns one of the harshest of lessons of being human: Namely, that to be alive means that one must know pain. Life *is* pain, according to an ancient Buddhist proverb. The ancient Hebrews came to believe that pain was an essential part of life, for *not to have pain* they believed, *is not to have been human.* In taking the bite of the fruit of the Tree of Knowledge, Adam might be said to have admitted the awareness of individual pain, and of personal suffering, into Eden.

Pain results, in part, from the multiple assaults on the individual's sense of self-hood. These assaults begin early in life. Now, reasonable levels of pain might be said to be necessary for human growth. For example, it has been argued that for the first few months of life, the infant views him-or herself as being the center of the universe. However, with the passage of time, the infant begins to encounter an inevitable degree of frustration. The parents, no matter how well motivated to meet the child's needs, fail to do so at the instant the s/he makes those needs known. This externally imposed frustration, as well as interactions with significant others and the natural development of the infant's brain, forces upon the infant an awareness: (a) that s/he is not the center of the universe, and (b) that his/her control over the universe is a little less than perfect.

This process of revising his/her view of the relationship between the "self" and the universe is a natural consequence of the process of development. Erikson's (1980) theory of ego development, although not specifically addressing spiritual growth, does provide a framework within which to view spiritual growth. Each of the eight stages of growth identified by Erikson is initiated by a developmental challenge, which the individual must master, in order to proceed to the next phase of life.

The demands of each of these developmental stages impacts on the individual's sense of "self-hood" or spirit. For example, the first stage of ego development postulated by Erikson (1980) was that of *basic trust/mistrust.* In the healthy family unit, parents provide an atmosphere of stability, that is, a stable, supportive, *relatively predictable* environment, one that allows the infant to establish a sense of *basic trust* in the world (Erikson, 1980). It is in this stage that the individual's sense of basic connectedness with his/her fellows is established. While the infant is able to tolerate some degree of instability, s/he still requires that, within certain limits, caregivers be present and able to meet his or her needs.

It is this predictability and support that provides the infant with a framework of stability within which further psychosocial growth might take place. But, parental support is only relative; of necessity the infant will experience some degree of frustration and disillusionment. In a very real sense, the experience of frustration might be said to form part of the foundation of spiritual growth. The infant's unavoidable frustration helps to stimulate a growing awareness of personal existence as a separate part of the universe. At the same time, the infant's frustration when needs are not instantly met forces the child to interact with significant others in his or her environment. Developmentally, the child is faced with the task of reconciling frustration at not having the needs of "self" instantly met by significant others. The child must reach the point where s/he can appreciate that, in spite of their faults, the parents will provide a "good enough" place for continued growth.

An unfortunate reality of life is that the individual's spiritual identity, that is "soul," is assaulted a thousand times each day. For example, during Erikson's (1980) stage of ego growth identified as *industry/inferiority,* the child is involved in an educational system that seems at times to be designed to crush the spirit. Fulghum (1991) provides a painfully graphic example of how, without meaning to do so, the modern educational system crushes the child's faith in "self." Ask the child in the kindergarten class to do something, Fulghum (1991) suggests, be it sing, draw, or dance, and "Their answer is Yes! Over and over again, Yes!" (p. 226). But, by the time these same students reach high school or college, when asked the same question, only a very small percentage will raise their hands. "What went wrong between kindergarten and college? What happened to 'YES! of course I can'?" the author asks (p. 227).

Through this process, it becomes possible to understand how, if we all begin life with a sense of "hope, faith and fortitude" (Fromm, 1968, p. 20), these traits are challenged, perhaps crushed, over the course of the lifespan. The assorted insults of daily living join forces to bring about both disappointment and obstacles to the individual's sense of spiritual wholeness. It is the individual's loss of faith that is, perhaps, most damaging to his or her adjustment. With the loss of faith, of trust, the individual comes to feel an empty void within (Tillich, 1957).

Perhaps his or her history was such that the individual never had an opportunity to experience anything other than an empty void or, perhaps, whatever spark of selfhood that once existed was smothered by forces beyond the individual's ability to cope. But, with this pain comes a moment of ultimate disillusionment, an awareness of the limits of personal power, and the futility of life (Fromm, 1968). In that instant, the individual realizes that not only is the universe not very supportive, it is often cruel and apparently irrational. The individual discovers that to live is to continue to suffer pain. This revelation, although it offers the opportunity for spiritual growth, does so at the expense of possibly shattering the individual's sense of "self." No person's worldview emerges unscathed from this moment of ultimate awareness of one's place in the universe. Upon achieving this ultimate insight, the individual reaches a decision point: She or he may come to reduce his or her "demands to what they can get and do not dream of that which seems to be out of their reach" (Fromm, 1968, p. 21), or the individual might strive to force his or her will upon the universe.

Surmounting this developmental roadblock is a difficult task for the individual, and many fail to successfully come to terms with this ultimate disappointment. One possible outcome is that, rather than accept personal limitations, the person becomes a "spiritual narcissist." If the individual becomes unable to acknowledge the possibility of a Power greater than "self," s/he will have no reason to deny "self" whatever pleasures life might have to offer. In all too many cases, if something is not found to fill the empty heart and soul of the individual, s/he may very well choose to do so with alcohol or drugs (Stratton, 1996; Graham, 1988; Frankl, 1978).

Admittedly, the acceptance of life with all of its inherent uncertainty, pain, and frustration, is often quite hard. It is easy for the individual to feel overwhelmed by the accumulated pain and frustration of daily life. An extreme method of coping with this pain is found when the individual comes to believe that s/he has no other option than to choose when to commit suicide (Stratton, 1996). Although this chapter is not devoted to the topic of suicide, the reader must recognize that there is a relationship between spirituality, substance abuse, and suicide. Within this context, the use of recreational chemicals might be viewed as the individual's seeking a "mini" death experience, through which s/he might try to control, or briefly terminate, internal pain. This view is consistent with that of the early psychotherapist, Karen Horney (1964), who viewed alcohol abuse as an attempt to "narcotize" internal pain.

Human Search for Soul

It is not by coincidence that Viktor Frankl (1978) concluded that substance misuse might be a response to a loss of direction within the individual. Based on his observations of human nature in the concentration camps of Hitler's Germany of World War II, Frankl came to deduce that after basic needs are met, the human animal engages in "a search for meaning—a search whose futility seems to account for many of the ills of our age" (p.17). Further, Frankl (1978) concluded that, for all too many people, there was no obvious meaning for personal existence. Indeed, the lack of personal meaning might be viewed as "a mass neurosis," which might very well be one factor for the apparent increase in recreational substance abuse.

Being (however imperfectly) aware of his or her existence, the individual becomes free to define a meaning for that existence (Frankl, 1978). In other words, the first step was self-awareness, followed by a lifelong process of searching for a meaning for personal existence (Frankl, 1978, 1962). One of the forces by which the individual shapes a sense of purpose in Frankl's eyes was that of *choice.* Even in the concentration camps of Hitler's Germany during World War II, Frankl (1962) found that

> there were always choices to make. Every day, every hour, offered the opportunity to make a decision, a decision which determined whether you would or would not submit to those powers which threatened to rob you of your very self. (p. 65–66)

From this perspective, alcohol and other drugs might be viewed as one of the powers that threaten to rob the individual of his/her "self."

Also inherent in Frankl's (1962) discovery that individual choice helps to shape his or her experience was the ability to *find meaning in suffering.* This ability is one of the forces that then motivates the individual to proceed on a process of spiritual growth. For just as the individual does not remain static across the lifespan, so too must the spirit constantly evolve to help him or her find meaning and purpose in the present stage of life. As the individual ages, s/he discovers that the answers and definitions of one era of life frequently are insufficient for the demands and pressures of later phases (Levinson and Levinson 1996; Levinson, 1986; Levinson, Darrow, Klein, Levinson, and McKee, 1978).

In other words, the now-aware individual must define the nature of the relationship between "self" and the Universe. This is a lifelong task. For at the moment of birth, the human animal might be viewed as starting a spiritual journey that will last for the duration of his or her lifetime (Norris, 1996). During this journey, the individual will repeatedly attempt to answer questions about the nature of "self" and the relationship of "self" to the external universe. This relationship between "self" and the Universe is defined by the choices that the individual makes, including choices about significant relationships. If, as Buber (1970) suggested, it is through our relationships that we distinguish or provide depth to our existence, then the chemical abusing or dependent individual has in effect selected a shallow relationship with a nonfeeling chemical by which to define personal existence.

Lamentably, the healthy spiritual process of growth is not one that might be prepackaged or taught to the individual (Norris, 1996; May, 1988). It involves an internal process of growing awareness and change, through which the individual's spirit is transformed with the development of new insights. These insights involve a radical change in perspective, which for many leads them to include the possibility of a "Higher Power" of some kind. Such a Being is viewed not as a part of the Universe, but apart from it, possibly surrounding it, and probably as having created it, depending on the individual's view of creation. This Higher Power is viewed as being superior to the individual in all aspects, forcing the individual to learn to relate to this Higher Power as being separate from, and superior to, the individual "self".

In psychological terms, the individual might be viewed as forming a series of internal maps, or schemata, in which his or her beliefs about the interrelationship between "self" and the external universe are organized. Over the course of the individual's lifespan, these internal schemata must be revised, as new information forces the individual to reexamine essential concepts. The world is found to consist of more than just the back yard, or the immediate neighborhood, or one's city of birth. Geographic relocation as the parents move from one home to another; an addition to, or loss from, the family of origin; the child's own growing physical and emotional competence are but a few of the forces which will challenge him or her to revise the maps or perspectives on the relationship between "self" and the external world.

The need for a sense of basic trust in the universe around the individual is one that is never fully outgrown. Even as an adult, the individual needs "to hold on to something solid" (Murphy, 1996, p. 18). One of the functions of the Higher Power is to provide something "solid" for the individual to relate to during life's journey. Indeed, in a very real sense, the individual's Higher Power might be viewed as an anchor point for individual spiritual growth over the course of one's lifespan.

The individual's spiritual voyage is of necessity a subjective experience (Frankl, 1978). The individual must search for the answers that help to define his or her own life, goals, and meaning. Prepackaged answers based on another's experience(s) or belief(s) seldom are specific enough to meet the needs of another individual. Unfortunately, in modern society there is a trend for many to relegate subjective perceptions or experiences to a lower level of importance than those that can be confirmed by "scientific" methods (Kaiser, 1996). This trend contributes to the present state of affairs, in which the individual is left to struggle with the most important questions of life on his or her own. (The essay by Charlotte Kasl later in this volume addresses some of these issues from a feminist perpective.)

It is a paradox that one of the essential elements of spiritual growth, namely *doubt,* is at one and the same time a strength and a weakness. *Doubt* allows for the development of faith, which is to say, the expression of belief in the face of uncertainty (Tillich, 1957, 1952). But, the enigmatic nature of spiritual growth, its very reliance on doubt as a motivating force, makes it a difficult process for many people. In the face of such *doubt,* many individuals come to believe that there is nothing beyond the "self" (Tillich, 1952). Lacking the ability to transcend personal boundaries, to accept the possibility that there is something of importance beyond the "self," these individuals come to place few (if any) limits on self-satisifaction. The individual becomes locked into a pattern of what Tillich (1952) termed "total doubt" (p. 48), or what Frankl (1962) might term "despair."

In such cases, the individual's own resources prove insufficient for continued spiritual growth, and she or he loses faith. As Merton (1955) observed:

> If...I trust only in my own intelligence, my own strength, and my own prudence, the means that God has given me to find my way to Him will all fail me. Nothing created is of any ultimate use without hope. To place your trust in visible things is to live in despair. (p. 16)

It thus becomes apparent that doubt, despair, the realization of life's futility, and ultimate disillusionment, *without the promise of hope,* all combine to make the individual vulnerable to the temptations offered by anything that promises to ease suffering. In other words, the individual, having found little meaning in personal existence, searches for something that might offer a promise of some measure of peace. It is at this point that the individual might come to accept the concrete, but very real temptation of recreational drugs. For, although alcohol and other drugs do not promise to provide an answer to life's questions, they *do* offer a concrete, predictable promise to narcotize the pain of daily living.

Of Humility and Control

The individual's attempt to use chemicals to "narcotize" internal pain might best be viewed as that person's attempt to reject internal and/or external reality, and through the use of chemicals to force one's will on the Universe. In other words, the individual seeks not acceptance of what *is,* but "what I want, when I want it." If the truth be told, this is a choice that we all adopt, to a greater or lesser degree. Total humility is difficult. For example, the student who uses his or her "lucky" pencil to take an examination, in the hopes that s/he will earn a good grade, or the sports figure who reenacts a special ritual before each game, might be said to engage in a behavior through which s/he hopes to force his or her will upon the Universe.

These are minor examples of a lack of humility, which apply to virtually all of us. But in this process, when taken to its extreme, lie the roots of both personality disorders and substance abuse and addiction. For, although personality disorders lie outside of the scope of this paper, one characteristic they share is that the individual adopts a rigid method of coping that s/he hopes will minimize internal and external stress (Shapiro, 1981). In other words, the individual adopts a personality structure through which s/he seeks, if not to impose one's will on the external universe, at least to do so on the internal representation of reality known as the "mind." It is perhaps not by coincidence that alcohol (and the other drugs of abuse), provides an *illusion of total control* over the user's feelings (Brown, 1985). Because of this characteristic of the drugs of abuse, there appears to be a relationship between the personality disorders and individuals who abuse or are addicted to recreational chemicals.

The authors of the Narcotics Anonymous "Big Book" observed that the addictive use of chemicals rests on the triad of: (1) a compulsion to use the chemical(s) of choice, (2) an obsession with further chemical use, and (3) a total self-centeredness on the part of the individual using the chemical(s) (*Narcotics Anonymous,* 1982). Further, the authors of NA's "big book" suggest that the individual's psychological defenses will work against his or her recognizing, and accepting, that the chemical(s) had come to dominate the individual's life.

In a sense, the individual's initial choice to indulge in recreational chemical use reflects his or her decision to give in to the delusion that there is *nothing* as important as the desires of the "self". In so doing, the individual elects to follow a course of action in which one seeks to impose his or her will on the universe. The danger of this process is that

> pandering to delusions of self-importance weakens the true self, and diminishes our ability to distinguish desires from needs (Norris, 1996, pp. 14–15).

In this manner, the chemicals quietly wreak havoc on the individual by making him or her incapable of distinguishing between what s/he *desires* from what s/he *needs* (Merton, 1995). Given this fact, it should come as no surprise to learn that clinicians encounter drug/alcohol-dependent individuals time and time again who speak of *needing* the drug, as if their very lives depended upon their having continued access to it.

Two of the hallmark defenses of a person locked in the grips of a substance use problem are *denial* of the drug misuse and, as stated earlier in this chapter, a measure of *self-centeredness*. Honesty and humility were recognized as the best defenses against these aspects of the addictive process. While honesty in a recovery program is essential, the importance of humility cannot be stressed too vigorously, for humility is "the last refuge in which the self becomes impregnable" (Merton, 1996, p. 293). Yet, paradoxically, it is this last refuge of the soul that is offered as one of the most important resources in the individual's recovery from alcohol and other drug problems. To understand how this last refuge of the self might form the foundation of the individual's recovery from substance use problems, one must appreciate the nature of humility itself.

Humility is, if not *the* most misunderstood word in the English language, at least one of the least appreciated. Far too many people believe that to be humble is to overlook one's strengths, in favor of one's shortcomings. This is, in reality, a form of *false pride* as deadly as keeping the focus only on the individual's strengths. One aspect of true humility, as was noted earlier in the commentaries on the Talmud, involves accepting what one has earned through one's labor with honor (Feinsilver, 1980). The individual comes to express his or her potential for growth through an acceptance of, and the expression of, "self," which is the essence of humility.

By extension of this argument, it might also be said that one should accept with honor those feelings that we experience as a result of our interactions with both internal and external reality. The opposite of this is the use of chemicals to impose on the "self" an artificial feeling of acceptance, of pride (which involves a degree of self-pleasure), for an external reality that is judged to be unacceptable to the individual.

Psychotherapy as "Soul" Therapy

The abuse of recreational drugs might be viewed as a form of narcissism that is satisfied through the misuse of chemicals. Unfortunately, that branch of scientific healing that supposedly is able to address such narcissistic self-indulgence, psychotherapy, has a poor success rate when attempting to "cure" the addictive disorders. It is suggested here that the very nature of modern psychotherapy is such that it is incapable of dealing with the widespread problem of recreational drug abuse. For, in a very real sense, the practice of psychotherapy itself might be said to have lost (for want of a better word) its own "soul," or spirit.

Most certainly, medical science does not know how to deal with the patient's religious beliefs. For example, although it is common for the physician to inquire as to a patient's religion, one rarely asks that person what his or her religious faith means to the individual (Sims, 1994). Indeed, a discussion of personal religious experience is avoided in most medical or psychiatric consultations. In today's technological world, it is easy to forget that the original definition of psychiatry, and its step-child, psychology, was that of *soul therapy* (Lothane, 1996). Indeed, the Greek word for the soul, *psyche* is the root of the word "psychotherapy" (Moore, 1996). Such therapy is based on the assumption that the soul is what makes us human (Moore, 1996).

But, in the latter half of the twentieth century, the behavioral sciences have embraced biochemical explanations of the various forms of psychopathology. In so doing, the science of psychotherapy has moved away from the treatment of that which makes us unique, *Spiritus,* to the treatment of medical diseases of the mind. A reflection of this process might be seen in how the narrative poetry of psychoanalysis has, in most journals devoted to mental health topics, been replaced by technical, mechanical descriptions of how the modern therapist might treat these diseases of the mind.

This is not to discount the advances made by science in the past century. Most certainly, the fruits of this branch of the tree of knowledge have brought with it a multitude of advances, each of which has reduced the level of human suffering. Modern insights into the biochemical foundations of brain function have produced new avenues of treatment for a wide range of emotional disorders. Unfortunately, in the process, the patient as a unique human being seems to have been replaced by his/her abnormal brain function(s).

Yet as we stand on the brink of the twenty-first century, one must wonder if, in its headlong rush to embrace that which is "new" and "scientific," Western civilization has not managed to lose touch with its roots, perhaps its very soul. For example, as we start the next millennium, clinicians have noted with dismay that few children or adolescents have been taught the proverbs and legends that guided our forefathers for so many generations (Peck, 1993). A small, but possibly significant, reflection of this process has been the growing emphasis on immediate gratification, rather than the enjoyment of the fruits of one's own labors.

In ages past, one might spend years, perhaps an entire lifetime, earning status and searching for a personal meaning to life. In contrast to this process, the present generation flitters from one media-generated illusion to the next, seeking to find gratification through a mindless identification with current materialistic trends. Yet, as the Lakota Wisdomkeeper Mathew King observed, without spiritual power, the mindless pursuit of materialism can only result in destruction (Arden, 1994). In this sense, recreational substance abuse might be viewed as a prime example of materialism. Misuse provides an illusion of immediate gratification of the individual's desires, without the need to compromise with the demands of everyday reality. It thus should come as no surprise, as Frankl (1978) noted almost a generation ago, that recreational substance abuse was one of the emerging popular trends.

The Role of Spirituality in Recovery

The spiritual perspective of substance misuse evolved more than fifty years ago, when a group of individuals came together, in order to identify what seemed to help them in their struggle to abstain from their drug of choice: alcohol. These were the earliest members of the organization now known as Alcoholics Anonymous (AA). Their knowledge of the seductive powers of alcohol came not from dispassionate study of the phenomenon of addiction, but from their own struggle to abstain from strong drink. In coming together, they sought not to identify the "cause" of addiction, so much as what common factors assisted their recovery.

In their discussions, the earliest members of A.A. discovered that, as their addiction to alcohol evolved, each person had made a series of choices that, collectively, centered his/her life around the continued use of alcohol. Alcohol became the "axis" (Brown, 1985) around which the individual centered his or her life. The process of recovery, likewise required that the individual make a series of choices to center life around something other than the continued use of alcohol. Drawing upon the teachings of a then-popular religious movement known as the Oxford Group, the earliest members of AA came to see that in the place of the continued use of alcohol, she or he had to commit his/her life to the process of further spiritual growth.

Through this retrospective reconstruction of what had proven essential to their individual paths to recovery, the earliest members of AA found that to abstain from alcohol, a spiritual rebirth was necessary. Out of this reflective process emerged the Twelve Steps of the AA program. Thus, one of the most profound insights that emerged from the earliest of AA meetings was the rediscovery that humans are a spiritual beings. Further, the earliest members of AA concluded that

> it is in the spiritual part of the addict that the disease takes root...[it] begins as a spiritual deterioration and, if left unchecked, worsens and gradually invades the mind, the emotions, and eventually the body. (Martin, 1990, p. 16)

There were several key elements of the spiritual growth program that emerged from this retrospective analysis of their recovery. First, in response to the individual's discovery of how little actual power he/she has over the universe, the Twelve Step recovery program offers the individual not more power, but the opportunity to become *humble.* The early members of AA noticed that they had several personality characteristics in common. Perhaps one of the most important of these personality characteristics was a certain lack of humility, as evidenced by their tendency to live by the philosophy "I want what I want, when I want it!" The AA Twelve Step program offered in place of this self-centeredness a sequential series of steps through which she or he could learn humility. By learning humility, the individual acquires power over his or her addiction.

One of the grim realities of human existence is to feel pulled in a dozen different directions at once, to attempt to meet the demands of daily living with personal resources that are often inadequate or ineffective. The individual accepts the "self" as being imperfect, although capable of growth. In contrast to this self-acceptance, the person who is vulnerable to the compulsive use of chemicals often feels threatened by this aspect of reality. She or he develops a sense of *false pride* as a defense against what are perceived as overwhelming personal defects. The earliest members of AA concluded that one of the challenges of recovery was that the recovering individual must learn that this is normal, and that one has to accept the multitude of imperfections that lie at the very core of our existence if the journey to recovery is to continue. In other words, the individual needs to learn that to recover from alcohol/drug use problems, it is necessary to give up on the search for perfection. The individual needs to learn how to live with the various imperfections, the divisions, that lie within each person's soul (Kurtz and Ketcham, 1992).

These are tasks that are not unique only to recovering persons. However, the chemically dependent individual might be viewed as seeking a "shortcut" to spiritual wholeness through chemical means (Peck, 1993; Kurtz and Ketcham, 1992). As time passes, the user may discover that alcohol, and by extension the other drugs of abuse, only offer an *illusion* of control. (Martin, 1990; Brown, 1985). In such cases, the individual might seek help for his/her chemical use problem, or might renounce the use of chemicals. Unfortunately, part of the nature of the addictive disorders is an element of denial, which all too often prevents the individual from being able to see that the "control" that s/he seeks through the use of chemicals is only an illusion, not a true god-like ability to control internal and external reality.

To combat this illusion of control, it is necessary for the individual to establish a relationship between "self" and a Higher Power. This is not to say that one must embrace formal religion. Rather, the Higher Power is embodied in a God *as the individual understands God.* The concept of a Higher Power, which is not incorporated into formal religious doctrine is, perhaps, best reflected by the Lakota Wisdomkeeper Mathew King:

> You can call Wakan-Tanka by any name you like. In English I call Him God or the Great Spirit. He's the Great Mystery, the Great Mysterious. That's what Wakan-Tanka really means—the Great Mysterious. You can't define Him. He's not actually a "He" or a "She," a "Him" or a "Her." We have to use those kinds of words because you can't just say "It." God's never an "It." (Arden, 1994, pp. 4–5)

In the Twelve Step program, religious doctrine as such is not forced upon the individual. The person is introduced to the concept of *spirituality* as a pathway to healing the spirit. The very word "healing" is derived from the Old English word, *haelen*, which means "to make whole" (Stratton, 1996). In this manner, the individual is gradually introduced to a community of fellow sufferers who have also fallen into the trap of using chemicals as a shortcut to being made whole.

This is not to say that religion is forbidden within the recovering community. Adherence to a religious doctrine, and participation in that religion, offers some advantages, for religion

> anchors our values by relating them not to the capricious play of purely human valuations, but to an objective source. It anchors them in the will of God, as disclosed in the goal underlying all existence (Bokser, 1966, p. 196).

The point is that spiritual growth is possible not only within the confines of religion, but also within a *community* of individuals with similar needs, desires, and interests (Stratton, 1996; Kurtz and Ketcham, 1992). Although they frequently overlap, there is a very real difference between spirituality and formal religion (Kurtz and Ketcham, 1992; Martin, 1990). This explains why formal religion is not automatically necessary for the development of the sense of relationship to one's Higher Power central to the Twelve Step program.

However, religious values and beliefs offer one avenue through which to search for a sense of meaning in the journey of life (Rosenberg, 1966). It is during the process of assessment (discussed earlier in this chapter and in other chapters as well, e.g., Albers) that the therapist explores whether the individual client is a member of an established religion or not, and then takes steps either to work within the framework of that religion, or introduces the individual to a program of recovery that utilizes spirituality, without participation in a formal religion.

The earliest members of AA found that they *needed* to acknowledge the role of a Higher Power in their recovery from alcoholism. The act of submitting one's self to a Higher Power is to make one's self humble before that Spirit. For example, Ferdinand M. Isserman (1966), in speaking of prayer, noted that through this act, one becomes humble in the presence of God, and submits to that will. Through this process, the individual acknowledges his or her role in the universe as subordinate to that of a Higher Power, placing personal desires on "hold" while seeking first to understand, and then follow, the dictates of the Prime Mover. The Lakota Wisdomkeeper, Mathew King, concluded much the same thing, when he stated that while talking *to* God was useful, *listening* to God was equally important (Arden, 1994).

Although it is not discussed within the Twelve Step program, part of what the individual seeks in putting "self" into a relationship with a Higher

Power seems to be what Merton (1961) termed *salvation.* Through this experience, the "self" is

> ...drawn up like a jewel from the bottom of the sea, rescued from confusion, from indistinction, from immersion in the common, the nondescript, the trivial, the sordid. (Merton, 1961, p. 38).

In effect, the individual is freed from the dictates of his or her individual ego, in order to seek a communion with his or her Higher Power. In the process of seeking this relationship with God, the individual renounces those things over which s/he had no real power, no real control, including recreational chemicals. In the process of seeking this relationship, in following the program for spiritual growth devised by the earliest members of AA, the individual finds a meaning to his or her life: To carry the message of recovery to those who still are trapped within the grasp of recreational drugs.

Therapeutic Implications

The integration of spirituality into the rehabilitation of a person with a substance use disorder begins with the process of *assessing* both the individual's personality structure and his or her spiritual beliefs. The two are often deeply intertwined. For example, in the experience of the author, individuals with Antisocial Personality Disorder often have problems with issues surrounding the theme of *control,* and view spirituality from the perspective of being controlled by, or of finding a way to manipulate, what s/he perceives as a Higher Power. At the same time, individuals who have a Borderline Personality Disorder tend to view their Higher Power with suspicion, which reflects the "good parent/bad parent" conflict that is at the core of this personality pattern. All too often, for such an individual, the Higher Power is viewed as being harsh and punitive.

The second step is the process of *integrating* psychological insights into a program of recovery that fosters the individual's spiritual growth. This step is often facilitated by having the individual become involved in a Twelve Step program. After this step is accomplished, the content of therapeutic sessions will often alternate between periods of time devoted to a discussion of the client's ongoing problems in living and the development of spiritual insights within the clinical session. The therapist needs to determine, to the degree that this is possible, at which of Erikson's developmental levels the client is fixated, and then begin the process of helping the individual resolve that conflict. At the same time, the therapist must work to help the client develop the spiritual insights that will enable him/her to continue to abstain from substance abuse (see Morgan, 1996).

For example, it has been the author's experience, in working with individuals with a Dependent Personality Disorder (DPD), that these patients frequently have concerns that seem to reflect unresolved issues of *autonomy/shame and guilt.* Further, clients with DPD tend to have trouble understanding the difference between *concern* for another individual's feelings and *responsibility* for that person's emotions. Because of the internalized image of a harsh, judgmental Higher Power often found within these individuals, it is necessary to teach them (a) that anger is frequently an appropriate emotional response, and (b) that there are ways in which to appropriately express personal anger.

Ultimately, spiritual growth is best fostered within a community (Kurtz and Ketcham, 1992). Unfortunately, the individual with a substance use problem is frequently alienated from his or her fellows (Martin, 1990). Thus, within the therapeutic session, it is often necessary to explore the individual's sources of resistance to joining a Twelve Step group such as AA. Some individuals, especially those who fear interpersonal closeness (such as individuals with an Avoidant Personality Disorder), might hesitate to join a Twelve Step group because of a fear of rejection. Others, especially the personality types that are strongly self-centered (for example, the Histrionic Personality Disorder, Antisocial Personality, or Narcissistic Personality patterns) might avoid Twelve Step group involvement because they find that such groups do not allow them to meet their narcissistic need to be the center of attention.

The ultimate goal of psychotherapy, and a spirituality-based recovery program, is to foster the process of healing. To accomplish this goal, it is necessary for the person with a substance use disorder to continue his or her own spiritual growth. Healing can only be accomplished within a community, in which all of those involved are seeking the same spiritual goals (Kurtz and Ketcham, 1992). Thus, an essential part of the process of recovery for the individual is to introduce him or her to the concept of spiritual growth as the "axis" around which recovery must center.

Speculative Questions

The utilization of a spiritual perspective in the rehabilitation of individuals with substance use disorders is still in its infancy. There is still a great deal to learn about the role of spirituality in the treatment of alcohol and other drug abuse, and addiction. Some ongoing questions might include:

(1) What assessment instruments will offer the best insight(s) into the individual's personality and spiritual resources?

(2) Is it possible to address the client's spiritual growth in a neutral manner, that does not force the therapist's personal values upon the client?

(3) If this is possible, how should the therapist attempt to develop a therapeutic environment that both fosters spiritual growth and does not force his or her personal values on to the client?

(4) How should the therapist respond to issues such as individual autonomy, or the right to choose not to become involved in a self-help group?

(5) How should the therapist deal with issues of client resistance?

Summary

Although the disease model of alcohol and other drug addiction is quite popular, human service and medical professionals do not understand that, unlike other forms of "disease," the substance use disorders have a strong spiritual component. Individuals who abuse, or who are addicted to, alcohol and other drugs tend to use personality defenses rarely encountered by rehabilitation professionals who work with other forms of illness. They might be said to have a vested interest, not in their recovery, but in the continued use of their drug(s) of choice.

The process of recovery involves introducing the individual to a program of spiritual growth which will challenge his or her defense mechanisms, and through which the person can begin to move beyond the point where chemicals are needed to cope. The Twelve Step program has emerged as a way of recovery that offers the individual a step-by-step program for spiritual growth, based on the experiences of the earliest members of this self-help movement. However, the assessment of the individual's level of spiritual maturity, and the integration of spiritual growth techniques into traditional psychotherapy, are still both in their infancy. There remains a great deal to learn about how to assess the individual's spiritual growth, and how to foster his or her growth in this often overlooked realm of existence.

References

Arden, H. (1994). *Noble red man.* Hillsboro, Oreg.: Beyond Words Publishing, Inc.

Bokser, B. Z. (1966). *The eternal light.* New York: Harper & Row.

Brown, S. (1985). *Treating the alcoholic: A developmental model of recovery.* New York: John Wiley & Sons, Inc.

Buber, M. (1970). *I and thou.* New York: Charles Scribner's Sons.

Doweiko, H. E. (1996). *Concepts of chemical dependency (3rd ed).* Pacific Grove, Calif.: Brooks/Cole.

Erikson, E. (1980). *Identity and the life cycle.* New York: W. W. Norton & Co.

Feinsilver, A. (1980). *The Talmud for today.* New York: St. Martin's Press.

Frankl, V. E. (1978). *The unheard cry for meaning.* New York: Touchstone.

Frankl, V. E. (1962). *Man's search for meaning.* New York: Touchstone.

Freedman, D. X. (1992). The search: body, mind and human purpose. *American Journal of Psychiatry, 149,* 858–866.

Fromm, E. (1956). *The art of loving.* New York: Harper & Row.

Fromm, E. (1968). *The revolution of hope.* New York: Harper & Row.

Fromm, E. (1965). *Escape from freedom.* New York: Avon Books.

Fulghum, R. (1991). *Uh-oh.* New York: Villard Books.

Graham, B. (1988). The abuse of alcohol: Disease or disgrace? *Alcoholism & Addiction, 8* (4), 14-15.

Hackforth, R. (1989). Phaedrus (in) *Plato: The collected dialogues* (Hamilton, E., & Huntington, C., (eds). Princeton, N. J. : Princeton University Press.

Hilts, P. J. (1994). Labeling on cigarettes called a smoke screen. *St. Paul Pioneer Press, 146* (5), 1A, 6A.

Horney, K. (1964). *The neurotic personality of our time.* New York: W. W. Norton & Co.

Hyman, S. E., & Cassem, N. H. (1995). Alcoholism. *Scientific American Medicine.* (Rubenstein, E., & Federman, D. D., eds.). New York: Scientific American Press.

Isserman, F. M. (1966). *The eternal light.* New York: Harper & Row.

Jacobson, S. (1995). *Toward a meaningful life—The wisdom of the Rebbe Menachem Mendel Schneerson.* New York: William Morrow & Co., Inc.

Kaiser, D. (1996). Not by chemicals alone: a hard look at "psychiatric medicine." *Psychiatric Times, XIII* (12), 41–44.

Kaplan, H. I., Sadock, B. J., & Grebb, J. A. (1994). *Synopsis of psychiatry (7th ed).* Baltimore: Williams & Wilkins.

Kurtz, E. & Ketcham, K. (1992). *The spirituality of imperfection.* New York: Bantam Books.

Lefkowitz, D. (1966). *The eternal light.* New York: Harper & Row.

Levinson, D. J., Darrow, C. N., Klein, E. B., Levinson, M. H., & McKee, B. (1978). *The seasons of a man's life.* New York: Ballantine Books.

Levinson, D. J. (1986). A conception of adult development. *American Psychologist, 41*(1), 3–13.

Levinson, D. J., & Levinson, J. D. (1996). *The seasons of a woman's life.* New York: Knopf.

Lieber, C. S. (1995). Medical disorders of alcoholism. *The New England Journal of Medicine, 333,* 1058–1065.

Lothane, Z. (1996). Psychoanalytic method and the mischief of Freud-bashers. *Psychiatric Times, XIII* (12), 48–49.

Martin, J. A. (1990). *Blessed are the addicts.* New York: HarperCollins.

May, G. G. (1988). *Addiction and grace.* New York: Harper & Row.

Merton, T. (1955). *No man is an island.* New York: Harcourt Brace Jovanovich.

Merton, T. (1961). *New seeds of contemplation.* New York: New Directions Publishing.

Merton, T. (1995). *Run to the mountain: The journals of Thomas Merton (Vol. 1).* (Hart, P., ed.). New York: Harper Collins.

Merton, T. (1996). *Turning toward the world: The Journals of Thomas Merton (Vol 4).* (Kramer, V. A., ed). New York: HarperCollins.

Moore, T. (1996). *The education of the heart.* New York: HarperCollins.

Moore, T. (1997). Mystic clouds & natural spirituality. *Orion, 16* (3), 30–33.

Morgan, O. (1996). Recovery-sensitive counseling in the treatment of alcoholism. *Alcoholism Treatment Quarterly, 13*(4), 63–73.

Murphy, C. (1996). A few loose ends. *The Atlantic Monthly, 278* (6), 18–21.

Narcotics Anonymous. (1982). Van Nuys, Calif.: Narcotics Anonymous World Services Office, Inc.

Norris, K. (1996). *The cloister walk.* New York: Riverhead Books.

Office of National Drug Control Policy. (1996). *The National Drug Control Strategy: 1996.* Washington, D. C.: U.S. Government Printing Office.

Peck, M. S. (1993). *Further along the road less traveled.* New York: Simon & Schuster.

Peck, M. S. (1997). *The road less traveled & beyond.* New York: Simon & Schuster.

Rosenberg, S. E. (1966). *The eternal light.* New York: Harper & Row.

Samet, J. H., Rollnick, S., & Barnes, H. (1996). Beyond CAGE. *Archives of Internal Medicine, 156,* 2287-2293.

Schlesinger, G. N. (1994). Truth, humility and philosophers. In *God and the Philosophers* (Morris, T. V., ed.). New York: Oxford University Press.

Shapiro, D. (1981). *Autonomy and rigid character.* New York: Basic Books.

Sims, A. (1994). "'Psyche—spirit as well as mind.'" British Journal of Psychiatry, *165,* 441–446.

Stratton, E. K. (1996). *Touching spirit.* New York: Simon & Schuster.

Tillich, P. (1952). *The courage to be.* New Haven, Conn.: Yale University Press.

Tillich, P. (1957). *Dynamics of faith.* New York: Harper & Row.

CHAPTER THREE

Healing the Addictive Mind

Lee Jampolsky

As a psychologist working with addiction, as well as in my own life, I have found that addictive behavior is not limited to a reliance on alcohol or other drugs. It is my belief that addiction to chemical substances is a metaphor for our current human condition. The roots of addiction can be seen in our search for happiness in something outside of ourselves, be it drugs, relationships, or new shiny cars. As long as we are looking for happiness in the world, rather than in our own minds, and towards a connection with something larger than ourselves, we may be in the throes of addiction. While our minds are in the vicious cycle of addiction, peace of mind remains out of reach.

Because I believe that we are all prone to thinking addictively, and because I believe that the answer to our addictive thinking is within a personal spiritual journey, I have written this chapter with a personal tone. My hope is that the result of this will offer not only an academic understanding of the problem but also a compassionate and personal set of solutions. I believe that approaching the problems of addiction in our culture must include not only an intellectual framework, but also an awakening of what exists in the heart.

This chapter includes some vignettes. All names, identifying information, and other factors have been changed. Some stories are composite sketches. Any resemblance that you may find between the vignette and somebody that you know is purely coincidental.

The Relationship between Spirituality and Addiction

I have come to a place, both within my intellect and my heart, where it is difficult to consider addiction without also considering spirituality. One represents the state of "woundedness," despair, and yearning, while the other calls to wholeness and healing with a voice of hope, fulfillment, forgiveness, and compassion.

Addiction, as I will discuss in this chapter, is a human condition to which each and every one of us is heir. The good news is that there is also something within us that is directed to connectedness rather than to an empty and purposeless existence.

Most of us find ourselves walking through our lives experiencing only fragmented moments of peace of mind. We spend our lives thinking that the next accomplishment, relationship, drug, or dollar will bring us the happiness and contentment for which we long. We end up like hungry tigers chasing our tails, running in circles, and becoming more frustrated and ferocious with each step.

A basic approach to working with addictions and the utilization of spirituality

It is my belief that inner peace is a matter of choice, if only we know what the choices are and how to choose. The goal of my work is simple: It is to assist the individual in recognizing and listening to the presence of love which, I believe, is in us all.

I became involved in this field, and later wrote the book *Healing the addictive mind* (1991), which serves as the basis for this chapter, after struggling with my own addictions, and after years of working with individuals and families struggling with theirs. I grew up in an alcoholic family and continue to work through many of the issues that this created. In my work I have found that most families are affected by addiction in some form. The patterns of behavior in families affected by addiction are, individually and collectively, both predictable and tragic (Black, 1982; Cermak, 1990; Steinglass et al., 1987; Wegscheider-Cruse, 1989). I also have witnessed that recovery from addiction can be a doorway to awakening to love, compassion, the awareness of the interconnectedness of life, and the kind acts that follow this awareness. This is precisely how I would define a spiritual path.

Unfortunately, I also have seen many people, including myself, simply trade one addiction for another and call it recovery, burying love deeper in darkness. After I no longer used alcohol and other drugs, I fell prey to workaholism. I have come to believe that what determines the difference between awakening to love (i.e., undertaking a spiritual journey) and trading addictions is the extent to which we examine our fundamental beliefs about ourselves and the world. For this reason much of my work and philosophy can be seen as humanistically and existentially based.

There have been many uses of the word *addiction*, most in relation to chemical dependency. One of my goals in my work is to have our culture become more aware of the breadth of addiction. When you see or hear the word *addiction*, I encourage you to begin mentally to replace it with the phrase, "pursuing happiness in things (people, places, substances) external to myself."

I believe that most of us, to some degree, have pockets of addiction in our lives. Regardless of what age you are, what letters you have after your name, or how much money is in your bank account, the extent to which we are stuck in our addictive patterns is the extent to which we inhibit our potential to love. If you have become tired of attempting to find hiding places from the world, long for relief from running faster on the treadmill, or realize that more does not equal happier, then I humbly suggest to you that your heart holds the answers and your spiritual journey has already begun.

The fallacy of looking outside ourselves for happiness

Addiction is a familiar word, yet what exactly does the word mean? It is safe to say that no addict woke up one morning and set out to become addicted. Addiction is more covert and sly, and seems to sneak into a person's life through the back door. Most people would not call themselves addicts, yet it is my observation that addictive behavior is prevalent in our society.

When we find ourselves frustrated, angry, and unhappy, we probably don't recognize that what is occurring could be the process of addiction. And if we don't recognize an addiction, we dig a deeper hole for ourselves in an attempt to escape the uncomfortable feelings. Individually and culturally, it is time to stop running away from addiction and to begin looking closer at just what addiction is.

I had been seeing Peter in my practice for about three months when during a session, he began crying uncontrollably. I was moved by the depth of his crying. The sounds that left his mouth sounded ancient, as though they had lain chained in dark isolation for centuries. Peter struggled to speak through his tears, as if the familiarity of words would bring him out of the pain that so enveloped him. But words would not come, and only the despair of deep loneliness filled the room. Then, for a moment, Peter emerged from the hold of his pain, as if gasping for air in a sea of unknown depth, and whispered from his tears the only words he could say: "I'm so afraid."

Peter had been addicted to cocaine for seven years. Prior to my seeing him, he had not used any mind-altering substance for one year. He had gone to a well-known 28-day recovery program. Peter was 32 years old, married, a lawyer, had plenty of money, lived in a beautiful home, and yet felt that there was "something missing." At the time Peter began to see me, he stated, "I have everything going for me and I don't use drugs anymore, and I'm still not happy."

Peter came to find that the "something missing" he described was the awareness and experience of love; in short, a spiritual journey. What kept him from love and his spiritual development was his constant pursuit of happiness in things external to himself, which in turn covered up his deep feelings of emptiness and aloneness. It was not until the session just described that Peter even knew that he felt alone and separate from everybody and everything. Cocaine had been a dam, holding back the waters of loneliness. His stopping the use of cocaine had been the first step, and now Peter was face-to-face with his worst fear: his aloneness.

Peter believed, deep down, as many of us do, that he was alone and isolated in a cruel and punishing world. From this largely repressed belief, Peter set out to fill this void of emptiness. He began looking outside of himself for things that he mistakenly thought would make him feel whole. In so doing, he began his downward spiral into addiction. It was in the session just described that Peter began to realize that neither drugs, nor money, nor relationships could fill the void, the emptiness that he felt. Only removing the blocks to love in his own mind could begin to heal him and return him to wholeness.

In the months following this session, Peter began to see that his addiction had nothing to do with weakness or willpower. He began to see that his addiction to cocaine was simply a part of his addictive search for satisfaction and gratification in things external to himself.

Many people in our society look at people addicted to alcohol or other drugs as weak and morally inferior. It was the great anthropologist Gregory Bateson who first suggested differently (1972). He painted a picture of the addict as a person who had a spiritual thirst, a sense of knowing that there was something more. The addict, Bateson said, found that alcohol or other drugs momentarily and partially filled this thirst (other chapters, such as Morgan's and Berenson's, also refer to Bateson's contribution). Peter, though in deep pain, began to reconnect with his feeling that there must be something more. Through recognizing this spiritual longing, he began to look inside himself.

Confusion about spirituality

Many of us in our adult lives have shied away from spirituality. For some, negative experiences with religion as children caused us to turn away from God. In my work, I always use language that the individual is comfortable with. A spiritual journey can begin with never mentioning the word *religion* or the word *God*. For this reason I define recovery from addiction as the process of awakening to love. This is the same way that I would define any spiritual journey. Opening the heart to love is the highest human experience and is what undoing addiction is about.

For example, Peter had found that the depth of his aloneness was shallow in comparison with the boundless depth of love. As I watched him surround himself with love, I was reminded of something that Hugh Prather once wrote: "Learning to love yourself is the definition of change."

Let's look more closely at the definition of addiction. Addiction is a compulsive and continuous searching for happiness outside of ourselves, despite the fact that contentment always eludes us. More precisely, addiction is a continued compulsive external search, despite the fact that such a pursuit always leads us into pain and conflict. If we are to reverse addictive behavior, we must begin to challenge the fundamental concepts of the ego (defined as the part of our mind that is based upon fear and separation), which are:

1. **Guilt**. Guilt is the belief that we have done something wrong, bad, and unforgivable. It is based upon the belief that the past is inescapable and determines the future.
2. **Shame**. As guilt increases, we not only believe that we have done something bad, we begin to believe that we are bad.
3. **Fear**. Because of guilt and shame and the resulting feelings that we have done something wrong and are something wrong, we then become plagued with a fear of punishment. For some this translates into the fear of God; for others this manifests itself in the belief that they don't deserve love.

Guilt, shame, and fear do a war dance together that leaves us with anxiety and feelings of emptiness, incompleteness, and hopelessness. The ego keeps us from examining itself too closely by making us believe that guilt and shame are so strong and pervasive that we could not possibly get beyond them. Because of fear, we run from looking within ourselves, and we begin to look to people, places, activities, and possessions for our happiness. It is in this external search for peace of mind that the ego pushes us toward our first steps in addiction.

The following quotes, from *Accept this gift: Selections from a course in miracles*, by Walsh and Vaughn (1992), are what I think addiction is about. They illustrate that when we continue to shift from one goal (relationship, job, drug) to another, despite the fact that our goals never satisfy us, we are caught in the cycle of addiction:

- Love and guilt cannot coexist, and to accept one is to deny the other.
- The end of guilt will never come as long as you believe there is a reason for it.
- You must learn that guilt is always totally insane, and has no reason.
- Only your mind can produce fear.
- You must have noticed an outstanding characteristic of every end that the ego has accepted as its own: When you have achieved it, it has not satisfied you. That is why the ego is forced to shift ceaselessly from one goal to another, so that you will continue to hope it can yet offer you something.

On happiness

The idle, external search for happiness is pervasive in contemporary society. You can't watch more than fifteen minutes of commercial television without a series of advertisements, telling you that you need some new and improved products in order to be happier. At a very early age, you begin to form the core of a fear-based addictive thought system, namely, that you are fundamentally inadequate as you are, and need something outside of yourself to make you whole.

It is crucial to question the fear-based belief system of the ego. The addictive thought system is seriously flawed and never gives us lasting peace of mind. In contrast with the addictive thought system, the love-based thought system tells us that our natural state of mind is one of wholeness and peace (Jampolsky, 1991).

You may have noticed that I use the word happiness and the phrase *peace of mind* interchangeably. To me, the word happiness does not denote a constantly smiling face, for we certainly have more than one feeling and one expression. Yet, it is possible to go through traumatic situations and still have peace of mind, and, in consequence, a sense of happiness. Tears and happiness are not mutually exclusive, if you are using the word to denote peace of mind. After all, if true happiness is not peace of mind, then what is?

Addictive Thought System

Love-based thinking recognizes a simple fact: I lack nothing in order to be happy right now.

I recently saw the movie *The Little Shop of Horrors*. The movie, perhaps unintentionally, provides a powerful and comical example of our addictive thought system. As the story opens, a young man finds a small and unusual plant, which he begins to nurture. One day the young man accidentally cuts his finger and finds, to his amazement, that the small plant thrives on his blood. Wanting to keep the plant healthy, he continues to feed it blood, but the plant wants more and more. The bigger the plant grows, the more it wants. The plant is never satisfied and only becomes louder and more obnoxious with increased feeding. Eventually the plant is a monstrous piece of botany demanding, "FEED ME! FEED ME!" This is what the ego, with its addictive thought system, feverishly states.

When did the addictive thought system start? It began precisely at the moment when we began to view ourselves as something other than whole, loving beings. It is a premise of my work that the experience of love is not something to be achieved; it is to be remembered. This is fundamentally what a spiritual path is. Who we are—love—has never left; it simply has been covered up by the addictive thought system. We did not become incomplete at some point in our lives; we simply forgot who we were, and so began searching outside of ourselves for happiness. The memory of love is only a thought away, and it awaits only our welcome.

Denial

In the early 1980's I was living on a ranch in Marin County, about thirty miles north of San Francisco. The only service on the ranch was electricity.

The water for the home came from a spring. The garbage that we accumulated needed to be either recycled, hauled to the dump, or put in the compost pile. I was in charge of the compost pile. I chose a spot for it near the house, close to where I liked to sit in the sun and read. About once a week I would take the garbage out and put it in the compost pile, diligently breaking up the larger pieces and mixing them into the earth. As time went on, I became lazy and would just bury some of the larger pieces, not taking the time to break the material apart and mix it into the soil. One day, while reading in my favorite spot, I noticed the place was starting to smell like a dump. My laziness in just burying my garbage had ruined my ability to relax and enjoy my peaceful spot. A farmer I am not, but I did learn one simple rule: Burying something and forgetting it does not work. One aspect of denial is thinking that if we bury our guilt, pushing it out of our awareness, we will be free of it. Not unlike my laziness with my compost pile, denial does not get rid of guilt. Denial produces fear.

The word denial is used frequently in chemical dependency programs. Part of the problem of chemical dependency is denial that there is any problem. I do not know any chemically dependent person who hasn't engaged in denial. Unfortunately, denial keeps the addict in an irrational frame of mind, allowing him or her to continue in addiction.

I do not believe that the process of denial in addiction is limited to the area of chemical dependency. With any addiction, in order for the ego to continue its obsessive quest for external gratification, our underlying wholeness must be denied. Addiction cannot exist where love and wholeness are truly acknowledged. In other words, the gift that addiction can bring is in the healing path of undertaking a spiritual journey.

Further, it is the denial of our underlying unity that is the foundation of addiction. If we experienced ourselves as whole, addiction would not occur, because we would feel complete, in and of ourselves. Unfortunately, we often remain blind to our own addictive patterns. Part of any therapy in regard to addiction needs to make a conscious effort to undo denial.

Projection

The ego's backward plan for our release from guilt has two key elements: denial and projection.

When you deny guilt and push it down, it starts eating away at you. The ego then looks for other ways to rid itself of guilt. In projection, the ego believes that if you unconsciously project your guilt away from yourself and onto someone else, you will magically be freed. Instead, you increase your feelings of guilt, fear, and inadequacy.

Projection, and the behavior that is a result of it, is best illustrated with a metaphor. Imagine that we set up a movie projector in order to view a film. The lights dim and the film begins. About ten minutes into the movie, you notice that I am fidgeting and appear uncomfortable. You ask me if I am okay, and I tell you that I don't like the movie. In fact, it is making me very uncomfortable. You know me as a rational person, so what I do next surprises you. I get up, walk over to the screen, and write on the screen, move it, even try to rip it. I don't like the movie, so I try to change the screen.

I suggest to you that each of us, sometimes on a daily basis, exhibits this insane behavior. Because we have a lot of company, nobody ever questions it. Let me begin to explain by asking you a question. If you don't like the movie, what are your more sane options? Though there are several answers, probably the most rational involve turning off the projector or changing the film. These answers reflect an understanding that the source of the image is not the screen. The image is projected onto the screen.

To understand how projection works in your daily life, imagine that the film projector is your mind and the film is your thoughts. Projection can seem complex, but is really quite simple. A few years back, I acquired a new playful puppy. He would run from room to room, playing with whatever he found. One day I heard him fiercely barking and growling, something that I had never heard him do before. When I found him he was in the bathroom; the door had partially shut, revealing a full-length mirror. He was standing there, feet firmly planted, hair on his back raised, growling at his image in the mirror. I thought it was pretty silly of him not to realize he was threatening to attack his own image. But, I guess that a lot of time I am as silly as he is: I growl at another, not realizing that I am seeing repressed parts of myself.

An Addictve Personality?

There have been endless arguments as to whether such a thing as an addictive personality exists (Bean, 1981; Ludwig, 1988; Peele, 1989; Royce and Scratchley, 1996). Though some of us may have a genetic predisposition to chemical addiction, I believe that we are all equally prone to addictive and conflicted ways of thinking, which lead to addictive patterns of behavior. We all equally yearn, on some level, for the spiritual experience of wholeness and love, and because of this we all may make the mistake of looking outside of ourselves for peace and happiness.

Serenity must come from within. It is my belief that there is only one opposing emotion to love, and that is fear. Fear is something that our egos made up, and fear is at the core of the addictive thought system. Based on fear, many other conflicted beliefs occur. I posit that there are four fundamental parts of the addictive thought system. They are fear, living in the past or the future, judgment, and a belief in scarcity. The following diagram illustrates the foundation of the addictive thought system:

The Addictive Thought System

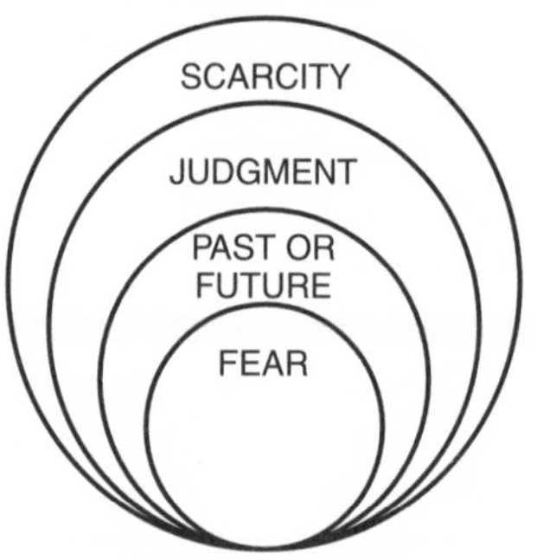

1. On fear

Projection leads us into a world where fear is constantly reinforced. We end up being afraid of love and freedom. Instead of inviting love into our hearts, we become hosts to guilt. We become like captive birds who never learned to fly, sitting in cages surrounded by bars of fear forged by our own thinking.

Miranda came to see me after she had split up with her husband of eleven years. Miranda had married after becoming pregnant at seventeen. Her father had sexually abused her as a child. She later admitted that she had seen pregnancy and marriage as the only way to get out of her abusive home. Though her mother never physically abused her, Miranda held tremendous anger and resentment toward her for not intervening with her father and providing a safe environment. She was sure that her mother must have known what was going on but remained silent. As a child Miranda learned that it was not safe to talk about feelings in her family, so she remained silent, alone with her fears.

Miranda went through her adult life playing out the silent and hidden feelings of her childhood. She always felt as though she were in an unsafe place, and was unable to confide in, or rely on, anyone. She had few friends and most of her coworkers saw her as distant, defensive, and aloof. Though Miranda wanted closeness with her husband, she felt she could not really trust him or anyone else. This, combined with her inability to speak of feelings, kept Miranda in a constantly lonely and fearful state.

Miranda came to see me at the request of her employer, because she had been regularly missing work and seemed visibly upset. Miranda, because of her family history, had a difficult time opening up to me. In the course of our early work together, she emerged as a woman who had never felt truly loved. In fact, she had never been told those three simple words: I love you. As a child she had become fearful and mistrusting; as an adult she knew no other way to be.

As our work unfolded, it became clear that there was a part of Miranda that felt guilty for what had occurred with her father. Irrationally, she wondered if she had done something to cause her father's behavior. She also felt guilty because a part of her was thankful to at least have had some attention. The guilt caused her to have many false and negative beliefs about herself. Miranda believed that she was sexually "dirty," and not deserving of a loving relationship with a man. Miranda was longing for love, yet her fear, guilt, and negative self-image kept her stuck in a cycle of either being defensive or isolating herself from others.

You may ask yourself what Miranda's story has to do with addiction. I chose to present Miranda's case because it illustrates the seeds of addiction. Another person could start out with a similar story and go on to use drugs as a way of isolating themselves. Yet another could fall into sexual addiction, having many sexual relationships, looking for affection in the only way familiar to them. In Miranda's case, she had continued to feel guilty and fearful, which led to isolating and defensive behavior, despite the fact that these behaviors led to continual unhappiness. On a behavioral and feeling level, this was addiction in the sense that she continued to act and think in the same ways despite the adverse consequences. The following diagram illustrates this addictive cycle:

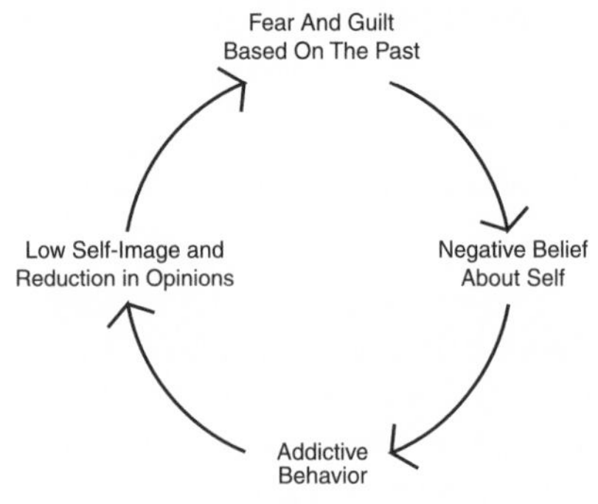

For Miranda this cycle looked like:

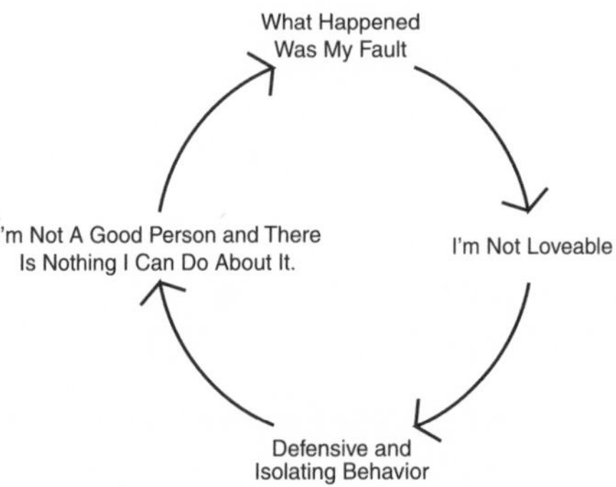

Miranda was slowly able to trust me and began talking in depth about her feelings, both as a child and as an adult. As she became less guilt-ridden and fearful, she became less defensive and broke her long history of isolation. Miranda began to experience love in her life. She had never been able to believe in God or a Higher Power, because she had always felt like she would be punished. As she trusted more, she was able to develop her spiritual side. Her heart went from being withered, cold, and isolated to full, welcoming, and open.

2. On living in the past or the future

In the addictive thought system, we believe that the past is our stockpile of ammunition to use in condemning both ourselves and others. We hold on to past grievances with other people and end up having anger and resentment eat away at us. We carry around past resentments that become like sandbags, keeping the flow of love out of our relationships.

I would estimate that the average adult spends much more than 50 percent of his or her time preoccupied with something in the future. Questions fill our minds: Will I have enough money to pay the bills? What if I fail? Will this person or that person like and accept me? The list goes on and on. Every time we become preoccupied with the future, we are creating an obstacle for love. Love lives in the present moment, absent of the past or the future.

There is nothing about a specific ailment or situation in and of itself that causes us to experience emotional pain. It is our perception, beliefs, and past experiences that determine if we feel pain.

3. On judgment

Look at judgment for what it is and what it creates. Judgment sentences you to guilt, low self-esteem, and feelings of inadequacy. If you are constantly comparing yourself with others, you can never allow love to set you free.

The flip side of negative judgment is acceptance and forgiveness. Where judgment builds a wall, keeping love out, forgiveness sends an invitation to love and puts wind in our spiritual sails. A quote from *A course in miracles* illustrates:

> When I have forgiven myself and remembered who I am,
> I will bless everyone and everything I see.

Judgment always sets conditions on love and perpetuates our addictive thinking. It says, "I will love you if I find you fit my expectations and if you pass my evaluations." A judgmental mind makes lists, often unconsciously, of passing criteria for love. In contrast, forgiveness sets no conditions. Forgiveness simply allows love to be itself.

We are always choosing between judgment and acceptance. With practice, we can just as easily choose to fill our minds with love-based thoughts, as we can choose the condemnation and judgment of the addictive thought system.

4. On scarcity

The addictive thought system constantly tells us that we are short on something: Not enough money. Not enough nice possessions. Not enough love. The addictive philosophy of "not enough" stems from one core belief: scarcity. Scarcity is the notion that we are always lacking something. Because of this belief, we become caught in endless pursuits to fill this perceived void. We think that our pursuits are valid, yet the following is really happening:

> Much of our emotional pain comes from thinking that we are lacking, less than whole.
> The ego tells us to search for things or relationships to make us feel a sense of wholeness.
> We embark on a search for what we mistakenly think will fill the void.
> In the end we still feel incomplete, and not knowing any other way to be, we start the process all over again.

The belief in scarcity is so pervasive in our society that we can hardly go through a day without being told in some way that we are not okay as we are. Television commercials tell us that a specific car or a certain kind of coffee or a particular cologne will make us fulfilled and content. We drive down the freeway, full of frustration from demeaning jobs, and see billboards of happy and affluent people smoking cigarettes or relaxing with bourbon. When listening to the news, I find that a large percentage of the stories are about people who felt so much like they were "not enough" that they committed crimes out of a sense of desperation and hopelessness.

With such external stimuli, it is no wonder that we continue in the mad illusion of thinking that something outside of us will bring us freedom and power. But, to think that our feelings of being "not enough" are the fault of the advertising industry would be naíve. What we see in the media is a reflection of our own collective state of mind.

Addiction as a Misdirected Spiritual Search

When we look into our minds, we can see the roots of addiction. I submit that most addictive behavior stems from a three-step process of addictive thinking:

1. I am not okay the way I am. There is a void in me that needs to be filled.
2. There is something or someone external to myself that will fill this void.
3. My happiness is dependent on finding this substance, possession, or person.

The feeling of yearning for something more is, as has been suggested, a misdirected spiritual longing. We are like a child who has wandered away from home and gotten lost. All that is on the child's mind is returning home, yet if gone long enough, he or she may forget the faces of his or her parents and the safety of home. We have wandered away from wholeness and love. In the process we have forgotten who we are and have gotten lost. The more we have searched outside of ourselves, the more lost we have become. It is only in the quieting of our minds that we can come to know ourselves.

I worked with Alan, a cocaine addict, when I was directing an outpatient hospital treatment program for chemical dependency. Alan returned for a visit about a year after finishing the program. I knew he was doing fine when he said, "I really appreciate all that you people said to me. But, you know, all of our talking would not have kept me clean. Even after stopping the drugs, I still felt like there was something missing. I wasn't sure what it was. One day I just sat down on my bed, shut my eyes, and asked what I was missing. If I had been looking in the window at myself, I would have said that I was nuts. I had never prayed, meditated, or any of that stuff. I didn't hear any words to answer my question, but an overwhelming sense of peace and calm came over me. It was the first time that I recall ever feeling at ease with myself. It was a new feeling, yet it felt ancient at the same time. So what I'm trying to say is, thanks. The talking was important in getting me to look at myself and what I was doing. But it was in the quiet, beyond the words, that I began to find my self."

I knew that Alan had begun to find what he had been yearning for all along: self-love and self-acceptance.

The two forms of communication

The addictive thought system is a loud and unrelenting voice. Yet beneath it is the quiet, calm, and ever-present voice of love. Our first step in undoing the addictive thought system is to make an effort to listen to the serene, peaceful voice of love. The intention to listen to love is a powerful tool. Like a river, it will eventually overcome any obstacle.

Communication can seem very complicated, yet it is actually quite simple. It is my belief that there are really only two forms of communication.

The first form is that based on love, where you extend love and compassion to yourself and others. The second form of communication is that based on the addictive thought system; you act defensively, yet deep down yearn for love. In short, the two ways of communicating are (1) extending love, and (2) making a call for love.

When you interact with other people operating from the addictive thought system, their defenses and attitudes may make it seem like they are porcupines: When you try to get close, their quills prick you painfully. Those stuck in the addictive thought system are so afraid that they build walls around themselves. If others attack these walls out of anger, they only reinforce their walls, making them thicker. Taking a jackhammer to addictive behavior does not work; love is the only force that can penetrate the walls of the addictive thought system. This is important to remember when undertaking therapy with a patient entrenched in addictive behavior and thinking. This is not to say that confrontation has no place, but that the individual must experience loving compassion beneath any intervention.

Both in families and in the consulting room, being loving does not mean being only sweet and nice, tiptoeing around issues that are in need of being addressed. Stating how you feel, in a loving and nonjudgmental way, allows defenses to quietly crumble.

What the addicted person is actually saying is that he or she is scared and in need of love: nothing less, nothing more. The more we can hear this call for love, instead of identifying with the verbal assaults and negative behavior, the greater chance we have of breaking through the walls of addiction.

From a place of peace, the mind can begin to allow the warmth of love to melt away illusions of fear and guilt. We cannot heal the addictive mind while it is entrenched in fear and conflict. It would be like trying to get out of a Chinese finger puzzle: The harder you pull, the tighter it becomes. Trying to get over fear from a place of fear does not work.

It is impossible for your mind to serve two goals at once. For example, I may say that I want peace of mind while still holding a grudge over something that happened last week or last year. If I see any value in holding a grudge, my goal cannot really be peace of mind. Peace of mind is impossible as long as we still see value in the fear-based thinking of the addictive thought system. One purpose of this book is to help you increase your commitment to love. As you begin to want only love, you will begin to see only love. The love-based thought system is just that simple. The only thing that the love-based thought system asks of you is that you lay down the defenses of the addictive thought system and extend the invitation to love.

The Love-Based Thought System

Many of us grew up in families where the unspoken message was: "I'll love you if you do what I want you to do." The "I'll-love-you-if..." message causes an individual to think either that he or she is undeserving of love, or else that he or she must please others in order to be loved.

Those of us who received this message began to believe that, if we showed our parents all of ourselves, including our dark and hidden thoughts, then we would be rejected. Consequently, we learned to keep certain segments of ourselves hidden, in the hope that we could be fully loved.

When we feel that we must keep aspects of ourselves hidden in order to be accepted, the result is that we never quite feel deserving of any love and support that we do receive. Groucho Marx once quipped about this feeling,: "I wouldn't want to belong to a club that would have me for a member." If we want to undo the addictive thought system, we must begin to realize that we are fully lovable the way we are, because we are love itself.

Utilizing spirituality in personal and therapeutic intervention

I enjoy finding fine old wood furniture that has been covered with layers of paint. When I come across a piece, it is not the layers of paint that I concern myself with, it is the beautiful oak, pine, or mahogany that lies beneath the old and cracked paint. As I gently strip off the paint, being careful not to damage the wood, what is beneath is revealed. Stripping off the paint is a long and tedious job. There are times when the wood actually looks worse than when I started, and I am tempted to abandon the project. Sometimes I need to simply have faith that with a little more work I will see the original and beautiful wood. Once the paint is off, I usually need to care for the wood, because it is parched and vulnerable to damp or dry air. After applying a little oil, I end up with a gorgeous piece of furniture.

And so it is with moving from fear to love. Do not only concern yourself with the layers of fear and darkness, cracked by years of guilt and judgment. Look beneath and imagine the beauty that waits to be uncovered. Know that it is not necessarily going to be an easy or painless process, but that it will be rich in its rewards. When I am done stripping furniture, I don't go through the scrapings of paint on the floor; I throw them away. They have no use to me. In the same way, let go of fear. Throw fear away like old paint; it has no use to you in love-based thinking.

In the addictive thought system we compulsively search for happiness in people, things, and substances; that process always results in a vicious cycle of fear. In the love-based thought system we look within, going through and beyond fear to find love. As we see love in ourselves, we begin to see it elsewhere. A child's eyes, a friend's touch, even a group of people we have never met—all become reminders of love. We see love everywhere because it is everywhere. Once love is awakened in our hearts, we see that there is no place untouched by love. We can deny the presence of love, but that does not make it disappear. It waits patiently for us to uncover our eyes and open up our hearts. When we see darkness and hate, it is like we are seeing old paint on furniture. We always have the choice of whether to see darkness or light, in the same way that we can choose to see the paint or the wood.

The first step toward increasing our experience of love is to begin to train our minds to overlook the illusions of darkness—the paint—created by the addictive thought system. Love lies just beyond. Begin to trust in a deeper part of yourself; give it a chance to emerge and be itself. To trust calls for a leap of faith, for fear tells us that if we look within we will not like what we see, and certainly nobody else will. We must begin to trust in our inner life, in our inner guide, for this is the way to uncover the memory of love.

On the present moment

People seem to be always struggling with time, constantly running to beat the clock. When we first meet another person, we may tend to size up him or her in terms of what he or she has done or not done in the past. When we respond to a job advertisement, we send in a resume: a list of our past. In fact, we may tend to determine our own self-worth by looking at the chronicle of the past that we keep filed in our mind. As a society and as individuals, we look to what we have done or haven't done in the past instead of who we are in the present.

When we become focused on the present, the window of our perception radically shifts. We begin to see the world and ourselves in a fresh light. There is a sense of newness, release, and relief. There are no outside measuring sticks in the present moment to determine self-esteem; there is only love shining in and around us. As we make this shift in our perception of time, a sense of peace enters into our life.

Not too long ago, researchers became interested in peak performance. Scientists and psychologists interviewed and observed athletes who seemed to achieve optimal levels of performance. Much of what was learned from these athletes was later applied to non-athletes' lives. And it seems that one thread runs through the ability to reach optimal levels of performance, be it in athletics, relationships, or work: When we are focused on the present, we move, think, and perform at higher levels than when we are preoccupied with negative thoughts or images of the past or future.

On acceptance

The basic tenet of the addictive thought system is judgment: The belief that constantly analyzing, comparing, criticizing, and condemning are traits that bring security and peace. In contrast, the love-based thought system sees that peace of mind is obtained through the art of practicing acceptance.

In much of my clinical training, there were certain assumptions made by clinicians that were rarely questioned. For one, there was an assumption that the individuals who came seeking treatment were having some problems in certain areas of their life and that they desired change. We saw ourselves as "agents of change" and would try to help change the patient into a "higher functioning" person. I do not question that most, if not all, people in some way want change; I am positing that there may be more than meets the eye in how we achieve change. I have come to see that a certain phenomenon must occur before deep change—that is, change that occurs on both the behavioral level and the feeling level—can occur. I call this phenomenon the paradox of change.

In order to truly change, we must first accept ourselves just as we are, without reservation. We must be able to see beyond our dysfunction and see our essential wholeness. If we do not approach ourselves with an attitude of acceptance and love, we beat ourselves up. And as long as we beat ourselves up, positive deep change is impossible. The only change that occurs by condemning yourself is that you end up feeling worse. The paradox of change is that we can't effect deep change until we first accept ourselves just as we are.

To my mind the various Twelve Step self-help groups, such as Alcoholics Anonymous, work not so much because of what is said during the meetings, but because of their attitude of acceptance. The attitude is, "We accept you as you are today, and should you want to look at various aspects of your life, we're here to help you through it with love, without judgment."

Here are a few thoughts about the nature of acceptance of yourself and of others:

- Our energy is exhausted when we judge, analyze, compare, and criticize. Conversely, we feel enlivened when we extend acceptance.
- Peace of mind comes from accepting who we are rather than evaluating and punishing ourselves for what we have done. Likewise, peace of mind also comes from accepting others.
- Acceptance is based on the present moment. Judgment is based on the past.
- Acceptance does not mean condoning negative behavior. It simply means that to change our own negative behavior (or to encourage another to change) we must see that there is a worthwhile person beneath the behavior.
- Peace of mind comes from accepting things that are not within our power to change. This also means recognizing that we cannot control other people.
- Acceptance does not know anything about expectations. Acceptance is not attached to future outcomes.

On abundance

Even though we may not remember them well, I believe that all of us have had moments in our lives where we felt complete and fulfilled, moments where there was no perception of lack, only wholeness and love. In these moments, we spontaneously break through the confines of the ego's belief in scarcity and become aware of the truth of who we are.

The love-based thought system recognizes that the ego's thought system is insane, and only leads us into conflict. Abundance is the simple recognition that what is of value does not decrease in value over time and does not need to be guarded. What is of value grows in value when it is given away. When we embrace abundance, we determine what is valuable in a completely different way than when we view the world through the lens of scarcity.

It may sound as though abundance suggests that people stop work or do nothing. This is not true. I had the good fortune to spend some time with one of the great teachers of abundance, Mother Teresa. She certainly can't be accused of doing nothing. And, at the same time, when starting up a mission, she didn't think in terms of scarcity, saying, "Oh, we can't do this because there is not enough money." Mother Teresa knew that loving and kindness are all that is truly important, and that all else falls into place from this. It is not a pretty room or fancy food that creates healing; it is love. Mother Teresa certainly worked very hard, but she was working from the place of abundance, knowing what she had to give, and not from scarcity, wondering what she would lose. The love-based thought system, which includes an attitude of abundance, can heal the addictive mind.

Cognitive Differences between Fear-Based and Love-Based Thinking

By now the differences in the two modes of thinking should be fairly straightforward. To clarify further:

The ego sees problems and obstacles in every situation.

Love-based thinking sees opportunities to learn in every situation.

Addictive thinking holds on to fear, irrationally believing that fear serves some use.

Love-based thinking recognizes that healing is releasing fear.

Addictive thinking holds onto the negative past, thinking that grudges and guilt serve a purpose.

Love-based thinking sees that healing is letting go of the past.

The ego tells us that seeing lack, fault, or unworthiness in some one else makes us feel all the more powerful.

Love-based thinking states that healing is recognizing the worth in everything and everybody.

The ego equates judging yourself with healing yourself.

Love-based thinking equates loving yourself with healing yourself.

The addictive mind tells us that we are separate and that our thoughts don't make a difference.

Love-based thinking tells us that the most powerful healing force is a loving and forgiving thought that joins everyone.

Below you will find a comparison of the two thought systems. It should be noted that positive thinking by itself does not necessarily bring about change. You must also identify the negative belief, that is, the addictive belief, that is keeping you from being able to embrace the truth. Thus, if you find yourself in conflict, your first task is to identify the addictive belief. Your second task is to replace it with love-based thinking.

Beliefs of the addictive thought system

1. I am alone in a cruel, harsh, and unforgiving world. I am separate from everybody else.
2. If I want safety and peace of mind, I must judge others and be quick to defend myself.
3. My way is the right way. My perceptions are always factually correct. In order to feel good about myself, I need to be perfect all of the time.
4. Attack and defense are my only safety.
5. The past and the future are real and need to be constantly evaluated and worried about.
6. Guilt is inescapable because the past is real.
7. Mistakes call for judgment and punishment, not correction and learning.
8. Fear is real. Do not question it.
9. Other people are responsible for how I feel. The situation is the determiner of my experience.
10. If I am going to make it in this world, I must pit myself against others. Another's loss is my gain.
11. I need something or someone outside of myself to make me complete.
12. My self-esteem is based on pleasing you.
13. I can control other people's behavior.

Beliefs of the love-based thought system

1. What I see in others is a reflection of my own state of mind. There is an underlying unity to all life. I lack nothing to be happy and whole right now.
2. My safety lies in my defenselessness, because love needs no defense. Acceptance is what brings me peace of mind.
3. My self-worth is not based upon my performance. Love is unconditional.
4. Forgiveness, with no exceptions, ensures peace.
5. Only the present is real. The past is over and the future is not yet here.
6. In order for me to change my experience, I must first change my thoughts.
7. Mistakes call for correction and learning, not judgment and punishment.
8. Only love is real, and what is real cannot be threatened.
9. I am responsible for the world I see, and I choose the feelings that I experience. I decide upon the goal I would achieve.
10. To give is to receive. For me to gain, nobody can lose.

11. I am complete right now.
12. My self-esteem comes from loving and accepting myself as I am today, and then sharing love and acceptance with others.
13. I can't change others, but I can change how I perceive others.

Irrational beliefs of the addictive mind

1. My self-esteem is dependent upon my being approved of by everybody on this planet.
2. If I am to consider myself worthwhile, I must excel, achieve, win, and display glowing competence at all times, in all places, and at all costs.
3. All things that go wrong in my life are caused by other people. These people need to be blamed and punished.
4. If external situations in my life are not exactly how I want them to be, I must feel tense, worry endlessly, and expect a disaster to occur within seconds.
5. If something negative happened in the past, I should be very concerned about it repeating itself in the future. It will help if I keep dwelling on the possibility of it occurring.
6. If I avoid painful issues and stuff down my emotions, I will be safe and happy.
7. I am weak and need to be dependent on somebody or something else.
8. I should be very involved in, and upset about, other people's problems.
9. There is one right way to view the world
10. I am limited in what I can do and the happiness that I can experience.

Affirming who you are

In closing, my hope is that this chapter has given the reader food for thought in both the personal and the professional domains of addiction. It is my deepest hope that the power of unconditional love will find its way to every heart.

We, individually and culturally, spend a great deal of time unconsciously reinforcing the addictive thought system. We engage in endless negative self-talk, focus on blame and criticism in our relationships and society rather than on solutions and personal action. It seems that we rarely hold anything positive and true in our mind for more than a few seconds. When we look in the mirror, we may have an easier time seeing a person we are critical of than seeing the light of love shining back at us.

This is all because, in the cycle of addiction, our beliefs about who we are become distorted. It is up to each of us, you and me, to start giving the cultivation of love as much time as we have given to fanning the fire of fear.

References

Bateson, G. (1972). The cybernetics of the "self": A theory of alcoholism. In *Steps to an ecology of mind* (New York: Ballantine). [Originally published in 1971, *Psychiatry, 34*, 1–18.].

Bean, M.H. (1981). Denial and the psychological complications of alcoholism. In M.H. Bean and N.E. Zinberg (Eds.), *Dynamic approaches to the understanding and treatment of alcoholism* (pp. 55–96). New York: Free Press.

Beattie, M. (1987). *Codependent no more.* San Francisco: Harper/Hazelden.

Black, C. (1982). *It will never happen to me.* Denver, Colo.: MAC Publishing.

Brown, S. (1985). *Treating the alcoholic: A developmental model of recovery.* New York: Wiley.

Cermak, T. L. (1990). *Evaluating and treating adult children of alcoholics.* Minneapolis: The Johnson Institute.

Jampolsky, L. (1991). *Healing the addictive mind: Freeing yourself from addictive patterns and relationships.* Berkeley: Celestial Arts.

Ludwig, A. M. (1988). *Understanding the alcoholic's mind: The nature of craving and how to control it.* New York: Oxford University Press.

Peele, S. (1989). *Diseasing of America: Addiction treatment out of control.* Lexington, Mass.: D.C. Heath.

Royce, J. E. and Scratchley, D. (1996). *Alcoholism and other drug problems.* New York: Free Press.

Steinglass, P., Bennett, L. A., Wolin, S. J., and Reiss, D. (1987). *The alcoholic family.* New York: Basic Books, Inc.

Wegscheider-Cruse, S. (1989). *Another chance: Hope and health for the alcoholic family, 2nd Edition.* Palo Alto, Calif: Science and Behavior Books.

CHAPTER 4

A Systemic View of Spirituality: God and Twelve Step Programs as Resources in Family Therapy

David Berenson

Perhaps the most underutilized resource in family therapy today is God.

In our society, to even assert that God exists is frequently dismissed as a matter of private belief or as belonging to the province of religion and not relevant to the practice of family therapy. We live in an age where the prevailing "enlightened," scientific world view is, as Nietzsche proclaimed, "God is dead," and we practice therapy within a mindset still heavily influenced by Freud's attitude that all religious or spiritual experiences are illusions and wish-fulfillments and that there is "no knowledge derived from revelation, intuition, or divination" (Freud, 1933, p. 159). As therapists, we may actively reframe, positively connote, restructure, or prescribe, but most of us do not function clinically with a confidence that there is always available to us a loving, divine presence that can dramatically heal emotional and relationship problems.

There is a certain fear and trembling as one starts to address the topic of God, perhaps because it seems intrinsic to spiritual inquiry, but also from trepidation about how one will be received: "Did you hear about him? I think he's gone off the deep end and become a religious fanatic," or, certainly less likely among therapists: "What he's saying is blasphemous and dangerous. It does not conform to standard religious dogma." Within the family therapy field, there have been attempts by two of the field's originators to deal directly with the issue of the sacred, or spirituality: Gregory Bateson, in the years before he died, was working on a book which was completed by his daughter, Mary Catherine Bateson, and published under the title *Angels fear: Towards an epistemology of the sacred* (1987); and Murray Bowen addressed the topic of spirituality at the Georgetown Family Symposium in 1980, but remained virtually silent on it afterwards. There has been a notable lack of response within the family therapy community to both attempts, perhaps accompanied by private dismissals that these are the preoccupations of a dying man and a man growing older. Mary Catherine Bateson (1987) described her father's hesitancy to publicly address the topic of the sacred:

> He had become aware gradually that the unity of nature he had affirmed in *Mind and Nature* might only be comprehensible through the kind of metaphors familiar from religion; that, in fact, he was approaching that integrative dimension of experience he called the sacred. This was a matter he approached with great trepidation, partly because he had been raised in a dogmatically atheistic household and partly because he saw the potential in religion for manipulation, obscurantism, and division. The mere use of the word religion is likely to trigger reflexive misunderstanding. (p. 2)

It is easy to dispense with the word religion, and substitute the word spirituality for it. For many this is more than a semantic trick. Spirituality, as opposed to religion, connotes a direct, personal experience of the sacred unmediated by particular belief systems prescribed by dogma or by hierarchical structures of priests, ministers, rabbis, or gurus. We could say that spirituality is to conventional religion as systems thinking is to linear, cause and effect thinking. It is now even becoming fashionable in certain circles to proclaim oneself spiritual, but not religious.

Is it as easy to dispense with God, both the word and the reality it represents? People have certainly tried. Bateson (1979) spoke of the sacred, of "the pattern which connects," and of "self-healing tautology." The theologian John Macquarrie (1987) proposed the term "holy being." Eastern religions and proponents of the New Age speak of the Self, of Higher Self, and of Higher Consciousness. Alcoholics Anonymous uses the term Higher Power interchangeably with God. We might even use the somewhat awkward term "properties of whole systems." None of these alternatives, though, brings forth the awe, power, and majesty that have been associated with the word God and the presence that it can evoke.

For many, however, the word God does not call forth love, peace, and joy, but rather conjures up images of a smug piousness, of a guilty hypocrisy, of a syrupy-sweet tone of voice that may cover a vengeful intolerance, of convoluted dogma, and of boring sermons that may coexist with frenzied declarations of blind faith. If one clinically examines the content of peoples' professed belief in God, looking also at their suppressed or repressed emotions and their current and childhood relationships, there is evidence for Freud's (1927) conclusion that the belief in God is "born from man's need to make his helplessness tolerable and built up from the material of memories of the helplessness of his own childhood and the childhood of the human race" (p. 18). Hans Küng (1981), the theologian, has accepted much of Freud's critique of the belief in God. He pointed out that:

1. A believer's image of God may spring not from original insight and free decision but from a vindictive or kind father image imprinted at an early age.
2. Early-childhood experiences with adults who appear as "gods" may be transferred to God both positively and negatively.
3. The image of a vindictive Father-God may be deliberately misused by parents to discipline their children with long-term negative consequences on their religious attitudes.
4. Religion and sexuality may be knit together in such a way that what appear to be religious conflicts are really only fixations of the earliest experiences in the family (p. 310).

Küng also stated, however, that "religion, as Freud shows, can certainly be an illusion, the expression of a neurosis and psychological immaturity (regression). But it need not be...Belief in God can certainly be very greatly influenced by the child's attitude to its father. But this does not mean that God cannot exist" (p. 300). He also took Freud's (1927) criticism that religious ideas are "fulfillments of the oldest, strongest and most urgent wishes of mankind" (p. 30), and stood it on its head, pointing out that "the believer in God can say the same" (p. 300). Küng concluded that atheism may be as much based on wishful thinking or projection as theism, and that Freud indeed may have had repressed religious feelings, which he used his atheism and belief in science to try to overcome.

Freud argued that religion is a defense against sexuality, while Jung argued that sexual imagery can be a defense against, or manifestation of, essentially spiritual or religious feelings. Looking only into one's psychology or subjective experience for definitive evidence for or against the existence of God sometimes seems to lead to an infinite regress, a maze of feeling, defense, and interpretation where one frequently winds up resigned to a leap of faith either into theism or atheism to put an end to the confusion and uncertainty. It is understandable that we treat the existence of God as a matter of private, and perhaps arbitrary, belief since there appears to be no evidence to decide in any other way.

Systems Thinking and Therapy: A Way Out of the Maze?

As it has evolved, family therapy has become a fascinating amalgamation of abstract theory and pragmatic practice. New clinical innovations are frequently justified by reference to cybernetics or general systems theory, while there is also a strong emphasis placed on tangible, demonstrable clinical techniques and results. Thus, Humberto Maturana gets adopted within the family therapy field because of his theoretical elegance, and Milton Erickson gets adopted because of his clinical skill, even though neither is a family therapist. This mixture of theory and practice provides specific tools that we can use to expand our understanding of God and spirituality:

1. The Theory of Logical Types and the principle of metacommunication. Whitehead and Russell's (1910) Theory of Logical Types, as well as Information Theory, were used by Bateson (1972) as "guides" in his development of the categories of Learning I to Learning IV, while the Theory of Logical Types and Group Theory were used in a similar way by Watzlawick, Weakland, and Fisch (1974) as underpinnings for their distinction between First and Second Order Change. Whitehead and Russell stated that "whatever involves all of a collection must not be one of the collection" (p. 37). This statement begins to give us some assistance with the question of God. God has been described as the "all that is" or the "class of classes" or the "context of contexts," and it is a category error to attribute to the whole, God, characteristics that apply to the parts, individual members of a class, set, or collection. While God, as the set itself or the set of sets, may provide the possibility for the set of humanity and for individual human beings to exist, God cannot accurately be described as having the identical qualities as the particular members of the set, nor can individual human beings be described as having the same attributes that the set as a whole possesses. Human essence may be similar to divine essence (human beings being made in the "image of God"), but specific human beings are not God, nor is God a human being.

We can approach this problem less abstractly by using the principle of metacommunication. While most competent family therapists are not very conversant with the Theory of Logical Types, they do know how to metacommunicate, to communicate about communication and relationships. They may talk to a couple about how they interact with each other, or coach an individual on differentiating from her family of origin, or work as a team to generate an appropriate counterparadox for a family. Metacommunication is inherent in family therapy in general as well as in structural, Bowenian, strategic, and systemic therapy in particular. Effective metacommunication has at least two results: It allows more detachment and clarity of perception for members within a system about the qualities of that system, and it allows the generation of new possibilities, probabilities, and actualities that could not be predicted by looking at the system's past. Thus, if we can metacommunicate effectively about humanity's communication with and about God, we may attain more perspective on the current human condition and possibly bring forth a vision of a new transcendent reality to be actualized.

2. The use of process. Family therapists are not unique among therapists in their understanding that therapy moves through certain stages and phases, that it has a beginning, middle, and end, whether it be a single consultation or a multi-year psychoanalysis. There is an underlying process that can be described. Arthur Young (1976), the inventor of the Bell helicopter and a systems theorist and philosopher, has developed an explicit and comprehensive metatheory of process which proceeds through specific steps or stages and has been applied to both physical evolution and to the evolution of consciousness. It is possible to use this understanding of process to describe the evolution of humanity's conception and perception of God or, perhaps more accurately, the co-evolution of humanity and God.

3. The importance of relationship. What is unique about family therapists is the primacy they give to altering relationships as the method of change, whether the relation is between two members of a family, between an individual and his family of origin, between a therapist and the family system, between a therapeutic team and the family system, or between an individual and her thinking and feeling systems. When I was a medical student observing Nathan Ackerman demonstrate family therapy, I was struck by how he told us to look "between" rather than "at" people. Twenty years later, reading Martin Buber (1965b), I was struck by his statement that both the individual and society are essentially illusions. "Each considered by itself is a mighty abstraction. The individual is a fact of existence in so far as he steps into a living relation with other individuals. The aggregate is a fact of existence in so far as it is built up of living units of relation…I call this…the sphere of 'between'"(p. 203). Buber gives ontological priority to that which family therapists give clinical priority.

The importance, perhaps even primacy, of relationship can assist us with respect to the question of God. Rather than attempting to describe the evolution of God, or the evolution of humanity's conception of God, or the co-evolution of humanity and God, we can seek to describe the evolution of the relationship between humanity and God. We even might go a step further and describe God itself (himself or herself) as immanent or inherent in relatedness or the "between."

4. Alcoholics Anonymous and other Twelve Step programs as paradigmatic and pragmatic demonstrations of spirituality. Having used elements of family and general systems theory to develop a new conception and perception of God, I will seek to use the history and practice of Alcoholics Anonymous and similar self-help groups as models for practical application of spiritual principles. To merely make assertions about the existence or nature of God is in the tradition of speculative theology and philosophy which, unless it engenders specific new empowering experiences and insights, is not particularly useful and is perhaps even detrimental if it leads to substituting theoretical intellectualizing for direct action. In providing clinical evidence to demonstrate God as "the between," we will need to go beyond the boundaries of family therapy, since up to the present family therapy has largely ignored spirituality and also because individual and family therapy have inherent structural limitations that make it difficult to fully access a spiritual reality within the therapeutic framework. I would even argue that Twelve Step programs are themselves systemic therapies with a unique contextual structure that allows for the effective treatment of addictive disorders in a manner that other therapies cannot.

The Evolution of Humanity's Relationship with God

Using the principle of metacommunication, it is possible to describe the evolution of the relationship between humanity and God. The description should be equally applicable to understanding the internal process of the prevailing myths or metaphors of God, to the actual history of humanity's notion of God, and to the evolution of an individual's sense of spirituality. Much as it is said in biology that ontogeny recapitulates phylogeny, we can say that the unfolding of an individual's spiritual experience is isomorphic with the evolution of both the spiritual metaphors and the religious history of humanity.

I will describe the evolution of humanity's relationship with God as an eight stage process, starting with an initial oneness with the divine at the first stage, proceeding in the next stages toward differentiating a totally separate and conscious sense of self until there is complete alienation from God at the fourth stage, then a turn toward reintegration with a regaining of the oneness at the seventh stage, and finally a transcendence of that oneness in the emergence of the divine as "the between" or relatedness at the eighth stage.

The following diagram portrays this process of the fall and return:

8. God as the Between

1. God in the World — 7. Oneness With God

2. God Above the World — 6. "I Am God"

3. God Outside the World — 5. God As the Universe

4. "God Is Dead"

1. God in the World: Owen Barfield, a British lawyer, writer, and philosopher, developed the term "original participation" to describe the relation between "primitive"human beings and their world which, as seen by them, was enchanted with everything, including what we now see as inanimate objects, possessing spirit or divinity. The story of the Garden of Eden, as well as the creation myths of other cultures, also reflect this primordial oneness where God dwelled in the world. Barfield (1965) wrote:

> The essence of original participation is that there stands behind the phenomena, and on the other side of them from me, a thing

> which is represented of the same nature as me. Whether it is called "mana," or by the names of many gods and demons, or God the Father, or the spirit world, it is of the same nature as the perceiving self, inasmuch as it is not mechanical or accidental, but psychic and voluntary. (p. 42)

Thus, human essence, nature essence, and divine essence are seen as one and the same. The film *The Gods Must Be Crazy* provides some sense of the quality of participating consciousness and the difference between it and our modern consciousness in its depiction of the contrast between the way of being of the Kalahari bushpeople, on the one hand, and other Africans and Europeans, on the other hand. There is a naturalness, a gracefulness, that the Kalahari possess that is strikingly lacking in the supposedly more civilized.

Morris Berman (1981), in his book *The reenchantment of the world*, described the evolution of science, technology, and capitalism as intrinsically connected with Weber's "disenchantment of the world" or Schiller's "disgodding" of nature. There is a shift from an initial harmony or oneness with nature to a separation from nature in an attempt to control it. Berman described the difference between these two modes of consciousness: "The 'primitive' may often be frightened by his environment or by things in it, but he is never alienated by it...We, on the other hand, by denying both the existence of spirits and the role of our own spirit in our figuration of reality, are out of touch with it" (p. 142).

On an individual level, the sense of participating consciousness manifests through what Freud (1930) described as an "oceanic" feeling, "of an indissoluble bond, of being one with the external world as a whole" (p. 65). His psychoanalytic explanation of the feeling is that it is a remnant from the infantile period that exists before "one can differentiate between what is internal—what belongs to the ego—and what is external—what emanates from the outer world" (p. 67).

2. God above the World: As the sense of oneness with the world was lost, there was still retained a relationship of personal communication with divinity. Rather than being present in the world all the time, the gods and goddesses of Greece and the God of the Hebrews came to be seen as residing above the world, whether on Mt. Olympus or in Heaven, actively looking after the world and periodically intervening in it.

Julian Jaynes (1976) argued that the Greeks of the Iliad and the Hebrews of the Old Testament literally heard the voices of the gods and goddesses or of God as auditory hallucinations telling them what to do. Jaynes stated that they were ruled in everyday life by unconscious habits and in encountering anything new by voices and visions. This mode of knowing persists up to the present both in certain types of religious experiences as well as in schizophrenic hallucinations. This is not to suggest either that religious visions are delusional in nature or that schizophrenics really possess a religious wisdom, but that both visions and hallucinations are expressed in this particular mode which we can describe as fusional or dyadic.

Rather than the oneness that the primitive experiences with nature or that the fetus experiences in the womb, in the second stage of process there is a symbiotic, fusional relationship between a rudimentary I and an Other, whether the Other is God or the infant's mother. With fusion and the associated psychological defense mechanisms of projection and identification, the Other is greatly loved as well as greatly feared, appearing both as benevolent and vengeful.

3. God outside the World: When the prophets of Israel no longer heard the voice of God, they wrote down the Law, and when Ulysses, as perhaps the first character in Western literature to have a well-developed sense of a separate I, became self-determined in his actions, he no longer had to rely on the voices of the gods for guidance as did the heroes of the *Iliad*. From a religious perspective, one may see this shift as a continuation of the "fall," as part of the descent into sin, and from a scientific or humanist perspective one might take this as progress, as humanity growing up and taking back the fire from the gods. In either case, they are value judgments about the necessary, and perhaps inevitable, evolution of human consciousness and its relation to God. As there is an increase in the separate sense of self, of I-ness, there is an increased ability to take willful, premeditated action and a decreased sense of contact with the sacred.

In the third stage of process, the predominant mode becomes triadic rather than dyadic, with both internal triangles, thought mediating between the I and its flow of experience, and external triangles, manifest in relationships either specifically as the Oedipal triangle, or more generally as interlocking triangles within the family system.

The transition from the unconscious sense of self of the second stage of process, in which there are not clear distinctions from other human beings and from God, to the preconscious sense of self of the third stage, where other people and God are perceived as separate and external, can be seen as having taken between 2000 and 2500 years—from ancient Greece and Israel up to the Europe of the Enlightenment, in the seventeenth and eighteenth centuries. It was only toward the end of this period that the accepted worldview or paradigm matched the shift in consciousness that had been occurring.

Küng pointed out that Descartes, Copernicus, Kepler, Galileo, and Newton were all representatives of mathematical-mechanical natural science as well as believers in God. However, their God had largely evolved from one who actively participated with humanity and nature to one who was the "Creator—however remote—and Ruler of this world machine" (p. 90). "The ancient-medieval idea of a God above the world" had shifted to "the modern, enlightened idea of a God outside the world," (p. 90) and the sense of a personal God to an impersonal Deity. God had changed from what Pascal had called the God of Abraham, Isaac, and Jacob to the God of the philosophers. This deism "developed consistently into a scientific atheism, which did not need God either physically for the explanation of the world or even morally for the conduct of life" (Küng, 1981, p. 91).

4. "God Is Dead": This aphorism of Nietzsche both describes and evokes the quality of modern consciousness as it has completed its evolution from participating consciousness to isolation and separation. The totally conscious, and self-conscious, self of the fourth stage can more easily attempt to dominate and control nature, now seen as a machine from which God has been removed, at the expense of an unprecedented alienation.

Nietzsche sought to describe the emotional consequences that accompanied the change in intellectual outlook. His evocation of the modern human condition:

> Is there any up or down left? Are we not straying as through an infinite nothing? Do we not feel the breath of empty space? Has it not become colder? Is not night and more night coming on all the while?...God is dead. God remains dead. And we have killed him...What was holiest and most powerful of all that the world has yet owned has bled to death under our knives. Who will wipe this blood off us? (translated by Kaufmann, 1950, p. 81)

It is certainly possible to dismiss Nietzsche as overwrought, romantic, and neurotic. However, it is not as easy to dismiss Auschwitz and the evil it represents and engenders. Elie Wiesel (1987) wrote:

> Defying all analogies, Auschwitz institutes itself as a point of reference...[it] symbolizes the culmination of violence, hatred and death (p. 4)...Never shall I forget that night, the first night in camp, which has turned my life into one long night, seven times cursed and seven times sealed...Never shall I forget those flames which consumed my faith forever. Never shall I forget that nocturnal silence which deprived me, for all eternity, of the desire to live. Never shall I forget those moments which murdered my God and my soul and turned my dreams to dust. (p. 43)

It seems almost unbearable to let in the full intensity of the horror and evil of Auschwitz as a metaphor for the modern human condition of which Buber (1965b) said:

> This condition is characterized by the union of cosmic and social homelessness, dread of the universe and dread of life, resulting in an existential condition of solitude such as has probably never existed before to the same extent. The human person feels...exposed by nature—as an unwanted child is exposed—and at the same time a person isolated in the midst of the tumultuous modern world. (p. 200)

There seem to me four categories of reaction or response that human beings can have to this oppressive condition:

A. *Fundamentalism*—As a way of denying the full impact of evil and the sense either of complicity or of powerlessness that accompanies the death of humanity's relationship with God, one can seek to cling more tenaciously to outmoded childish fantasies of religion: of a Father-God who will protect his children against destruction, of a Messiah who will come physically for the first or second time to save the world, of supernatural forces that will intervene to violate or reverse physical laws. Fundamentalism, however, need not only be religious; it exists whenever anyone embraces a dogma that provides a consolation, absolving one of participation in the evil and holding out the promise of a utopian, externally imposed solution to the current human condition. Thus, there is humanist fundamentalism that promises a better world if we just interact rationally, political fundamentalism that proclaims that everything will be better after the revolution or when my particular cause is triumphant, scientific fundamentalism with its blind faith in dogmas based on mechanistic reductionism, and even psychotherapeutic fundamentalism which paradoxically finds it consoling either to embrace the dogma of unlimited therapeutic growth or the dogma of the impossibility of fundamental change.

B. *Nihilism*—Rather than seeking to escape the sense of meaninglessness and emptiness inherent in modern life by adopting a fundamentalist position that seeks to reestablish a lost idyllic past or to create a utopian future, nihilism seeks to avoid the nothingness by embracing it. Nietzsche accurately foresaw that, with the death of the relationship with God and the collapse of the system of morality that was based upon religion, there would be an upsurge of nihilism. He saw nihilism as "the conviction of the nullity, of the internal contradiction, futility and worthlessness of reality" (Küng, p. 388). It, like fundamentalism, can take a number of forms: the bored, intellectual cynic; the yuppie driven by an insatiable drive to achieve more and more success; the sociopathic personality; adolescent Satanism; certain types of addiction; outbreaks of random and senseless violence; political terrorism; domestic violence and abuse; and the institutionalized violence and vengeance of Nazism. What becomes particularly appealing to some, and dangerous to everyone else, is when the energy of nihilism is combined with the rhetoric of fundamentalism; Hitler, Stalin, and Jonestown demonstrate the danger of this combination.

C. *The attempted exercise of willpower*—With the collapse of fundamentalist morality and in the face of nihilism, existentialists have embraced the exercise of will. Nietzsche spoke of the "will to power," Heidegger in *Being and time* of "resoluteness," and Sartre in *Being and nothingness* of "fundamental choice." Perhaps the epitome of this mode of willfulness is the Sisyphus of Camus with his scorn as he is walking down the hill to push the rock back up it.

The difficulty with the defiant attempt to impose one's will is that it reinforces exactly what is contributing to the current human dilemma: the conscious, isolated self, who is now totally separated from any sense of the divine. Bateson (1972) pointed out that "surrender to alcoholic intoxication provides a partial and subjective shortcut to a more correct state of mind" (p. 309). The sense of participating consciousness that is accessed, albeit in a distorted form, in active addictions may be, in many respects, epistemologically, ontologically, and theologically more "correct" than the separate sense of self that is trying to control the addiction. Thus, a crucial step in the "hitting bottom" or "deflation at depth" which is central to AA's process of recovery is seeing the bankruptcy, futility, and impotence of the will.

D. *Rebirth or resurrection of the relationship with God*—The only remedy for the death of God may be the birth of a new sense of, and relationship with, God. The difficulty is for that sense to be truly new, not a projection of past fundamentalist ideas or based upon the exercise of willpower. Martin Buber (1965a) powerfully brought forth the essence of this gap where the old relationship or dialogue with God has died, and the new one has not yet been born: "Illumination cannot be accomplished in any other place than in the abyss of I-with-me…it is in its most real moments not even a monologue, much less a real conversation…all speech is exhausted; what takes place here is the mute shudder of self-being" (p. 137). The family therapist Thomas Fogarty (1977) has described this phase as getting in touch with one's inner emptiness, Alcoholics Anonymous as coming to see that one is powerless, the Zen Buddhists as the period of the Great Doubt, and the Christian mystics as the Dark Night of the Soul.

While Buber evoked the quality of the process of hitting bottom, he also placed it against a wider context, what he called the Eclipse of God. He wrote: "Something is taking place in the depths that as yet needs no name…The eclipse of the light of God is no extinction; even tomorrow that which has stepped in between may give way"(Buber, 1952, p. 129).

Once the death of the old concept of God is complete, at the end of the fourth stage of process, a new sense of God can emerge, ending the period of the eclipse of God. Depending upon the intensity of the experience of hitting bottom, there may be generated a new concept of God at the fifth stage, a direct experience of God within, or as, the self at the sixth stage, a oneness with God at the seventh stage, or a relationship with an absolute, loving presence at the eighth stage. Having completed the fall, one can begin the return.

5. God as the Universe: In the third stage, God came to be seen as transcendent or outside the world; in the fifth stage God is seen as immanent or inherent in the world. While the materialist notions of eighteenth and nineteenth century science removed God from the universe, some twentieth century scientists in fields such as quantum mechanics and astrophysics have, to some extent, restored God to the universe, though the impersonal nature of the Deity remains. In contemplating the very small realm of the atom and the very large realm of the cosmos, feelings of awe, humility, and wonder are generated but not necessarily feelings of love, bliss, and gratitude, and this God can as easily be called Nature. Einstein described his conception of God: "I believe in Spinoza's God who reveals himself in the orderly harmony of what exists, not in a God who concerns himself with the fates and actions of human beings" (quoted in Küng, 1981, p. 628).

6. "I Am God": If the discovery at the fifth stage is that God is immanent in the world, the discovery at the sixth stage is that God is immanent in the self, perhaps even is the self. The expression, "I am God," can be uttered either by the mystic, such as the Sufi Al-Hallaj Mansur whose ego is dissolving into the divine, or by the spiritual dilettante whose ego is inflated by discovering a divine spark within himself. There is a similarity to the second stage of process, or God Above the World, in that there are strong feelings of encountering a divine presence, but also a fundamental difference in that there is not literally an external voice of God that is heard, but instead there may be a sense of listening to inner voices.

The conventionally religious view holds that God is totally separate from the self, while some proponents of a New Age spirituality hold that the self is God, sometimes basing their position on Carl Jung (1928), who described God as an "autonomous psychic content" (p. 239) and also stated that the unconscious or psyche cannot be distinguished from God. Buber (1952) vehemently criticized this position, essentially holding, as we might say today, that Jung was not thinking systemically, that he was seeing God as an individual phenomenon rather than as a function of the between. Buber wrote:

> For if religion is a relation to psychic events, which cannot mean anything other than to events of one's own soul, then it is implied by this that it is not a relation to a Being or Reality which, no matter how fully it may from time to time descend to the human soul, always remains transcendent to it. More precisely, it is not the relation of an I to a Thou...Jung conceives of God not as a Being or Reality to which a psychical content corresponds, but rather as the content itself. (p. 79–80)[1]

7. Oneness with God: This is the ultimate state reported by mystics where there is no separate I left to fuse with God. It has been likened to a drop having fallen into the ocean. If the fifth stage of the evolution of spiritual consciousness is characterized by conditions associated with a sense of awe and wonder and the sixth stage by strong feelings of compassion or beautiful sadness and bliss or joy, the seventh stage has an all-pervasive ground of well-being, peace, and love that transcends specific emotions. Franklin Merrill-Wolff (1973), a mystic with a background

[1] In fairness to Jung, he spoke differently about the subject of God in his personal life than when he saw himself speaking as a psychologist. There is the famous interview with the BBC where, when asked whether he believed in God, he replied, "I know. I don't need to believe." (McGuire and Hull, 1977, p. 428), and in another interview, "These two terms are psychologically very much related—which doesn't mean that I believe that God is the self or that the self is God. I simply state that there is a psychological relation between them" (McGuire and Hull, p. 327).

in philosophy, wrote a book describing this state which he titled, *The philosophy of consciousness Without an Object*. J. Krishnamurti (1979) also spoke of this shift to a state of consciousness without subjects or objects and called the state meditation or choiceless awareness: "In the flame of meditation thought ends and with it feeling, for neither is love…Out of emptiness love is" (p. 52).

Since conceptual categories completely break down at the seventh stage, it is equally possible to assert that God is nothing and that God is everything. This domain can be brought forth by the declaration of tautology variously expressed as: "I am that I am"; "The Lord is One"; "God is love"; "There is no God but God"; "Thou art that"; or, "What is, is."

With the achievement of oneness there is restored the sense of God In the World, with key differences that one is still capable of performing the mental operations of previous stages and that one is aware of the oneness. Another way to state the distinction is that, at the first stage, the self is itself unaware of itself, at the fourth stage, the self is alienated from itself, and at the seventh stage, the self is itself aware of itself. The state of oneness is not at all similar to a feeling of fusion; paradoxically, when the ego or separate sense of self is seen to be an illusion, one is able to be more self-determined and responsible in one's actions. Yet it is not the final step. Buber (1952) described himself as having been a mystic for a number of years, but as having gone beyond that, to seeing that God is inherent in dialogue or relationship.

8. God as Relatedness or the Between: At the eighth stage of process we arrive at a new, systemic conception and perception of God which again can only be expressed paradoxically: God is immanent within I-Thou relationships; yet entering into dialogue or relation also can provide a sense of a transcendent, absolute presence. To be completely relating in the here and now brings forth a sense of the Beyond, and being aware of the reality of the Beyond brings one into more intimate relation with others. This relationship with God does not remove one from the world, but brings one into more immediate contact and connection.

The "between" presents itself when there is a balance between inside and outside, between the internal and the external. This notion of God transcends both the conventionally religious view of God outside the self and a psychological view of God as the self.

It seems to me that God as dialogue or relatedness (between) can manifest in four ways:

A. Between an individual and a divine presence— Bill Wilson, the cofounder of Alcoholics Anonymous, described the experience that allowed him to stop drinking:

> My depression deepened unbearably and finally it seemed to me as though I were at the very bottom of the pit. I still gagged badly on the notion of a power greater than myself, but finally, just for the moment, the last vestige of my proud obstinacy was crushed.

> All at once I found myself crying out, "If there is a God, let Him show Himself! I am ready to do anything, anything!"
>
> Suddenly the room lit up with a great white light. It seemed to me, in the mind's eye, that I was on a mountain and that a wind not of air but of spirit was blowing. And then it burst upon me that I was a free man. Slowly the ecstasy subsided. I lay on the bed, but now for a time I was in another world, a new world of consciousness. All about me and through me there was a wonderful feeling of Presence, and I thought to myself, "So this is the God of the Preachers." A great peace stole over me. (Alcoholics Anonymous, 1957, p. 61)

We can use Bill's experience to exemplify a number of the characteristics that distinguish this sense of spirituality from the previous stages of process:

1. God in the World—The person who still has an intrinsic oneness with the sacred cannot become depressed. In *The Gods must be crazy*, when the bushman was imprisoned, he stopped eating and peacefully awaited his death but did not express any unhappiness. This contrasts with Bill's alienation, depression, and despair, which set the stage for a new spirituality.
2. God above the World—Bill did not literally hear the voice of God. His writing, "It seemed to me, in the mind's eye," indicates an awareness of the metaphorical nature of his experience.
3. God outside the World—"For a time I was in another world, a new world of consciousness." Bill's system of concepts, his view of the world that had kept God outside it, was temporarily suspended, and he immediately became aware of a divine presence that conceptual thinking obscures. It is interesting to note that, when Bill returned to his ordinary state of consciousness, he began to doubt his experience, thinking that maybe he had been hallucinating, thus potentially placing God again outside his world.
4. God Is Dead—Bill had been alienated from religion for most of his life, and for him God was indeed dead, with no fundamentalist ideals to console him. In both his attitudes and behavior he had certainly been nihilistic, and he had what he subsequently termed a "near-fatal encounter with the juggernaut of self-will" (*Alcoholics Anonymous*, 1953, p. 37). He, having admitted defeat, not being able to turn to fundamentalism, nihilism, or willpower any longer, was able to be open for a rebirth of a new sense of the sacred.
5. God as the Universe—Because of the pain associated with his bottoming-out process, Bill did not spend much time contemplating either the nature of the universe or a new intellectual conception of God as a modern scientist, systems theorist, or theologian might. He just stopped resisting the notion of a power greater than himself, in part because a friend of his had suggested, "Why don't you choose your

own conception of God?" (*Alcoholics Anonymous*, 1976, p.12). His God, or Higher Power, was certainly experienced as directly and personally loving, not as impersonally immanent in the universe.

6. I Am God—The strong feeling of ecstasy that Bill reported is characteristic of the sixth stage of process. However, a crucial distinction is that Bill did not see the ecstasy as the product of his psyche; he found himself addressed by a presence that was "all about me and through me," both without and within. Subsequently, a cornerstone of the AA message has been that the individual alcoholic is "not God," that claiming God-like powers, particularly that of control, is potentially disastrous (Kurtz, 1982).

7. Oneness with God—When Bill speaks of the ecstasy subsiding, of being in a new world of consciousness with a great peace stealing over him, he is describing this state in much the same way as did Merrill-Wolff (1973). The focus is now not on the intense feeling of ecstasy, but on the all-pervasive state of peace. Bill's description in itself cannot be used to make a distinction between Oneness with God, the seventh stage of process, or God as the "Between," the eighth stage. For that we will have to examine some of the other manifestations of God as the Between and see how Alcoholics Anonymous and other Twelve Step programs exemplify them.

B. *Between human beings*—The traditional mystic finds God in solitude; the person with a perception of God as the Between finds God in relating to others. If one looks into Scripture, one can find precedent for God manifesting as a function of an I-Thou relatedness between people. Jesus said, "For where two or three are gathered together in my name, there am I in the midst of them" (Matthew 18:20), and Jesus' statement that, "The Kingdom of God is within you" (Luke 17:2, *King James Version*), is perhaps more accurately translated, "The Kingdom of God is in your midst" (*New American Standard Bible*). Rather than a psychological phenomenon found within people, in their hearts, the Kingdom of God can be seen also as an inter-human phenomenon found between or among people, in their midst.

The history and practices of Alcoholics Anonymous demonstrate this notion of spirituality residing between people. The beginning of AA is dated, not from the transformative experience that allowed Bill to stop drinking, but rather from the day that Dr. Bob Smith, the cofounder of AA, had his last drink. Bill's "hot flash" was seen as less important than the six hour dialogue that Bill and Dr. Bob had when they first met. The partnership between Dr. Bob and Bill, rather than Bill's insights or charismatic leadership, is considered to be the source of AA. Thus, Alcoholics Anonymous has avoided many of the traps and pitfalls that have beset other spiritual movements which place authority and leadership within a single individual rather than within a relationship that serves as a conduit for a transcendent power.

In practice, Alcoholics Anonymous and similar Twelve Step programs are strikingly non-hierarchical. There are no permanent leaders, meetings are chaired by a secretary who has a maximum of a three month term, and meetings are usually led by a nonprofessional volunteer speaker, who tells his or her story of recovery and then calls upon others to share. The atmosphere of honesty, authenticity, and openness allows a sense of spirituality to develop that is not easily accessible in individual or family therapy because of the unavoidable issues of hierarchy, authority, and transference that are inherent in consulting a paid, professional therapist.

If newcomers to the program have difficulty with the notion of a personal Higher Power, they are frequently invited to see the group itself as a Higher Power, thus allowing a contextual shift away from placing power within the individual self. They are also encouraged to select someone from the group to be their sponsor, a way of modeling and passing on an I-Thou relationship. The sponsor is not seen as being superior to the newcomer but as someone who is deepening his or her own sobriety by working the Twelfth Step of AA, carrying the message to other alcoholics. There is a lore passed down from sponsor to sponsor, and we can see this as the between, or context replicating itself through the particular individuals participating in the sponsoring relationship.

C. *Between feminine and masculine*—At the core of the new spirituality is what has been called the return of the Goddess (Whitmont 1982). Riane Eisler, in *The chalice and the blade* (1987), has presented evidence that, during the period of human history which I have termed God In the World, the Goddess was worshiped as the supreme aspect of divinity, and that the "'feminine' power to nurture and give [was] the normative ideal, the model to be emulated by both women and men" (p. 28). She further pointed out that "the primacy of the Goddess—and with this the centrality of the values symbolized by the nurturing and regenerating powers incarnated in the female body—does not justify the inference that women here dominated men" (p. 27). Matrilineal societies were not matriarchal; rather the relationship or partnership between female and male was valued as important. Starting in the period we have termed God Above the World, the partnership model has been replaced with what she calls the "dominator model—in which human hierarchies are ultimately backed up by force or the threat of force " (p. xix).

As Eisler stated, "our reconnecting with the earlier spiritual tradition of Goddess worship linked to the partnership model of society is more than a reaffirmation of the dignity and worth of half of humanity" (p. 194). It may indeed be central to the future of all humanity as we shift from a dominator view of both human relations and spirituality, symbolized by the blade, back to a partnership view, symbolized by the chalice. The Hasidim speak of the *Shekinah*, God's glory, essence, or presence on earth, as being feminine and in exile, like a homeless woman wandering, the earth. Perhaps one of the main tasks of our age is the reunion of the masculine aspect of divinity, God or spirit, with the feminine aspect, Goddess, *Shekinah*, or soul.

An obvious area where the relationship between feminine and masculine is expressed is in sexuality. Religion and sexuality have conventionally been seen as separate and incompatible, but Elaine Pagels (1988), among others, has pointed out that this has not always been the case, that, for example, the view of sex as wicked and sinful was adopted by the early Christian church only after some conflict. This split between spirituality and sexuality is consistent with other types of dualistic thinking, such as the split between mind and body, or between heaven and earth, that have become prevalent in Western scientific and religious thinking, and sexual expression may emerge as one of the main arenas where these splits are healed.

The relationship between masculine and feminine as a manifestation of spirituality need not manifest only externally. Jung (1946,1963) pointed out that there is an "internal marriage" between masculine and feminine, or animus and anima. This internal marriage leads to a *mysterium coniunctionis*, a direct experience of a numinous spiritual reality.

The recent history of AA and other Twelve Step programs reflects this increased emphasis on the feminine and on the importance of relationship. While there has always been a feminine tone to AA's emphasis on accepting one's powerlessness, of seeing the futility of dominating, controlling willfulness, and shifting to a willingness to be receptive to the care of a power greater than oneself, the AA program was until recently a program primarily run by men for men. The last few years have seen an influx of women into the Alcoholics Anonymous program, but more strikingly, they have also seen the emergence of the Adult Children of Alcoholics movement, with its initial, predominantly female leadership, and a flowering of other Twelve Step programs that have a high percentage of women participants and that frequently focus on relationship issues.

D. *Between human beings and Supreme Being*—At first glance the relation between human beings and Supreme Being may seem the same as the relation between an individual and a divine presence. A key distinction is that encountering a divine presence is experiential, while the relation between beings and Being is contextual. An experience of the sacred opens one to a domain that Bateson (1979) and Maturana (1988) may be referring to when they speak respectively of the "pattern which connects" and the "coordination of actions." There is an interplay and intercommunication between human beings, the parts, the finite, and Supreme Being, the whole, the infinite, that leads to coherence, cohesiveness, congruence, and connectedness.

As an individual allows a sense of spirituality to permeate his or her life, as individuals relate to each other as an I to a Thou, and as God is reunited with Goddess, there is the emergence of the All That Is which connects and coordinates, empowering individuals to discover and fulfill their unique destinies. It manifests in two ways: synchronicity and synergy.

Etymologically, synchronicity comes from the Greek *syn*, together, and *chronos,* time, thus literally being a co-incidence or occurring together in time. Jung (1952) described synchronicity as an a-causal connecting principle. As one opens to a spiritual reality, there is a dramatic increase in the number of synchronicities or meaningful coincidences that start occurring. Bill Wilson (*Alcoholics Anonymous*, 1957) described a number of synchronistic events that occurred around both his transformative experience and his first meeting with Dr. Bob, and frequently people will describe an uncanny set of coincidences that led up to or followed their attendance at their first Twelve Step meeting.

Synergy is derived from *syn* and *ergon*, work, thus being a working together. The terms synergy or synergism have been used in biology and medicine to indicate "the action of two or more substances, organs, or organisms to achieve an effect of which each is individually incapable," but more strikingly synergism in theology is "the doctrine that regeneration is effected by a combination of human will and divine grace" (*American heritage dictionary*, 1969). Thus, synergy, is found both between human beings working together toward a common purpose that could not be achieved through their isolated pursuits, and between humanity and divinity, wherein finite human beings interpret and implement the divine pattern. This relation between human beings and Supreme Being can also be called co-creation.

A typical AA meeting frequently manifests this sense of synergy or inherent order. The speaker, or the first person to start the discussion, may start somewhat hesitantly, saying he or she is not sure what to say, but will then get the call of the spirit, and as others start to share, there is an almost palpable sense of the between that emerges. There is a strong sense of dialogue and relatedness, even though people do not directly address each other during the meeting. Buber (1965a) captured some of the essence of dialogue, observable in AA and similar contexts where human beings are co-creating with Supreme Being:

> All who are joined in a genuine dialogue need not actually speak; those who keep silent can on occasion be especially important. But each must be determined not to withdraw when the course of the conversation makes it proper for him to say what he has to say. No one, of course, can know in advance what it is that he has to say; genuine dialogue cannot be arranged beforehand. It has indeed its basic order from the beginning, but nothing can be determined, the course is of the spirit, and some discover what they have to say only when they catch the call of the spirit. (p. 87)

Conclusion

This article has perhaps been foolish in rushing in, ignoring Gregory Bateson's implicit warning about fearing to tread and Ludwig Wittgenstein's (1922) admonition: "Whereof one cannot speak, thereof one must be silent." Yet Wittgenstein also declared that, "There is indeed the unsayable. This shows itself; it is the mystical," and Bateson (1987) claimed "not uniqueness but membership in a small minority who believe that there are strong and clear arguments for the necessity of the sacred, and that these arguments have their base in an epistemology rooted in improved science and the obvious" (p. 11).

My endeavor to explicitly delineate eight stages in the evolution of humanity's relationship with God carries with it the risk of turning God into a thing, an It, rather than a presence, a Thou. In addition this article has perhaps become a fairly lengthy monologue about the importance of dialogue.

One fortunate byproduct of the article's length is that it forecloses further discussion of the application of spirituality in clinical practice, of using God as a technique. My main point is that God, or more accurately God, Goddess, All That Is, is not just a technique, interesting philosophy, or clinically useful hypothesis, but is in truth a "meta-objective" actuality that goes beyond our usual notions of subjective and objective.

Family therapists are in a unique position to appreciate a very real resource that is neither "out there" nor "in here" but is between, among, and beyond.

References

[Alcoholics Anonymous]. (1953). *Twelve steps and twelve traditions*. New York: A.A. World Services.

[Alcoholics Anonymous]. (1957). *Alcoholics Anonymous comes of age*. New York: A.A. World Services.

[Alcoholics Anonymous]. (1976). *Alcoholics Anonymous*. (Third Edition) New York: A. A. World Services.

Barfield, O. (1965). *Saving the appearances*. New York: Harcourt Brace Jovanovich.

Bateson, G.(1972). *Steps to an ecology of mind*. New York: Ballantine.

Bateson, G. (1979). *Mind and nature: A necessary unity*. New York: E.P. Dutton.

Bateson, G., and Bateson, M.C. (1987). *Angels fear: Towards an epistemology of the sacred*. New York: Macmillan.

Berman, M. (1981). *The reenchantment of the world*. Ithaca, N.Y.: Cornell.

Bowen, M. (1980). Presentation, Georgetown University Family Symposium.

Buber, M. (1952). *Eclipse of God*. New York: Harper and Row.

Buber, M. (1965a). *The knowledge of man*. New York: Harper and Row.

Buber, M. (1965b). *Between man and man*. New York: Macmillan.

Eisler, R. (1987). *The chalice and the blade*. New York: Harper and Row.

Fogarty, T. (1977). On emptiness and closeness. *The Family, [Journal of the Center For Family Learning]*, Rye, N.Y., vol. 2, no.1.

Freud, S. (1927). *The future of an illusion. Standard Edition* 21:3–56.

Freud, S. (1930). *Civilization and its discontents*. Standard Edition 21:59–147.

Freud, S. (1933). *New introductory lectures on psychoanalysis*. Standard Edition 22:3–180.

Jaynes, J. (1976). *The origin of consciousness in the breakdown of the bicameral mind*. Boston: Houghton Mifflin.

Jung, C. G. (1928). *The relations between the ego and the unconscious*. Collected Works.

Jung, C. G. (1946). *The psychology of the transference*. Collected Works, 16.

Jung, C. G. (1952). *Synchronicity: An acausal connecting principle*. Collected Works, 8.

Jung, C. G. (1963). *Mysterium coniunctionis*. Collected Works 14.

Kaufmann, W. (1950). *Nietzsche: Philosopher, psychologist, antichrist*. Princeton: Princeton University Press.

Krishnamurti, J. (1979). *Meditations*. San Francisco: Harper and Row.

Küng, H. (1981). *Does God exist*? New York: Random House.

Kurtz, E. (1982). Why AA works: The intellectual significance of Alcoholics Anonymous. *Journal of Studies on Alcohol*, 42, 38–80.

Macquarrie, J. (1987). *In search of Deity: An essay in dialectical theism*. New York: Crossroad Publishing.

Maturana, H. (1988). Reality: The search for objectivity or the quest for a compelling argument. *Irish Journal of Psychology*, 9, 25–82.

McGuire, W. (Ed.), and Hull, R. F. C. C. and Manheim, R. (Trans.) (1977). *C. G. Jung speaking: Interviews and encounters*. Princeton: Princeton University Press.

Merrill-Wolff, F. (1973). *The philosophy of consciousness without an object*. New York: Julian Press.

Pagels, E. (1988). *Adam, Eve, and the serpent*. New York: Random House.

Watzlawick, P., Weakland, J. and Fisch, R. (1974). *Change: Principles of problem formation and problem resolution*. New York: Norton.

Whitehead, A. N., and Russell, B.(1910). *Principia mathematica*. Cambridge: Cambridge University.

Whitmont, E. (1982). *Return of the Goddess*. New York: Crossroad.

Wittgenstein, L. (1922). *Tractatus Logico-philosophicus*. London: Routledge.

Young, A. (1984). *The reflexive universe: Evolution of consciousness*. Portland, Oreg.: Robert Briggs Associates.

CHAPTER 5

Overcoming Cultural Points of Resistance to Spirituality in the Practice of Addiction Medicine

David E. Smith

and Richard B. Seymour

Great strides have been made in the treatment of addiction in recent years. These include advances in the understanding of brain chemistry and receptor-site science, the adoption of many new treatment procedures, and advances in understanding the nature and treatment of relapse. Addiction medicine (addictionology) has become an accepted medical field, represented by the American Society of Addiction Medicine (ASAM), and is included in medical school curricula for primary care and nonspecialist physicians. One of the greatest advances, however, has been the coming together of addiction and treatment and the recovering community, represented not only by Alcoholics Anonymous, but by a growing number of fellowships and programs representing a wide spectrum of addiction recovery concerns.

The availability of long-term recovery has legitimized treatment by giving patients a posttreatment goal involving abstinence and supported recovery. The interaction between treatment and recovery, however, has created a demand for recovery formats that take into consideration and alleviate a variety of cultural and professional points of resistance. In dealing with these problems, there needs to be increasing collaboration between those in the addiction medicine field and the progenitors within the recovering community (see Morgan's chapter 1 for insight into the need for collaboration in addiction studies).

The influence of the recovery group process has exerted a major influence on addiction medicine in general and on the Haight Ashbury Free Clinics (HAFCI) in particular. Darryl Inaba, Pharm. D., director of HAFCI's drug treatment program, estimates that as many as fifty different Twelve Step meetings a week occur at the various sites of the Haight Ashbury Free Clinics.

In fact, the quiet revolution of Twelve Step recovery, using culturally relevant models, whether they be church, clinic, or residential program, has saved many lives and has done much to counter the therapeutic pessimism and despair which dominate so many inner city, and even suburban, communities ravaged by the drug epidemic.

The Nature of Spirituality

In writing about addiction, recovery, and spirituality, it seems fitting to begin with what these terms mean to the authors. In this context, *addiction* is a disease, in and of itself, characterized by compulsion, loss of control, and continued use in spite of adverse consequences. The disease is progressive and, without treatment, often fatal. Addiction is incurable. No individual who has passed the threshold of the disease can go back to nonaddictive use; any attempt to resume use will result in the further progression of the disease. Addiction can, however, be brought into remission through abstinence from all psychoactive drugs, including marijuana and alcohol, and adherence to a program of supported recovery.

Recovery involves the acceptance of one's helplessness over the disease of addiction and adoption of a system of behavior that involves the development of personal spiritual maturity. Although there are recovery programs and fellowships that claim there is no need for a spiritual component in recovery, the authors believe that such a component is necessary for effective and long-lasting remission from addiction. This belief is based on the conviction that, by their nature, human beings are entities composed of interpenetrative and interactive physical, psychological, and spiritual aspects, and that the disease of addiction, like the human beings that it afflicts, has a tripartite nature and manifests physically, psychologically, and spiritually. Therefore, addiction has to be addressed in all three aspects for effective treatment and recovery.

Alcoholics Anonymous (AA) and other related Twelve Step fellowships have been labeled by some as religions because they involve a spiritual dimension in their approach to recovery. Such a label is unfounded; spirituality is not religion. Religions, at their best, include elements of spirituality, but spirituality is an element that transcends the limitations of individual religion by being an aspect of life itself.

In the authors' view, *spirituality* is primarily involved in a process of connectedness and relationship, that is, the relationship of an individual to something that is larger and more encompassing than the self. That "something" may be the group or fellowship, God as one may understand and interpret God, an amorphous loving presence, or any interpretation of a higher power, or anything beyond one's individual ego. Addiction has often been called a "disease of terminal uniqueness," or a "lonely disease." This is because the addict in the throes of denial is incapable of responding to anything or anyone beyond his or her own ego-conception of self. The awakening of spirituality makes it possible for addicts to escape from the prison of their own ego. The concept of surrender involved in this, and the misinterpretation of spirituality as religion, or some specific religion, lies at the heart of much resistance to the process of recovery, particularly within cultures that identify Twelve Step recovery with a specific white, male, Christian mindset.

Addiction: A Multicultural Problem in Need of Multicultural Solutions

Just as addiction is a global, rather than a national or regional, phenomenon, so addiction problems in this country are multicultural in their effect. Although characterized as a "melting pot," the United States is actually a multicultural society composed of people of many different races, religions, and backgrounds. Even the European American, seen by many as the dominant culture, is made up of people of many nationalities and ethnic groups far too numerous to list, with Catholic, Orthodox, white Anglo-Saxon Protestant, Moslem, and other religious backgrounds.

Internationally, one cannot simply take a treatment program that is successful in New York or Seattle, replicate it out of whole cloth in Florence or Addis Ababa, and expect the replication to fly. While the technical aspects of drug dependence may be similar, addiction takes place and is treated within a cultural milieu. The whole fabric of successful treatment needs to be woven around cultural realities.

The same can be true for individuals. We were not produced on an assembly line like so many interchangeable units, and our treatment outcome improves when there is a spectrum of care available. The same is true for both treatment and recovery within our multicultural society.

The relative efficacy of Twelve Step recovery in addiction medicine

In this society, Twelve Step fellowships, such as Alcoholics Anonymous, Narcotics Anonymous, and Cocaine Anonymous, are increasingly seen as the primary means to ensuring long-term abstinence and sobriety through addiction recovery. At least one government supported symposium has taken place with the goal of improving the general understanding of Twelve Step fellowships, not only within the medical, law enforcement, and judicial communities, but also among school counselors and clergy, indeed among all individuals who come into contact with possible addicts and are in a position to refer these individuals into potentially lifesaving supported recovery.

In the course of the symposium, hosted in 1990 by Robert L. DuPont, M.D., former Director of both the National Institute on Drug Abuse (NIDA) and current President of the Institute for Behavior and Health, it became clear that although there is no hard data, due in part to the Twelve Step tradition of anonymity, many thousands of addicts have come to enjoy increasing years of sobriety and well-being as a result of their use as recovery support. That symposium has led to the publication of a book, *A bridge to recovery: An introduction to Twelve Step programs* (DuPont et al., 1992), that provides many insights into the nature of Twelve-Step recovery fellowships.

It has been suggested that Twelve Step fellowships and their success provide credibility to addiction treatment as the bridge between active addiction and active recovery. While this may be increasingly true for the so-called mainstream of white, European American cultures in this country, it may be less true for other cultures within our society.

Several years ago, Smith and colleagues (1993) and Buxton and colleagues (1987) presented papers enumerating and discussing a variety of "points of resistance" to the Twelve Step recovery process. The focus of those papers was on points of resistance within the so-called mainstream of society, and they concentrated on individual and cultural concerns. Some of the concerns that result from different cultural orientations echo those of individuals. In general, these involve both real problems that need to be addressed if these cultures are to benefit from Twelve Step recovery fellowships and a cluster of misconceptions, misinterpretations and misperceptions about addiction medicine, and Twelve Step recovery and its fellowships.

In describing the problems facing the African American community, Pastor Cecil Williams of Glide Methodist Church (discussed in detail below) noted some of the concerns encountered in developing the Black Extended Family Project, and also some of the ways in which these problems can be solved through understanding and adaptation of the program to meet specific cultural needs. In that a vital link is developing, and must be retained between addiction medicine treatment and spiritual recovery, the authors will look at some of the areas of concern and discuss ways and means of addressing the problems that they involve. The first of these is the perception by non-European Americans that the Twelve Step fellowships are exclusively white, mainstream fellowships.

An exclusively white, male, Christian, middle-class focus?

History tells us that the first Twelve Step fellowship, Alcoholics Anonymous, was born in 1935 through an interaction between Bill W., a down-on his-luck stockbroker from New York, and Doctor Bob, a surgeon living in Akron, Ohio (AA, 1957). Both of these men came from white, middle-class backgrounds, as did most of the formative members of AA, who helped to develop the "steps" and "traditions" that gave the fellowship and its successors their basic form and character. The original ideals and concepts for the new fellowship were rooted in the Oxford Movement, a Christian fellowship that later became known as Moral Rearmament. When AA first became interrelated with treatment for alcoholics, it was through the Minnesota Model, developed at Hazelden (an early treatment center in Minnesota) with at least partial initial sponsorship from the Catholic Church (McElrath, 1987). The writing style found in the *Big Book* (AA, 1976), originally published in 1939, can also be seen to reflect the white, male, middle-class, Christian origins and values of its authors. (Again, for more detail regarding this history, see Morgan, chapter 1.)

With such beginnings, one would expect there to be an ongoing adherence within AA and other Twelve Step fellowships to Christianity and white middle-class values, to the exclusion of other cultures. And yet, from its beginnings, elements within the "group conscience" of AA began working to broaden the scope and flexibility of the fellowship. Early on, AA members began to distance themselves from the Oxford Movement, remaining friendly but moving toward a more eclectic spirituality that did not specify Christian dogma. In *Alcoholics Anonymous comes of age* (AA, 1957), Bill W. speaks of how the Twelve Steps of recovery were rephrased in their development, using more inclusive terms and concepts such as "a higher power" and "God *as we understood him*."

Alcoholics Anonymous may have had its specific beginnings in the Oxford Movement and the personal interaction between Bill W. and Doctor Bob, but its basic tenets reflect a spectrum of cultural antecedents, a number of which are discussed in *Drugfree: A unique, positive approach to staying off alcohol and other drugs* (Seymour and Smith, 1987). Throughout history and within various cultures, attempts have been made to deal with addiction and associated human problems. The most generally successful of these have involved in some way the development of individual spiritual maturity within a supportive environment. The authors see the Twelve Steps developed by Alcoholics Anonymous, and adapted by other recovery fellowships, as a blueprint for developing spiritual maturity, similar in intent to such entities as the Buddhist *Four Noble Truths* and *Eightfold Path*, the Hindu *Vedas*, and the Zen *Oxherding Panels*.

While the history of AA in the United States has primarily involved European American culture, the nature of the Twelve Steps and the precepts that underlie the various "fellowships" can be seen as much more universal. The AA approach is both basic and flexible, lending itself to a wide range of interpretation and applications. In his book, *Physician, heal thyself!* Dr. Earle M. (1989) discusses his personal experiences with AA chapters in other cultures throughout the world. In his travels, Dr. Earle encountered Buddhist, Moslem, and other AA chapters that had adapted Twelve Step insights to their own cultural needs and points of reference.

Individuals with certain religious backgrounds may have particular problems relating to certain tenets of the Twelve Steps. (See the chapter by Rabbi Carol Glass for an example.) Many Buddhists, for example, venerate the Buddha as a fully enlightened being to be followed and emulated, but do not see him as a "higher power." These Buddhists, not utilizing a concept of God or a higher power in their cultural background, see their faith as a philosophy and a way of life rather than as a religion. Points of reference need to be established in order for Twelve Step recovery to become meaningful for these individuals.

Spirituality in Twelve Step fellowships: Public policy and cultural issues

Alcoholics Anonymous and the other classical Twelve Step fellowships are spiritual programs. Spirituality is at the core of their effectiveness as a means to ongoing sobriety and recovery. That fact cannot be denied. This does not mean, however, that AA and the other recovery fellowships constitute a religion.

While it is true that Alcoholics Anonymous came into this world trailing clouds of Christian rhetoric, AA is no more a religion than is so-called secular humanism, though there are those who would call secular humanism a religion, too. As "proof" that AA is a religion, some point out that the word "God" appears from time to time in the Steps and in the *Big Book*. The phrase "In God We Trust" also appears on our monetary currency. Does that make the United States government a religion? And is the Treasury Department its church? The thought gives rise to interesting speculation.

In his article, "The twelve steps: A political time bomb," Lewis Andrews (1991) raises the issue of Twelve Step religiosity in terms of AA's vulnerability to constitutional restriction under the separation of church and state. He points out that while in the past most AA meetings were held in churches, or private clinics and hospitals, today they are increasingly to be found in such public institutions as schools, universities, community health centers, town meeting halls, prisons, and juvenile halls. While many would applaud this increasing secularization of scope, some who identify Twelve Step recovery as a religion see its appearance in public institutions as a violation of the constitutionally guaranteed separation between church and state. The situation becomes more volatile as increasing public sector entities that have some involvement in the referral of alcoholics and other addicts see Twelve Step fellowships as the preferred mode of recovery. That was, indeed, the gist of the referral symposium led by Dr. DuPont in 1990.

Given the politics of the day, Andrews foresaw the possibility of public funding being denied to hospitals and other publicly funded institutions that refer or even advocate the referral of clients to AA, or allow meetings to take place within their precincts. He also foresaw curious realignments of forces for and against the Steps, with the conservative "prayer in the classroom" minions lining up behind "recovery" to do battle with rigidly brittle ideologues within the American Civil Liberties Union. While the religiosity of Twelve Step fellowships may become a point of constitutional law, it is a point based on basic misunderstandings of the Steps.

One of these misunderstandings is the misconception that Alcoholics Anonymous and the other Twelve Step recovery fellowships are cohesive entities that have clear-cut rules and regulations for their memberships. For purposes of discussion, we will refer below to AA, as our general comments are similar for the other primary recovery fellowships. In actuality, although AA has a national council and an office with the primary task of publishing and distributing materials, it is primarily an idea that has been adopted and adapted by largely autonomous groups of recovering people throughout the world. Its program for recovery, consisting of the Twelve Steps and supplemented by the *Big Book* and other publications, is referred to within the fellowship as a "suggested" course of action and is open to wide interpretation. According to the AA Third Tradition, "the only requirement for AA membership is a desire to stop drinking" (AA,1952).

The focus of Twelve Step recovery is spiritual, just as the focus of most addiction treatment approaches involves some combination of physical and psychological factors. Spirituality and a spiritual focus also infuses most of what we call religion, but religion is more than spirituality, and it is the "more than" that comes into constitutional conflict. Religions are by their nature exclusionary. No matter how broad their frame of reference, someone is left out. School prayer issues revolve not around whether people have a right to prayer. We all have a right to pray *as we see fit*—or not to pray, if that is our conviction. The unspoken issue in school prayer involves the ascendancy of one religion, recognized by the government, to the exclusion of others, and that *is* a constitutional issue.

By contrast, the Twelve Step recovery process is spiritually inclusionary. Within the basic desire to stop drinking (and using), a full spectrum of spiritual options is open to the recovering addict. The autonomy of individual groups is upheld by the Twelve Traditions. These form the bylaws of Twelve Step recovery and differ as little as the Twelve Steps do between fellowships. The traditions also ensure that AA-based fellowships have no opinion on outside issues, and religion is an outside issue. The core of the Steps is spiritual and relative. The truth of this is born out by the variety of cultures, including those in Eastern Europe and Asia, embodying a wide variety of religions and religious beliefs, as well as degrees of atheism and agnosticism, wherein the Twelve Step movement has taken root and begun to flourish.

While there are many meetings that have a distinct Christian orientation that goes far beyond joining hands and reciting the Lord's Prayer, there are many others that do not. Definitions of God and a "higher power" can and do include an open range of options. In his book, Dr. Earle M. (1989) describes meeting groups for atheists, agnostics, and freethinkers and discusses his own activities in developing programs, such as The Forum, for individuals who were uncomfortable with what they perceived as religious language in the steps. Essentially, religiosity and a belief in God as represented in any particular religion is unnecessary for the workings of Step related recovery. Belief in a power outside oneself that is capable of bringing one to sanity, however, is necessary in terms of addiction, even if this power is characterized as the meeting group itself.

In reaction to Twelve Step recovery, programs such as Rational Recovery have appeared that strongly oppose the tenets of AA, particularly the insistence on belief in a higher power. These claim success in helping individuals stop drinking and using, but the authors feel that these programs miss the point of why belief in a higher power is important to recovering people in Twelve Step programs.

Addiction can be seen as a *disease of self-centered fear* that depends on isolation and deeply held positive convictions regarding the nature and effects of the addict's drugs of choice. That isolation renders the addict incapable of understanding the disease and its personal effects. This is the basis of denial. No matter how helpful addiction treatment may be, the problem of relapse remains acute, so long as the addict attempts to fight the addiction on personal will power alone. That addict is fighting a losing battle, locked in emotional gridlock in a state of "white knuckle sobriety," where increasing anxiety from the stress will inevitably result in relapse. The reason for this is that positive convictions about use are buried within the individual's spiritual belief system, where they can only be reached if the addict is willing to accept that there is something outside his or her own immediate being that can lead him or her to sanity, i.e. a power higher than oneself. (A similar discussion occurs in Jampolsky, chapter 3.)

Surrender and powerlessness

The concept of surrender, given its many war-related connotations of occupation, rape, loss of freedom, etc., is hard enough for anyone to accept, but particularly hard for cultural groups that have, over time, suffered more than their share of occupation and loss of freedom.

African Americans, for example, may feel that they have been in a state of individual and cultural powerlessness for many generations, and have no desire for further surrender. Native Americans have similar difficulties with that aspect of Twelve Step recovery, as it runs counter to tribal mores of self-reliance and stoicism.

Adolescents, although their cultural cohesion to adolescence is transitory, are in the process of developing their own individuality and are often loath to accept the appearance of giving up something they have so recently gained.

Moslems may have the least problem with the concept of surrender. "Islam" means, literally, "submission to God's will" (Guralnik & Friend, 1962).

Members of the recovering community, however, in using the term "surrender," speak about "joining a winning team" and urge newcomers to "hang out with the winners." In admitting powerlessness over the disease, addicts are in effect gaining the power, through enlisting the support of their Higher Power and the fellowship itself, to be responsible for their own recovery. A misunderstanding of this process can lead to an interpretation that people in Step-related recovery are somehow "copping out" from personal responsibility. The point is, however, that while the addict may not be responsible for having a disease that involves physiological and possibly genetic, psychological, and overweening environmental components, in Twelve Step fellowships the addict is most certainly responsible for his or her own recovery.

Points of resistance among health professionals

Some cultures are heavily invested in treatment approaches to addiction that do not recognize recovery and its promises as the goal of addiction treatment. These treatment approaches may be based on the concept that addiction is not a disease but a cluster of symptoms and behaviors that are secondary to preexisting psychopathology. In these terms, addiction is not a viable object for primary treatment, but rather something that will clear in the course of psychotherapy and recovery, and therefore is not a viable primary goal.

Even though the efficacy of Twelve Step recovery is generally recognized by addictionologists, the treatment community in the United States is still somewhat divided on this issue. There are individual physicians and academics who will argue that the whole concept of addiction is an artifice, that drug and alcohol abuse in all its forms is a moral issue, to be dealt with primarily through the courts and the criminal justice system.

One way in which professional resistance is being countered in this country is through medical education. For example, providing medical students with firsthand knowledge of Alcoholics Anonymous and Narcotics Anonymous has been a goal at the University of Nevada since 1974, when substance abuse education was added to the medical curriculum. Today, this exposure includes attendance at one AA/NA meeting in the second year and four in the third year, with appropriate class work to meet educational objectives. These objectives include: learning what happens at AA/NA meetings and becoming familiar with the importance of a home group; understanding the role of sponsors, and the pitfalls as well as benefits of working with the Twelve Steps; and, appreciating the value of service, as the recovering addict carries the message of recovery to other suffering alcoholics and addicts. Students also learn the differences between spirituality and religion, the importance of the Twelve Step "traditions," and the problems and paradoxes found in recovery fellowships. The goal of the program is to produce physicians with positive attitudes toward Twelve Step fellowships and sufficient skills and knowledge to support clients in recovery programs (Chappel, 1990).

In France, where the *Toxicomanes*, or physicians dealing with chemical dependency, are heavily invested into a psychotherapeutic approach, there is professional denial that Twelve Step programs exist, or if they do, are at all effective with French clients. Several toxicomanes maintain that, even if they themselves championed Twelve Step recovery and attempted to refer clients into recovery programs, the French, with their heritage of individual freedom and idiosyncratic behavior and belief, would never abridge their freedom by joining such fellowships as AA. Health professionals in such wine-producing, and consuming countries as Italy, Spain, and France also expressed concern over the issue of addicts needing to maintain abstinence from all psychoactive substances. Wine, they maintain, is a food and should not be included in such a blanket prohibition.

Acceptance of Twelve Step recovery overseas has differed from culture to culture, from country to country, in some cases from community to community. In Scandinavia, such countries as Finland, Iceland, and Sweden have experienced phenomenal multiplication of existing AA groups over the past twenty years, while others, such as Denmark and Norway, have experienced a decline in groups over the same period (Stenius, 1991). With the advent of *glasnost*, narcologists in what is now the former Soviet Union discovered AA. Since that time, treatment has been increasingly linked with Twelve Step recovery in Russia and other eastern European republics (Zimmerman, 1988).

Black Extended Family Project

The Black Extended Family Project (BEFP), a collaborative effort between Haight Ashbury Free Clinics and the Reverend Cecil Williams's Glide United Methodist Church in San Francisco's Tenderloin District is a good example of how the precepts of Twelve Step recovery can be adapted to the needs of African American cultures. There, African American cultural mores and traditions are taken into consideration and made primary to recovery. The support system involves knowledge of, and pride in, the African American heritage and makes use of the spirituality inherent in that heritage to redefine its goals and activities.

The HAFC/Glide program represents an important collaboration, which has made possible an effective intervention into the inner-city crack cocaine crisis. The key to this intervention has been the adaptation of Twelve Step principles of recovery to the African American inner city culture. In the HAFCI/Glide program, the basic practicalities of recovery are utilized in a model that is uniquely meaningful in terms of the African American experience.

AA's *Big Book* uses the terms "spiritual experience" and "spiritual awakening," manifesting in many different forms, to describe what happens to bring about a personality change sufficient to induce recovery. While some of these may involve an "immediate and overwhelming 'God consciousness,'" most are what William James called an "educational variety" of revelation, developing slowly over time (James, 1969). (See Kasl's chapter 6 for a personal description of such an awakening.) According to a *Big Book* appendix on spiritual experience, the core of this process is the tapping of an "unexpected inner resource" by members who presently identify this resource with "their own conception of a Power greater than themselves" (AA, 1976).

Many members of the black community afflicted with crack cocaine addiction have been raised in the church. There is a tradition of revelation, with many being saved and now believing they are sinners because they have used and sold crack cocaine to their own people. God has been described in a strict denominational sense. Spiritual awakening in a recovery model in a church program may produce conflict with traditional religious definitions, particularly the third step: "Made a decision to turn our will and our lives over to the care of God *as we understood him*." Religious leaders, such as Reverend Williams, have played a leadership role in presenting a model of recovery theology that helps to mobilize the church as a sleeping giant in order to better respond to the nation's drug epidemic. In his model, Pastor Williams employs self-definition within a spirituality of recovery.

BEFP terms of faith and resistance

In working to develop the Black Extended Family Program and publishing "Facts on Crack," Cecil Williams took a hard look at what he saw as shortcomings in the traditional Alcoholics Anonymous recovery model when applied to the African American community. It was clear to him that few African American addicts turned to AA and other existing Twelve Step programs for recovery. Evidently, he concluded, some of the traditional values contradicted African American values. Instead of attacking traditional Twelve Step approaches, as "Rational Recovery" and other variant recovery programs have done, Williams looked to the roots of recovery and adapted an approach that was in keeping with African American values.

First of all, he saw recovery as both a "miracle of healing" and a "movement for social change for our people." African Americans are a "communal" people, identifying strongly with an extended family and membership in the African American community, unlikely to respond to the perceived AA focus on individualized efforts toward abstinence and recovery. Collectively and as individuals, African Americans have experienced a history of being "anonymous" and "powerless." Williams points out that, "To a black person who has felt invisible and unheard all of his or her life, being anonymous is already a familiar way of life." While the anonymity in Twelve-Step programs is meant to protect members' everyday lives, "many of those who come to Glide have no everyday lives. They don't have homes, jobs, or reputations to protect." Anonymity for these is yet another way to remain a nonperson, faceless and hidden from society. What was needed by the addicts at Glide was not anonymity and surrender, but recognition, a voice, a recognized heritage, and taking responsibility within a spiritually extended family dedicated to recognition, self-definition, rebirth in recovery, and community.

Acting on these insights, Pastor Williams initiated a list of ten "Terms of Resistance" that are repeated at Glide recovery meetings, just as the Twelve Steps are at a traditional meeting:

1. **I will** gain control over my life.
2. **I will** stop lying.
3. **I will** be honest with myself.
4. **I will** accept who I am.
5. **I will** feel my real feelings
6. **I will** feel my pain.
7. **I will** forgive myself and forgive others.
8. **I will** rebirth a new life.
9. **I will** live my spirituality.
10. **I will** support and love my brothers and sisters. (Williams, 1992)

Although the words may be different, echoes of the Twelve Steps can be heard throughout the Terms of Resistance. The First Step admission of powerlessness has been converted to "gaining control," but such a seemingly diametrical departure from the surrender of the first step may be necessary for African Americans and others with a long history of servitude and even slavery. When a black person hears the First Step admission of powerlessness, it is often interpreted as "one more command to lie down and take it." Yet, the first three steps correspond to the shift from inner directed fear to outer directed recovery that the recovering African American addict makes in gaining control, through a recognition of heritage within the extended family of recovering brothers and sisters. In effect, the overall process of self-exploration, spiritual house cleaning, forgiving oneself and others, on through awakening to and living one's spirituality, can be seen at heart as the traditional path of recovery given an African American cultural interpretation and lived within that context. There is very little difference between "support and love my brothers and sisters," and the Twelfth Step's "carry the message" and "practice these principles in all our affairs."

Cecil Williams presented the core sense of what was needed and what the Glide Church program provides by saying: "What we need to recover is to speak up, to tell our stories, to claim the truth about our lives before anyone and everyone."

Learning More about Addiction and Spirituality

A question at the core of this book is how we can, as professionals, learn more about the great range of potential and needed knowledge regarding addiction and spirituality. To the authors' minds, the best way to learn is to "go forth."

Some of the wise kings in history made a practice of traveling incognito among their subjects in order to get a true picture of conditions within their various domains. Similarly, in our own cultures, individuals seeking to learn more about their milieu have gained knowledge by engaging those who are on similar paths.

Addiction professionals need to learn all they can about both the process and the practice of recovery, and may accomplish that by engaging in a dialogue with the recovering community both at a conceptual level and by attending meetings. Similarly, interaction with church and civic groups, such as the HAFCI/Glide collaboration, can broaden the ability to both understand and work with the cultural and spiritual dynamics involved in the practice of recovery.

Conclusion

It is the authors' opinion that a spiritual program of recovery can be the key means in converting treatment into a drug-free life, so long as it continues to work toward inclusion of all those in need of its support. Even though Twelve Step recovery, as a spiritual program, is open and inclusive in its nature, its origins and predominance in white, male, Christian, middle-class society can make it appear exclusionary to members of other cultures. In lecturing about this to mostly white audiences of health professionals, Rafiq Bilal asks, "What if it were the other way around? What if you, an addict seeking support for your recovery, walked into a room full of African Americans and yours was the only white face? How would you feel?" (Bilal, 1992).

The distance between cultures may seem like a chasm at times, but it is being bridged by such projects as the Black Extended Family, providing both recovery and a means to developing cultural parity. Society is changing rapidly, and thankfully, recovery has the flexibility to change along with it. The autonomy guaranteed by the Twelve Step traditions makes it possible to be innovative and adaptive. Many special groups within AA have learned that, if there is no meeting that fits their special need, then they can go out and start their own meetings.

New fellowships have been born when people within existing fellowships decided that adaptation was called for, even beyond loose confines. It was thus, in the mid-1950s that young recovering drug addicts, who felt that their specific needs were not being met in AA with its focus on alcoholism, founded Narcotics Anonymous. Since that time, a plethora of other fellowships, including Cocaine Anonymous and Marijuana Anonymous, have been born.

The challenge is to adapt this process of recovery to all cultures and races, to counter stereotypes that recovery only works with certain groups. Relative to public policy, when addiction occurs in a white middle-class population it is called a disease and the response is appropriate treatment, whereas when addiction occurs in lower socio-economic non-white populations it is often called a crime with the response being prison. The Glide/Clinic model demonstrates that when the recovery program is adapted culturally, it can work for all populations and provide a link between treatment and a life of sobriety and recovery for its constituents.

References

Alcoholics Anonymous. [AA]. (1952). *Twelve steps and twelve traditions*. New York: Alcoholics Anonymous World Services.

Alcoholics Anonymous. (1957). *Alcoholics Anonymous comes of age: A brief history of A.A.* New York: Alcoholics Anonymous World Services.

Alcoholics Anonymous. (1976). *Alcoholics Anonymous: The story of how many thousands of men and women have recovered from alcoholism,* Third edition. New York: Alcoholics Anonymous World Services.

Alcoholics Anonymous. (1985). The Bill W.—Carl Jung Letters. *Best of the Grapevine*. New York: The A.A. Grapevine.

Andrews, L. M. (1991). The twelve steps: a political time bomb. *Professional Counselor*, pp. 28–34.

Bilal, R. (1992). Personal communication.

Brissette, C. (1988). Personal communication.

Buxton, M. E., Smith, D. E., & Seymour, R. B. (1987). Spirituality and other points of resistance to the Twelve-Step process. *Journal of Psychoactive Drugs*, 19(3), 275–286.

Chappel, J. N. (1990). Teaching medical students to use Twelve-Step programs. *Substance Abuse, 11*, 143–150.

DuPont, R. L., McGovern, J. P., & Brock, P. (1992). *A bridge to recovery: An introduction to Twelve-Step programs.* Washington, D.C.: American Psychiatric Association Press.

Guralnik, D. B. and Friend, J. H. (Eds.). (1962). *Websters new world dictionary of the American language*. Cleveland: The World Publishing Company.

HAFCI (1990). Cocaine: Treatment & recovery, African American perspectives on crack: vol. 2, tape 2. D. Inaba and W. E. Cohen (Eds.), *The Haight Ashbury Training Series*, San Francisco / Ashland, The Haight Ashbury Drug Detoxification, Rehabilitation & Aftercare Project and Cinemed, Inc.

James, W. (1969). *The varieties of religious experience.* New York: Crowell-Collier (Originally published in 1902).

M. E., (1989). *Physician, heal thyself! 35 years of adventures in sobriety by an AA 'old timer.'* Minneapolis: CompCare.

McElrath, D. (1987). *Hazelden: A spiritual odyssey*. Center City, Minn.: Hazelden.

Seymour, R. B. (1992). Panel presentation at "To Heal a Wounded Soul" conference at Glide Church, San Francisco.

Seymour, R. B. and Smith, D. E. (1987). *Drugfree: A unique, positive approach to staying off alcohol and other drugs*. New York: Facts on File Publications.

Smith, D. E., Buxton, M. E., Bilal, R., and Seymour, R. B. (1993). Cultural points of resistance to the Twelve Step recovery process. *Journal of Psychoactive Drugs, 25*(1), 97–108.

Stenius, K. (1991). Introduction of the Minnesota Model in Nordic countries. *Contemporary Drug Problems, 18*, 151–179.

Zimmerman, R. (1988, November). Alcoholism treatment—Soviet style. *American Medical News*, pp. 21–22.

CHAPTER 6

Many Roads, One Journey: One Woman's Path to Truth

Charlotte Kasl

I claim to be a passionate seeker after truth, which is but another name for God—Gandhi

In 1977, after finishing the course work on my doctorate in counseling at Ohio University, I moved to Minneapolis, the land of ten thousand treatment centers. Minneapolis was "addiction haven," with specialized programs for women, lesbians, and Native Americans. These programs tended to be holistic and expansive in their approach, often taking into account issues of sexism, racism, and oppression. Words like shame, codependency, and family systems peppered most professional conversations. Recovery was a buzzword, and the Twelve Steps were sacrosanct. The prevalence of incest and childhood sexual abuse was being uncovered, and in 1980, I joined a diverse network of professionals called the Incest Consortium, who regularly got together to help each other learn—people who worked with sex offenders, prisoners, young children, teenagers, and adult survivors.

Because I could recognize alcoholism and other drug abuse, I often referred clients to local treatment programs, who in turn referred their graduates to me. While I could see great value in Twelve Step programs, the parallels to patriarchal norms were disturbing. *Rules of patriarchy*: Be obedient, don't question, don't notice if you are being oppressed, let the dominant system define your reality, don't think for yourself, and turn your will over to an all-powerful male God rather than follow your inner wisdom. In the righteousness of AA, I also found a "blame the victim" stance. If addicts didn't succeed, it was their fault for not working the Steps hard enough. "Rarely have we seen a person fail who has thoroughly followed our path." I never heard anyone question the efficacy of the Twelve Steps, especially their application for people with different addictions, cultural backgrounds, religions, and customs.

While the AA approach was obviously a great support to many people, aspects of it seemed counter to the needs of women, especially those who had been abused or battered and needed to build their ego strength and feel positive about themselves. There was no focus on appreciating one's talents, strengths, and intellect. Even feeling powerful and happy was suspect, which was underscored for me one day when I walked into a Twelve Step group I was attending and said, "Hi, I'm Charlotte. I'm feeling good, life is going well, and I don't think I'll be coming to group much longer." This was heresy. The group's reaction presented me with a double bind. To be happy and feel good meant rejection from the group (because I was "in denial," or "in my addiction"). To be upset and unhappy brought inclusion, but at the terrible price of negating my power.

In reading all the approved AA and Al-Anon literature, I found no model of a healthy person. To be always "in recovery," always dependent on a group, never fully trusting your intellect, didn't match any model of power or maturity or emotional development as put forth by Erickson, Maslow, Fowler, and others.

My belief that a joyful life was expansive, creative, and considered all things possible until proven otherwise felt out of place in the world of addiction, where strong feelings and intellect were met with suspicion. My work as a Reiki healer (an ancient method for channeling life force energy) further widened the gap. I became a Reiki Master in 1983. In healing circles there was excitement, creativity, passion, and a belief that there are no limits to the possibilities for healing. I saw a woman healed of Lupus. I felt the power of energy coming through me in working with numerous people. I lived in two worlds.

This conflict led me to explore pathways to healing other than AA and the Twelve Steps, an exploration that proved crucial to the development of my life's work. From there I developed my own "sixteen steps of empowerment" and wrote my book, *Many roads, one journey: Moving beyond the Twelve Steps*(1992). But this work not only came out of my early professional experiences with counseling; the roots went way back to my childhood and my earliest searches for knowledge and truth.

My hunger for meaning in life, for something beyond the mundane rituals that cloaked my family, and so many others, is embedded in my history, which I will intertwine in my discussion on truth before describing the empowerment model.

Kahlil Gibran writes, "In your longing for your giant self lies your goodness, and that longing is in all of you." My belief is that overcoming addiction rests in seeking our giant selves, sorting through internalized messages from family, culture, and tradition, validating our strengths, learning to trust our internal wisdom, and focusing on our strengths and potential. Inherent in this journey is questioning, experimentation, disillusionment, doubt, and developing one's internal values and resources. It is a holistic approach that asks: Who are you? What do you need? What works for you?

Instead of hiding behind dogma or rhetoric, people are encouraged to become the authority of their own lives. Human relations that contribute to our spiritual development are based on authentic connections that bridge differences rather than homogenizing them. It takes two separate identities to create the kind of true union and intimacy that fill the longing for connection. Most importantly, healing is based on love, not fear.

Living by one's truth is laden with exquisite complexities. Truth can be ephemeral, elusive, complex. It can come like a bolt of clarity springing out of confusion. It can slowly emerge, stumbling, unsure, edging into focus. Truth is the child of silence, for we hear our voice of wisdom when we settle into a quiet receptiveness. Truth requires surrender of the inflated ego, controlled by "shoulds," traditions, fears, and stereotypes. It is the clear voice beneath our programming and conditioning, the river of spirit flowing through our heart and mind, connecting us to universal wisdom, to one another. (The notion of connectedness echoes through many of the chapters in this book.)

My first experience of being jolted by an "epiphany," or revelation, came at the age of four or five. My father was reading the paper and enjoying his daily glass of sherry. My mother was preparing dinner in the kitchen, and my older sister was just out of sight in the dining room, practicing the piano. As I stood in the living room, motionless, like a distant observer of our familiar, comfortable household, I felt an intense wave of longing for something more—something vast, penetrating, wondrous. I knew for certain that my destiny lay outside the safe walls of this home and all the homes in my neighborhood. My life would be different.

To live the truth means to know the truth, a challenge in a society rife with counterfeit gods. Material goods, beauty, wealth, and status are values that speak of obedience and conformity, not inquisitiveness, originality, and spirit. To settle into the kind of inner quiet that allows us to find the truth often requires withdrawal from the stimulation of computers, the Internet, Musak, television, junk mail, and committee meetings. It may also require a withdrawal from commitments. Many people struggle to find a balance between ministering to the homeless, hungry, helpless, or endangered and taking care of themselves. A truth that is wrenching for many people to say is, "No, I don't have the energy."

Our culture is not one that always values or rewards truth, as I found out at age five. As the excitement of Christmas intensified with the smell of cookies baking, hours spent looking in the Sears Christmas catalog, and my family's annual trip to see toys in Washington, D.C., I got to wondering about Santa Claus. Something didn't make sense. I crawled into the fireplace and looked up. Definitely too narrow for a fat man. I questioned my parents and Sunday school teachers: Does everyone have a chimney? (My Aunt Myrl didn't.) How many people are there in the world? Does Santa cover the whole globe? (No, my father said, some people don't have Christmas.)

I summarily deduced that Santa Claus was an impossibility, a fable that parents foisted on innocent children. Thrilled with my discovery, I rushed to tell Tina, a four-year-old who lived across the street. Much to my amazement, she turned ashen and ran home crying. My enlightenment was soon tarnished. "Tina's mother called," said my mother awkwardly. Her obvious discomfort turned my joy into a bleak emptiness in my gut. "Tina's very upset. She's been crying all afternoon because you told her there was no Santa Claus. Wherever did you get such an idea?"

"I figured it out," I answered. I felt a wave of indignation. Why did parents lie? Why did Sunday school teachers lie? Christmas was fine without Santa Claus. But my righteousness couldn't counter my feeling of loneliness and the thought that I was somehow bad. I had violated a tribal rule. That same conflict would take many forms in my life again and again; my power and intelligence would be pitted against the desire to belong and some vague notion of being a good girl, and later, a nice person. It would be many years before I found solace in writings on oppression and sexism.

The Santa Claus incident did not stop my questioning, but it dulled the joy of discovery and sent a stern warning: The truth is dangerous; people don't want to hear it. The incident also implied that I shouldn't see what I saw or know what I knew. I learned to feign innocence. Adults often thought my questions cute and precocious, but my questions mattered and I needed help. I wanted life to make sense: Why do we go to church? Why do girls have to wear skirts to school? Why are the acolytes all boys? Why is God in the sky? Why do women change their names when they get married?

While most adults were uncomfortable with these simple, natural questions, my father tried to give me serious answers. He was a scientist who valued logic and intellectual exploration, and I greatly appreciated his respectful intent. Unfortunately, many of my questions were not about science. They were about being a female in a social system he had internalized, which often resulted in unsatisfactory answers. "That's the way it is. It works best that way." Not for me, I'd think, feeling different and alone.

I found consolation in my grandmother, Charlotte Davis, a proud woman who'd graduated from the University of Michigan in 1986 with a degree in botany. She welcomed all of my questions about religion and social customs. Though she didn't have what one might call a conscious feminist perspective, her life was a testament to a woman's ability to maintain her identity. She had done so unwaveringly, while assimilating new ideas, shifting opinions, and looking to her own experience for answers.

The good intentions of my father and grandmother could not shield me from a culture that stifled girls' ideas and potential. By age twelve, a chronic affliction I called nervous stomach had settled in my gut and solar plexus. I had learned that to be loved and to belong to the tribe, I had to muffle my observations, hide my power, and temper my wisdom, all of which made me feel dull, alienated, and lonely. At fourteen, shortly after my grandmother died, I began suffering from depression. It choked me like a shroud for the next sixteen years.

My search for truth was further confused and obscured by religious practice, as taught in the Episcopal Church, which I attended in Alexandria, Virginia, in my preschool days, in Missoula, Montana, where I lived until age eleven, and in Ann Arbor, Michigan where I lived until my late twenties. My first inklings of spiritual experience were embedded in the sense of connection, kindness, and care I had often felt in Sunday school classes, in these liberal churches that focused on a loving God. Unlike regular school, no one was shamed and the teachers were always kind. But as I entered my teenage years, disillusionment crept in as I listened to the words I was chanting en masse with the congregation. "I'm not a miserable wretched sinner," I'd think. "I'm doing the best I can." "Why would I want to grovel around and gather up the crumbs from under thy table anyhow?" I began editing the offending words and felt a familiar gnawing in my gut as I stood mute amidst the mass of God's obedient servants. I wanted to belong, but I felt alone.

When I was eleven, a young minister visited our Sunday school class. "It's not when you're high on the ladder that you find God," he shouted, arms flailing, "it's when you fall, when you're on the ground." I hated what he said. It didn't make sense to me. "When you fall off a ladder, you skin your knees," I thought. Why couldn't God love me when I was happy, exuberant, successful? Was there no place for joy, wonder, and God to fit together? I revealed my concerns to our Sunday school teacher, a woman who had wanted to be a minister but had settled for a degree in theology. She didn't have any answers, but she let me know it was all right to be curious. I wasn't a cute child to her, I was a person with questions, questions that were probably similar to hers.

My father helped by offering liberal interpretations of the Bible. "It wasn't actually that water turned to wine or bread appeared mysteriously when Jesus gave the Sermon on the Mount," he would explain. "People would not have ventured out in that time without taking food and wine. It was that the crowd, deeply moved by the spirit of Jesus' words, opened their hearts and shared generously whatever they had." Explanations like this helped Bible stories seem less remote and impossible. Being spiritual wasn't about miracles, it was about love, generosity, goodness, feeling connected. Later, when I learned about indigenous spirituality, Buddhism, other eastern traditions, and the Society of Friends, known as the Quakers, I recognized a common thread binding them all together. Spirituality was both a mystical experience and a practical, earthly, daily way of living that included compassion, kindness, simplicity, truth, giving to others, and learning to love oneself and others more deeply. I came to see the spiritual journey as learning to live by the truth, to listen to my calling, and to have the courage to stand by my beliefs, even when it meant feeling different or separated from family, friends, and colleagues. Recently, with the help of the Dances of Universal Peace, and with tears of relief, I finally connected internally with the heart of what I believe is true Christianity—mercy and compassion and love.

My disillusionment with the Episcopal Church deepened as I witnessed the hypocrisy of religious rhetoric. The church preached compassion, mercy, kindness, and helping others, but my favorite minister was demoted to a small parish because he wasn't good at raising money. Another was fired because he brought alcoholics and poor people into Canterbury House, the auxiliary building where Episcopal college students often gathered. It seemed that compassion and mercy were reserved for starving children in Nigeria or Afghanistan, not for people we could see in our midst.

By the time I was seventeen, I felt the full force of the conflict between wanting the community of my church and feeling guilty for colluding with what I saw as hypocrisy. I was lonely for someone to talk with. One person said I was going through a normal rebellion and that "I'd understand later," the implication being that I would inevitably return to the fold. Leaving the church was painful because I had nothing to replace that kind of safety, acceptance, and community.

I shifted my focus to my piano studies and finding someone to marry. Intimate relationships came hard for me. Perhaps it was my restlessness, or longing for something more, that led me to be uninterested in several, very kind, good men with the potential for career and a solid family. I was also affected by my family, a family that knew how to cooperate, but not how to show hurt or anger or see the conflict. And, of course, although I had been shown genuine respect for my intelligence, and had a rebellious nature, I had internalized suffocating notions of what it was to be a woman. As a result, I did not have the skills to form an intimate relationship. I was a person with words and feelings, but not much of a voice when it came to asking for what I wanted. Because I had so little sense of my own self-worth, I pushed away men who were kind to me and was attracted to mysterious, difficult, distant men.

By twenty-four I had a master's degree in piano and had settled into a lovely home in Ann Arbor with a young professor of social psychology, whom I had married despite numerous signs that he could not show affection or be faithful. It was this period of life I would later recall when reading Al-Anon literature. I lost my identity, and in doing so lost my spirit and became depressed. What I needed was my voice, to ask for what I wanted, to believe I deserved respect. I became a good wife, a caricature of myself, acting out a role. I made clothes from designer patterns, had a sumptuous dinner ready by six every evening, threw elegant dinner parties, and gave piano lessons on the side. I also lay depressed on the living room couch most afternoons, ensconced in sleep, hoping I'd wake up to a world that included me. There were breaks in my gray, listless days. I started a doctorate in piano at Michigan State University and commuted to Lansing four days a week, but at the end of the term, without classes to shore me up, my depression grew even worse. Although my husband and I cared for each other at some level, our marriage was without connection, kindness, or love. There was him and me, but no there was no "us," no unity.

In the fourth year of our marriage, one night my husband didn't come home. I downed a bottle of sleeping pills and half a bottle of brandy. The next day, late in the morning, when I awoke, I didn't realize that I had gotten sick and vomited for hours in a blackout. All I knew was that no one had taken me to a hospital, my clothes felt tight, and my body felt mangled, attacked, broken. Later that day, as I dragged myself off the couch and came out of my stupor, I looked back on the previous night with a startling clarity, as if it had happened to another person. What a desperate attempt to get attention, I thought. What a terrible thing to do—taking all those pills. But that was me. I could have killed myself. Where had I gone?

The return to my own consciousness was as sudden and explosive as the eruption of a long-dormant volcano. "I'm a person; I have a life." Then another thought, almost comical, popped up: "Well, I've tried suicide and it didn't work, so I'd better figure out how to live." After just three sessions with a psychologist, I told my husband I wanted a divorce. House, security, and garden—it could all go. I would rather live in one room and work in a dime store than continue to be so unhappy.

So what was wrong with me in those days? Some might say I suffered from codependency. But I would rather say that I was a powerful woman in a patriarchal society, trying to fit a role that was counter to my spirit. *I wasn't sick; I was lonely for myself, isolated from community. I was a normal woman having a normal reaction to a depressing situation.* To fit in and be married, I lived in isolation and repressed all avenues to spirit and joy, namely my emotions, intelligence, creativity, perceptions, and wisdom. As a well-socialized female, I didn't ask for what I wanted and willingly accepted emotional starvation. I was suffering from internalized oppression.

So long as I hung onto the comforts of my emotional prison, I was destined to be depressed. That's why the thought of living in a single room and working in a dime store rang so sweetly. It was like a bell ringing in an empty sky, freeing me from fear. Some years later, Paulo Freire, author of *Pedagogy of the oppressed* (1972), gave voice to my inner struggle, a struggle that is inherent when we pit our authentic selves against the false selves demanded by society. I wasn't crazy; I was confused and frightened. Depression had enveloped me because I had given up my power of choice, had stopped speaking my truths. I had married to please my mother, then looked to my husband as the wise one. Outwardly passive, I had harbored a dark, festering anger deep within. My willingness to conform had taken me to the brink of death. Now, I would struggle as hard as it took to hang on to my identity and my life.

> The conflict lies in the choice between being wholly themselves or being divided: between human solidarity or alienation; between following prescriptions or having choices; between being spectators or actors; between speaking out or being silent, castrated in their power to create and re-create, in their power to transform the world. This is the tragic dilemma of the oppressed.
>
> The oppressed have adapted to the structure of domination in which they are immersed, and have become resigned to it and are inhibited from waging the struggle for freedom so long as they feel incapable of running the risks it requires...The oppressed suffer from the duality which has established itself in the innermost being. They are at one and the same time themselves and the oppressor whose consciousness they have internalized. (Freire, 1972)

At some level I knew that if I asserted my truths, I risked being called troublemaker, bitch, or man hater, the names used to keep women in their places. Freire's writings helped me see that what we call codependency is the double bind of women's oppression, which manifests itself as an addiction to security. Women are taught a lie, become immersed in that lie, and then feel incapable of running the risks it takes to extricate themselves. Fear sets in—paralyzing, blinding, debilitating. For most, it takes support from others and an understanding of the dynamics of internalized oppression to relieve the self-blame and guilt, which further debilitate and isolate women and other marginalized people. Fortunately for me, Betty Friedan's book *The feminine mystique* (1963) was published, followed by Robin Morgan's *Sisterhood is power* (1970). They were manna for the soul. I devoured them.

How does this discussion of oppression tie in with addiction and spirituality? Spirituality flows from truth. If we limit ourselves to sex-role stereotypes, or for that matter, to labels of any type, we deny many aspects of our potential—our ability to be passionate, tender, passive, assertive, fearful, wise, not knowing. In Aramaic, the language Jesus of Nazareth spoke, *ruakh* is the word for breath, spirit, and life. It's all one. To block access to our truths is to interrupt this flow of spirit/breath/life. Without the spiritual connective tissue assuaging us from alienation and loneliness, we are left empty, hungering. We become at high risk for addictions. Empty? Eat. Afraid? Drink. Sad? Fake a smile. Insecure? Find a prince.

From my early teens, I waged an internal war between my powerful, talented side and my value as a "girl," a female to be desired by a man. The price of having men like you, it was implied, was to dull the wildness of spirit. One could be mildly accomplished, although not in arenas that competed with men, but to seek brilliance and be centered on one's purpose was to invite being an "old maid." The injunctions—don't be too strong-minded, too passionate, too independent—all carried the unspoken completion, "for a man." They came in many forms, both overt and disguised. The most blatant was from my mother when, seeing that I was saving money at the age of twenty-one to buy a Steinway grand piano, she blurted out, "But what if you meet a man who doesn't want such a big piano?"

My own experiences and study of sociology, psychology, feminism, and oppression ultimately led me to believe that addictions must be seen in a cultural context, if we are to treat them effectively. (Many of the themes in this chapter echo the the cultural analysis in chapter 5 by Smith and Seymour). The hierarchical system that puts people in a double bind of compliance or defiance always creates inner turmoil. We comply at the risk of losing ourselves and defy at the risk of being censured and excluded. While I have observed this double bind in many situations, a most touching one was when I visited a Maori treatment program in New Zealand in 1994 on a five–week trip. The director, a Maori man named Tavi, had included native Polynesian dancing, history, and Maori language study as part of the treatment program. Although the program was successful and the clients found it far more helpful than traditional treatment programs for whites, the director of the umbrella organization, a white North American steeped in the AA tradition, constantly criticized the program for "not doing it right." Right for whom? His response reflected the narcissistic trappings of the program, which imply that if AA worked for one person—most often a white male of privilege—it should work for everyone. Tavi had recognized that his people's despair, alienation, and addictions were linked to the loss of their culture, language, and traditions. When he attempted to right the wrong done by society, to name the oppression and act to change it, he was censured by those above him in the hierarchy. This reaction, typical in hierarchical systems, put additional stress on Tavi, who was already attempting a difficult task on limited funds. To be effective in treating addictions, we must fit the program to the people, taking into account gender, culture, class, race, and individual needs.

Addiction, like anxiety, springs from alienation from self, along with a host of genetic and cultural factors. Spirituality means being ourselves—natural, unaffected, whole, connected to spirit and to the earth. Women need to affirm their power and intelligence. Men need the freedom to be vulnerable, sad, and afraid. Ethnic groups need to honor their heritage. We all need a safe place to explore the rage and grief we feel at having been violated, limited, and enticed into a lie.

While it is acceptable to have an addiction or to be forever in recovery, when we believe we can transcend addiction or heal with a different approach, we threaten the established order, which often sets us in conflict with ourselves and others. But, as Freire says, we must see the conflict "as a choice between being divided or being whole; between following prescriptions or having choices; between being spectators or actors; between speaking out or being silent." From this perspective, we understand addiction and dependency in a social context, rather than from an individual perspective. This is not to discount genetics and temperament; rather, to put them in a larger framework that gives us insight into the breadth of the problem.

Shortly after separating from my husband when I was twenty-eight, I had my first intense, passionate, sexual relationship with a man who shared my roots in the West and the mountains. I felt at home with him—loved, desirable, alive. While I had not overcome the deficits of my emotionally bereft childhood, I experienced a lightness of heart and a joy formerly unknown to me. It was a spring of romance, walks, flowers, friends, folk concerts, community, and reconnecting with parts of me that had lain dormant for many years. I also started playing the piano again and visiting old friends. I continued teaching piano and remained in the home I had shared with my former husband.

This period of sublime joy led me to believe that spirituality, happiness, and a free flow of sexual and life energy are crucial to our wholeness. This doesn't necessarily mean being explicitly sexual; it means being passionately in love with life. When we are filled with spirit, and the body, mind, and spirit are in balance, there is no room for addiction. My desire to bring joy and spirituality together was answered later when I learned about the Sufi tradition. The ecstatic poems of Rumi and Kabir were like hymns for my spirit.

> Every instant that the sun is risen,
> if I stand in the temple, or on a balcony,
> in the hot fields, or in a walled garden
> my own Lord is making love with me.
> I hear bells ringing that no one has shaken,
> inside "love" there is more joy than we know of,
> rain pours down, although the sky is clear of clouds,
> there are whole rivers of light.
> The universe is shot through in all parts by a single sort of love.

During my spring of awakening, I had another epiphany. I was to leave Ann Arbor and venture forth on my own. Much as I was in love, this was not the time for another relationship. I didn't know where I would go or what I would do, but I trusted absolutely that the answer would come. I immersed myself in life—staying open to people, music, books, community, and sexuality—and through a synchronistic series of events, I was led to move to London and study piano while living at a grand Victorian boarding-house for musicians.

The life-changing event that led to my move was a master class taught by Vladimir Ashkenazy, one of the greatest pianists of our time. I went to Daytona Beach to study with him while he was in residence with the London Symphony Orchestra for a month. He was unlike any teacher I had

had before. He made no assumptions about my limitations—I wasn't a student, or Charlotte, the average pianist. He delved into the music with me to find the voice, sound, and magic. We spent over an hour on one page of a Chopin ballade, flexing the phrases, going over one note again and again until finally he said, "Yes, yes, that's it. That's the sound." It was an enthralling glimpse at true passion, commitment, and being with someone who was his giant self. After four lessons, the concept of my potential was reawakened and greatly expanded. My deeper level of attunement to sounds, phrases, and colors made it possible to be fascinated and engaged for six hours of practice a day, easily.

What I learned from my lessons with Vladimir Ashkenazy and my two subsequent years in London was that true passion, whether sexual or musical, is one with spirituality. In those two years, I never worried about eating too much (although we went to many sumptuous restaurants—it was still the years of "Europe on five dollars a day"), weighing too much, drinking too much, or making love too much, because there was a balance between play and work, music, friendships, and lovemaking. I later integrated this knowledge with my addiction work, realizing that when the focus is on abstinence and deprivation, the addicted persons may stay sober, but they don't heal. Healing comes through the spirit, blessed by passion, joy, and purpose.

On one occasion a Japanese violinist, who had become a good friend, and I decided to play all the Mozart violin sonatas straight through. It took a major part of two or three days. Sometimes two Greek friends and I would play bridge late into the night with Paddy, the Irish bartender, and then walk in Holland Park to see the sunrise. It was a life without "shoulds". That experience of freedom led me to see that pleasure will not overtake our lives if it is not fueled by guilt, and that we need not fear joy and passion, when they serve a higher purpose or are enjoyed in balance. This experience translated itself into my belief that white-knuckle sobriety is unnecessary, that we can heal and transcend addiction, and most of all, that healing will not occur while we live in fear.

When I returned to the United States two years later, I found a position teaching piano at Ohio University in Athens, a picturesque town, reminiscent of New England, with white frame houses set in the rolling Appalachian foothills. I thought I had arrived at my life goal—a college teaching job in a beautiful community. But within the first year, I had a disturbing epiphany. On a clear fall afternoon, the air sharply delicious as I walked away from the music building to meet a friend for a late afternoon coffee klatsch, I stepped off a curb, heard the crunch of leaves under my feet, and the message came: "This isn't what you are meant to do forever. There is something else." "No!" I screamed inside. "Dammit, no!" But just as surely as I was standing there with the sun warming my back, I knew that I had been called to do something more, and I would follow. I had no idea what course of events would lead me to enroll in a doctoral program in counseling four years later, but again, I knew my job was to immerse myself in living and to open myself to the inner guidance that would come to me.

The willingness to hear and follow one's inner voice of wisdom was eventually to become paramount in my method of overcoming addiction. If we deny leadings that come from spirit we feel incomplete—strangers to our own lives, strangers to spirit. Many times a calling will come and we don't understand the reason why. This tests our faith and commitment. We can't bargain with the truth. Whenever I followed a leading that came to me, I had a feeling of motion, of going toward something rather than being trapped, of living with integrity rather than bargaining for security.

When we resist our truths because of fear or attachment to security, we are likely to experience a cosmic whack. I've had my share of those. For example, when I knew I should resign from teaching piano at Ohio University and change careers, yet delayed making that change, I ended up being fired while on leave of absence. It was a blessing in disguise that allowed me to teach my final year in the music department while taking courses free of charge in the counseling department. But it would have been so much better if I had had the courage to make the decision for myself. When we deny our power it can turn on us, either internally or externally. We get sick or depressed, or other people force us to move on.

The shift to counseling was less dramatic than it might seem. I had always been fascinated with psychology, or more precisely, with what made people act the way they do. From my teenage years, when I kept journals addressed as "Dear Friendly", through my college experience when I took a minor in sociology and psychology, I loved speculating with friends on motivation, learning, and relationships. As a piano instructor, I became more interested in teaching students who were stuck or having a hard time. It was a challenge to see where the blocks were—in the mind, heart, or the ability to listen, feel the beat, or develop the physical dexterity. This led me to teach courses in pedagogy and performance anxiety.

During this time, I fulfilled another life dream by adopting a three-year-old little girl—the first-single parent adoption by the Athens County Children's home. This signified the end of waiting for the right person to come along and planted me firmly on the path of seeking in life what I wanted, without depending on others. I had a rich community of other young parents, who swapped children and got together for picnics, camping, volleyball, and support groups.

I also found a spiritual home in the form of a three-year stint on the United Campus Ministry Board. It filled my yearning to be part of a spiritual community that lived by its values. The ministry provided a center for radical groups: draft counseling, abortion counseling, and women's workshops. I was also involved in feminist groups on campus and came to realize that feminism was a spiritual movement about wholeness, equality, fairness, and justice, not just for women, but for all people.

In the counseling program, I took a course on alcoholism based on the traditional stance that Alcoholics Anonymous was the one and only way to sobriety. While the course was invaluable in helping me recognize chemical dependency, it also echoed old feelings of being forced into an ideological box with no questioning allowed. This came to the fore one day when I openly challenged the dogma of Twelve Step. Shortly before class, while rummaging around in a secondhand salvage store, I had glanced at my watch and mumbled something about being late to class.

"What class?" a man nearby asked.

"It's a class on alcoholism," I answered.

"Oh, I've had that problem," he said. "Quit five years ago."

"Really?" I asked, curious about how he became sober. "Did you go to AA?"

"Naw. I just quit."

"All on your own?"

"Yep, it was ruining my life. I crashed up the car, lost a couple jobs, and my wife nearly left me. I'll never touch that stuff again."

"You didn't have counseling or anything? No AA?"

He shook his head, No.

"I just knew if I didn't quit I'd probably die."

As thrilled as I had been as a child to realize there was no Santa Claus, I rushed to class to let them know that AA wasn't necessary for everyone, after all. The professor caustically discounted my story. The man couldn't have been a true alcoholic, or else he would have relapsed. And if he hadn't relapsed, he probably would soon. Unlike the Santa Claus episode, I did not slip into shame or remorse. I just sat quietly, as if looking through a plexiglass wall at people in church, reciting tired phrases.

I had had a solid foundation in feminism and oppression. No one could convince me of the sanctity of the AA dogma. Any organization or model that posed itself as the one and only way automatically oppressed others. What I believed then, and still do, is that there is no one way people become addicted, no one way people get well, and no one prevention for addiction. There is love, power, joy, kindness, and walking a path of truth.

I loved being in the counseling program. I was given a teaching assistantship with a favorite professor and, while my questions about our textbooks, which often seemed classist, racist, and sexist, were disquieting to some professors, I felt liked and appreciated. In my last year of classes, I had an internship at the Ohio University Counseling Center. It was a rich experience that provided me an hour of individual supervision for every three hours of counseling.

After finishing my doctoral course work, it became clear that to grow I would need to leave Athens. This decision brought great sadness. I had loved Athens, with its rolling mountains, pastoral valleys, good friends, and community. I moved because I feared drifting into complacency. In Ohio, I had had one course on counseling women, taught by a man along with eight male supervisors. There was only one part-time female professor in my doctoral program. Rarely had issues such as incest, battering, and abuse been mentioned. I had more to learn about women's concerns, and I knew I couldn't do it in Athens. The first stepping stone would be a feminist women's therapy collective called Sagaris, in Minneapolis. It offered counseling services to women on a sliding fee basis, and many of the women coming for help were "in recovery" for addiction and were attending Twelve Step groups. Women at the collective were starting to focus on addiction, and many started attending Twelve Step groups for relationships, abuse, compulsive eating, and chemical dependency.

When I sought recovery data or outcome studies of treatment programs, I found very little, and none of it from AA organizations. Totally convinced of the rightness of their approach, they saw no need for documentation. Reading massive amounts of AA and Al-Anon-approved literature was itself an experience of literary starvation. The underlying fear of passion, power, joy, and celebration was reflected in the dull and righteous tone of the writing. Be careful, was the undertone. Don't get too exuberant, wild, or even happy. The chapter titled "To Wives" in the AA "Big Book" entitled *Alcoholics Anonymous*, advised women to repress their anger and never show fear or intolerance. They were covertly counseled to accept emotional deprivation, take full responsibility for the children, keep smiling, and cheerfully see their spouse though his drinking sprees, while avoiding being a nag or killjoy—the recipe that nearly killed me and has led to depression and addictions for countless women. Whatever happened to rigorous honesty? I wondered. The AA literature reminded me of my own depressing days of marriage, my need to fake happiness and play a role.

In the approved codependency literature, no one ever said living with a using addict is hell—be authentic, find your power, take good care of yourself, tell the truth, and don't be a martyr. Instead, women, who were presumed to be the "codependents," were chastised for being upset, angry, or wanting to leave a difficult situation. If you were sad, you should work the steps harder, or maybe do another fifth step. I came to see that if you came to a group feeling good, you were suspect and usually ignored, but if you came besieged with problems you would get a lot of attention. Hence, I came to believe it was crucial for women and other marginalized people to bond in power, to affirm their strengths and intelligence, as well as give support for life's difficulties.

When I participated in Twelve Step groups to have support to explore relationships, a step accompanied by mixed feelings, I refused to say I was powerless. I had been at the brink of death and had suffered from profound depression, anchored in an unremitting sense of powerlessness. While I understood the need for a first step—to acknowledge the power of an addiction and link it to the harmful consequences—the thought of saying I was powerless felt wrong. I understood why people said it, but I needed another way. Likewise, I abhorred labels of all kinds. I couldn't grasp the purpose of reducing the miracle of human life to a label, unless it was to control people. Repeatedly at gatherings, I could see people's energy wilt as they intoned "I'm an alcoholic, a codependent, a compulsive eater, an incest victim." Just as I had felt a great rebellion when people in church confessed to being miserable wretched sinners, I wanted to yell: "No, don't say that. You are a miracle of life, a wonder, magical. Look to your power and creativity."

I also took offense at some of the slogans and jargon of AA. Convenient phrases could bring people back to center, but saying "Keep it simple, stupid" felt crude and simplistic. Slogans like "Utilize, don't analyze" or "Your best thinking got you here" felt like abdicating the use of one's intelligence. In therapy sessions, I would recoil when women told me they were advised to "give up resentments," when what they were feeling was healthy anger associated with abuse and discrimination. I was aghast at the frequent appearance of the all-too-familiar "blame the victim" stance. If a woman gets raped, it's her fault; if the Twelve Steps don't work for you, either you don't really want to get well, or you aren't working them hard enough.

My most intense conflict with the AA approach was their inculcation of a belief system rooted in fear. There was the one and only way. If you don't follow the Steps, you can't get sober. If you don't go to group, you'll relapse. If you get resentful, you'll relapse. If you relapse, you'll die. People recited slogans and phrases devoid of authenticity. Like Catholics missing mass, people felt guilty and afraid if they missed a meeting or didn't do the prescribed readings. I often had a surreal feeling around "program people." There were lots of words and often very little genuine connection.

During this period of questioning, in 1980, I attended a three-week, life-changing spiritual training based on Ken Keyes' *Handbook to higher consciousness* (1995). He provided a profound combination of Eastern spiritual traditions mixed with humanistic psychology. I can't say enough about the skill and wisdom of the teachers and the program model. It was a freeing experience of living with people where there was no blame or shame; everyone was seen as running her or his own programming. We create our own suffering with our addictive demands, a translation of the Buddhist notion of attachment. I started to internalize how much we create our own reality, how love is the reality underneath our illusions, and how we are part of an interconnected web of life.

Shortly after returning, I found a spiritual home with the Society of Friends, commonly known as Quakers. Their philosophy validated my belief that, though our connection to spirit is sacred, the words that get us there are not. Quakers eschew dogma. They believe that the truth is more holy than any book or written word and that all people are equal in the eyes of God. There are no hierarchies in the Quaker meeting, and all decisions are made by consensus.

I also became increasingly interested in developmental models of human development: Maslow's hierarchy of needs, Erickson's developmental stages, James Fowler's levels of faith development, and Murray Bowen's assertion that differentiation, also a developmental model, is the foundation for intimacy and mental health. These models gave shape to my belief that all healing models need to support people as they move through developmental stages, rather than present a fixed approach. The concept of differentiation led me to see some major pitfalls in the AA model, in which people are not encouraged to internalize their own values or trust their own wisdom, and diversity is often seen as a threat.

In Twelve Step circles, I felt like a heretic in the midst of devoted loyalists. But I knew enough about social change to suspect there were others who felt as I did, who perhaps remained quiet out of fear. By 1980 I had left Sagaris to work on my own, and by 1983 I had graduated and passed the exam to become a licensed psychologist. As mentioned earlier, I became a Reiki healing master at the same time, providing a wonderful balance to academic work.

In 1985, at a lecture on codependency for 120 therapists and addiction counselors at Golden Valley Hospital in Minneapolis, I decided to model the adage "speak truth to power" by reading my version of the Twelve Steps. I called it "steps for empowerment." When I announced my intent, I felt a stinging silence in the room, followed by people picking up their pens and coming to attention. After my talk, sixty people asked for copies. At the National Women's Studies and Association of Women in Psychology meetings, large groups of women attended workshops I presented to explore the AA program. One woman shared my thoughts: "I feel like we're a bunch of heretics having a secret meeting." The conversations were often heated because people who liked AA felt threatened by questioning, as if it compromised their sobriety or made them wrong. That further strengthened my belief that AA doesn't help people differentiate, so that they can be fascinated with different ideologies and experiences rather than feel threatened and defensive.

I felt called to write a book on the subject, namely, of the need for empowerment and overcoming addiction, which I entitled *Many roads, one journey: Moving beyond the Twelve Steps* (1992). At the time, I was in the middle of writing my first book, *Women, sex and addiction: A search for love and power* (1989) and had interviewed numerous people who had repeatedly relapsed until they addressed issues of dependent sexual relationships, further suggesting that recovery from chemical dependency is a complex issue.

My exploration of people's ways of healing led me to interview rural Appalachian women, Native American groups in cities and reservations, African American treatment providers, rich white businessmen, and numerous others of different classes and ethnic backgrounds. If I learned one thing a thousand times, it was that the causes of addiction are many, and the path to healing varies dramatically based on culture, physical needs of the body, temperament, family background, and genetics. There is no one way. This belief led me to write an introduction for group meetings (presented below) that supports diversity.

Over a period of several years, the sixteen steps for empowerment evolved. Many copies were circulated as I handed them out at workshops or talks I was invited to give. One early version appeared in *Ms. Magazine* and elicited hundreds of letters in response. My final version appeared in *Many roads, one journey.*

I offer them here as a reflection of my journey—to be used, changed, or integrated with other models of healing. I start with a list of empowerment principles that underlie the steps, which are designed to help people evolve to their highest potential, enabling their creativity and potential for intimacy to flourish.

Fundamentals of Empowerment

1. Empowerment is based on love, not fear.

Fear may jump-start people into recovery, but love, and the promise of something better, provides the motivation to stay on a healing path. By focusing on what we have to gain, we start a shift in the survival brain that makes it worthwhile to let go of our addictions and destructive behavior.

2. Empowerment involves a holistic approach to a problem—body, mind, spirit, and community.

People's healing paths take many forms. Some focus on restoring balance to the physical body; others have therapy for childhood abuse, attend Twelve Step meetings, or learn to stay away from harmful relationships. Still others find support in meditation or community service. There is no one right way.

3. Empowerment encourages differentiation.

According to Eric Ericson, "Intimacy requires the ability to stand alone and risk forming one's own identity. It's the ability to retain one's sense of identity in close engagement with other people and other ideologies." A well-differentiated person can be a compassionate witness to others in distress, giving help when asked, without being emotionally drawn into their dramas. They are fascinated with different theories and ideologies and develop their values through experimentation and exploration, often synthesizing various approaches.

4. Empowerment encourages questioning and choices.

Paulo Freire writes, in *Pedagogy of the oppressed*, that "to block free inquiry is a form of violence." Questioning stimulates our inner world, helping us explore, adapt, and integrate wisdom. Questioning is a sign that people are finding their faith. Poorly differentiated people seek conformity, fearing those who question.

5. *Empowerment takes people beyond labels and models.*

Labels describe something about us, but they are not our essence or spirit. The ego grasps at labels to offset fear of the void, to create an identity, or to have an explanation for events that seem random and chaotic. It's important to identify our addictions, but not absorb them into our identity, just as it is important to take care of an illness without identifying with the illness. We may have an addiction, but we are not our addiction; we are all children of our Creator, sacred because we are alive. Likewise, a model of healing is a structure that can give support, but it must never supersede a person's own sense of integrity. No one should ever be coerced, manipulated, or forced to speak words or participate in rituals that violate their beliefs.

6. *Empowerment teaches us to trust our wisdom.*

We ask: What is true for me? What do I feel? What do I want? We may draw ideas from books or listen to teachers, but ultimately we develop a faith and belief system that is intensely personal, deeply felt, not easily shaken, and rarely a subject of intellectual debate. Ultimately, all models and dogma dissolve into hearing our truths unfold from within, moment to moment, as we stay present to ourselves and others. Our bodies become attuned to living with integrity, which creates a deep inner resonance when followed, and a painful dissonance when ignored or violated.

7. *Empowerment supports creativity, passion, and joy.*

Passion, not to be confused with being "revved up" by artificial means, is the power of our life-force energy flowing vibrantly through us, allowing us to feel connected to the beauty and wonder around us. Most people are constantly censoring their flow of ideas, feelings, and emotional responses to loss or success. The resulting "congestion" keeps them separated from their giant selves. In workshops I demonstrate this principle by striking a Tibetan bell near the microphone, then stopping it abruptly before the vibrations have completed their natural cycle. People feel disturbed and often hold their breath. Then I ring it again and let it flow until completion. People's response is to relax, breathe deeply, and feel peaceful.

To summarize: Empowerment encourages us to explore all of who we are, fearing nothing, stopping nothing, while being a fascinated observer. We are in our life but not of it. Empowerment is based on a profound kindness and compassion for ourselves and others. Instead of trying to get rid of parts of ourselves, we get to know them so they can be transformed. Our power comes from knowing ourselves deeply, listening for the voice of wisdom within and having the courage to live in accordance with it. Empowerment is one with the spiritual journey because it is an ongoing search for the truth, as it manifests moment to moment in our lives.

Many roads, one journey: We gather together

Based on the diversity of people's needs in treatment, I wrote an introduction for group meetings that affirms all people's ways. Here are excerpts from "We Gather Together," and the sixteen steps for discovery and empowerment as they appear in *Many roads, one journey*. I encourage you to use them, change them, and find the words that sing in your own heart. It is love and healing that are sacred, not the words.

Many Roads, One Journey

"Our purpose in meeting together is to support and encourage each other in moving beyond addiction, dependency, and internalized oppression. The only requirement for membership is a desire to maintain sobriety as we each define it.

"We come together from many backgrounds, and we can learn from each other's ways and experiences. None of us has the answers for another person. We do not impose our beliefs on others or expect others to tell us the way. We have faith that through determination, sharing our stories, supporting each other, and understanding the impact of our social system on us, we can each discover our personal path toward healing and sobriety.

"Growing and becoming strong is a balance between self-acceptance and a firm commitment to sobriety. We overcome addiction and internalized oppression so we can honor and enjoy the life we have been given. This process is not about moral worth. We are all sacred children of Creation this moment. These steps for discovery and empowerment are designed to create a healthy, aware Self which, over time, will help crowd out compulsive, addictive, or dependent behavior. We believe that through bonding with others, speaking genuinely from our hearts, forgiving ourselves and others, finding purpose, helping create social change, and accepting the imperfections of life, we will replace our addictive behavior with fulfillment and joy.

"The journey is sometimes difficult, sometimes smooth. This is natural. We are open to all avenues of healing and support each other in seeking our personal paths. Several things you may want to remember as you use these steps:

- There is no perfect path, only the path we choose one day at a time.
- While we are aware of the powerful nature of addiction, our collective will and commitment to sobriety and growth is even more powerful.
- Change takes time and is made of many small steps.
- Many people have healed from addiction and internalized oppression."

Sixteen steps for discovery and empowerment

While the steps are presented linearly, I think of them as circular. Often people select one step that speaks to them and use it for a period of weeks or months. I include quotes from people who have been in sixteen-step groups who responded to a questionnaire on the efficacy of the steps.

> **(1A) We affirm we have the power to take charge of our lives and stop being dependent on substances or other people for our self-esteem and security.**

> "After going through treatment nine times and failing to stay sober, I started believing that I actually was powerless. I needed something to tell me I could do it, not that I couldn't. When I tell AA people I don't think I'm powerless, I get a lot of raised eyebrows and 'looks' but I will never say I'm powerless again."

For people who have been oppressed and marginalized, it is crucial to affirm their inner power. A basic tenet of oppression is to destroy the will, so it can be usurped by those in control. In my own life, after suffering years of debilitating depression, saying I was powerless in any context felt like pulling a plug and draining my energy. I needed to remember my power. An incarcerated woman wrote to me after reading this step, saying it was the first time anyone ever told her she had power of her own. It was the catalyst to hope. Her prison counselor encouraged her to use the sixteen steps, and she has successfully left prison and functioned on her own for several years. Others found it useful to retain the word powerlessness in reference to drugs or other people.

> **(1B) Alternative: We admit we were out of control with/powerless over _________ yet have the power to take charge of our lives and stop being dependent on substances or other people for our self-esteem and security.**

> **(2) We come to believe that (choose one) God/Goddess/Universe/Great Spirit/Higher Power awakens the healing wisdom within us when we open ourselves to that power.**

> "For years I've believed in inner wisdom and have…needed to learn to trust it, as this step reminds me to do."

This step affirms that a sacred spirit or life-force energy is within us and around us. It suggests an active union between ourselves and the power/intelligence of the universe. Through faith and opening ourselves we tap into the power of the universe, draw it in, and use it to awaken our inner capacity for healing.

> **(3) We make a decision to find our authentic selves and trust in the healing power of the truth.**

> "I just love the word 'authentic'. This step reminds me to stop and really feel out what I am doing, saying, and thinking. Is it what I really mean?"

I remember the sudden clarity I felt when I realized that all we need to do in life is tell the truth and trust the outcome. We don't need to figure people out, take care of them, or analyze them. While it isn't easy to sort out the internal messages—what is authentic, and what is the voice of the trickster?—it makes the path simple. To find the truth implies that we reach deep and name our dreams, passions, creativity, and strengths. We develop an artful sense of timing. It is a challenging step, because it affirms questioning and defining our own values, which could require that we speak truth to power, even when it creates personal risk.

(4) We examine our beliefs, addictions, and dependent behavior in the context of living in a hierarchical, patriarchal culture.

This step puts addiction and dependency in a cultural context. I often believed that feminism saved my life. When I learned that social factors and negative stereotypes were at the root of my depression, fear, and dependent behavior, I no longer felt alone. I could recognize the internalized voices of oppression for what they were—the counterfeit voices of culture and authority, like unwanted intruders dampening my spirit, keeping me "in my place." I wasn't sick; I was oppressed. This step leads us to discern between our authentic voices and the voices of oppression—the shoulds, guilt, fears that control our lives.

(5) We share with another person and the universe all the things for which we feel shame and guilt.

No matter what the source, unacknowledged shame and guilt are like toxic pollution in our systems, blocking our clarity and freedom. Whether we have hurt someone else, or been abused, secrets become shame. To tell them is to start the process of releasing them. This step can be done in a group setting or with a trusted friend, but can also be seen as an ongoing process.

(6) We affirm and enjoy our strengths, talents, and creativity, remembering not to hide these qualities from ourselves or others.

> "In our 16-step meeting, each person would say something good about themselves…the next part was to say what we appreciated about the person to our right or left. This celebration of ourselves was uncomfortable, loving, and wonderfully healing."

If our talents come from our Creator, then to celebrate them is to celebrate creation. Humility is about accepting our gifts, enjoying them, and using them in the service of humanity. We neither adopt an arrogant stance about our talents and achievements, nor do we fall into the trap of false humility by muffling our intelligence, passion, and strength to avoid threatening others' egos.

(7) We become willing to let go of guilt, shame, and any behavior that keeps us from loving ourselves and others.

One of my difficulties with the Twelve Step model is that it is based on fear and control rather than love. In this model, the explicit goal is to love ourselves and others. To do this we need to look at the blocks that get in the way. To release them is the essence of healing and growth.

(8) We make a list of people we have harmed and people who have harmed us, and take steps to clear out negative feelings by making amends and sharing our grievances in a respectful way.

This step helps us repair relationships and clear out all "unfinished business" in a balanced way. Because I saw many women and people of color blame themselves for being abused, this step suggests that we make amends when appropriate, but we do not blame ourselves for having been abused or violated. While we are all responsible for creating a good life, many people trap themselves with self-blame about abuse as a means of controlling their grief. When we hold others accountable for inflicting harm, we step into our power and free ourselves from shame.

(9) We express love and gratitude to others, and increasingly appreciate the wonder of life and the blessings we do have.

While adversity tests our character and strength, love penetrates the armor around our hearts and opens us to love. To have our hearts pierced by love also opens us to our heartaches and grief. Love is the great healer, the connection to our spirit and soul. If God is love, then showing our love is a form of prayer that blesses both the giver and receiver. Likewise, when we remember our blessings and become mindful of the beauty and wonder around us, we elevate our consciousness to a higher plane. This is not to deny trouble or take a Pollyanna approach, rather to remind ourselves of all our blessings.

(10) We continue to trust our reality and daily affirm that we see what we see, we know what we know, and we feel what we feel.

"This step has helped me separate from a destructive relationship."

Trusting our own perceptions is the antidote to internalized oppression, which trained us to see ourselves through the eyes of those who confined us to our limited roles. With this step, we build a healthy ego and develop self-trust. In healing from my codependency, it was crucial to start trusting my reality and not need it validated by others. In my research on existing sixteen-step support groups, this step, along with the twelfth, were considered the most helpful to people in dependent or abusive relationships.

(11) We promptly acknowledge mistakes and make amends when appropriate, but we do not say we are sorry for things we have not done, and we do not cover up, analyze, or take responsibility for the shortcomings of others.

This step is particularly relevant for the codependent part of ourselves that gets enmeshed with others' journeys. It is important to say we're sorry when we have harmed or hurt another. It is also important not to deplete our energy and fuse with another person by analyzing or covering up or making excuses for their behavior. Figuring others out is often a defense against seeing the reality of a situation , expressing our feelings, or taking action.

(12) We seek out situations, jobs, and people who affirm our intelligence, perceptions, and self-worth and avoid situations or people who are hurtful, harmful, or demeaning to us.

"This is the step of all steps for people who are very dependent on others or have been in abusive relationships. It affirms you can let go of people and know you're okay."

This step encourages people to make connections between behavior, thoughts, relationships, and energy levels. It is like tuning into our life-force energy and being mindful of how we let it flow, give it away, or take it from others. This step is based on the premise that light energy creates more light energy. It encourages people to be around people who are supportive and helpful. For many it was a completely new concept. You could choose who was nurturing and fun to be around. You weren't obliged to "fix" everyone.

(13) We take steps to heal our physical bodies, organize our lives, reduce stress, and have fun.

Many people do not realize the connections between lethargy, depression, cravings, and a body that is out of balance—a common symptom of addiction and living in this stressful culture. Many people have cravings, not because of psychological trauma, but because their bodies are depleted of various hormones and vitamins, and they don't get exercise or proper nutrition. This aspect of recovery is one of the most neglected in the addiction field. The other part of this step is to keep life simple and organized, and to remember that laughter and pleasure spark our energy.

(14) We seek to find our inward calling and develop the will and wisdom to follow it.

First we listen to the guidance within; then we find ways to live by our inner truths. Finding our inner voice is a process that involves deep levels of listening. Living by our truths takes will, strength, and often acceptance of the unknown.

(15) We accept the ups and downs of life as natural events that can be used as lessons for our growth.

My subtitle for this step is: Lighten up. It matters, but it's not serious. This step was designed to mitigate against what I dubbed recovery narcissism—also New Age narcissism. While it is important to be aware of inner signals, many people start seeing themselves as a project in need of constant vigilance and repair. It is important not to 'pathologize' life by becoming analytical and narcissistic about every little mood change, conflict, or problem that comes our way. It's a matter of balance. Our focus needs to balance between inside us and outside us. Yes, our dramas matter, but in the cosmic scheme of things, they're not serious; they come and go. We need to find our essence underneath our dramas.

(16) We grow in awareness that we are interrelated with all living things, and we contribute to restoring peace and balance on the planet.

In speaking of creation theology, Matthew Fox says, "It's not enough to awaken the heart and right brain if you don't also put that energy to work relieving the suffering of the world." Ultimately, we need to step beyond our labels of addiction and codependency and to reconnect with the broader community. We are magical creations of life, all of us, and ultimately our inner spirituality is reflected in all that we do for others and for the global community.

Afterword

"You have named what I was feeling. You have given me words."

I have received nearly two thousand letters in response to the sixteen steps for empowerment and the book *Many roads, one journey*. The responses fall into several themes. The book and the steps gave voice to dissatisfaction and dissonance with traditional AA and other Twelve Step groups; they helped people feel they were not alone, and not crazy. Both book and steps validated what they had been thinking and freed them to be more creative on their recovery/discovery journey. Another common response was that it released people's guilt for wanting to leave a group, or having already left. Yet another response was that it provided a welcome alternative to the Twelve Step model.

The sixteen steps have been used for all forms of addiction and codependency, as well as for survivors of abuse. There have been approximately three hundred sixteen-step groups formed around the country; many have come and gone. Some were study groups, or time limited groups. They have been incorporated in several treatment programs. Countless other people used the steps on their own, not so much to overcome addiction, but as support for their powerful selves. One woman at a workshop showed me the dog-eared copy she had carried in her wallet for nearly five years.

The steps have led to new connections in my path. I was invited to visit a Maori treatment program in New Zealand, a sweat lodge with a group of Native Americans near Bozeman, Montana, who used the steps, and a women's group in Vermont. One man, a counselor, told me recently that he didn't like the sixteen steps when he first heard them but some years later pulled them out of a drawer when he was counseling a woman who was not staying sober in AA. When he saw the delight on her face and how they helped her, he realized that the sixteen steps spoke in a language that was useful to many.

There are clearly many roads on our journey to love and healing.

References

Fox, M. (1988). *The coming of the cosmic Christ: The healing of Mother Earth and the birth of a global renaissance*. New York: Harper & Row.

Fox, M. (1983). *Original blessing*. Santa Fe, N.M.: Bear.

Freire, P. (1972). *Pedagogy of the oppressed*. New York: Herder & Herder.

Friedan, B. (1963). *The feminine mystique*. New York: Norton.

Kasl, C. (1992). *Many roads, one journey: Moving beyond the Twelve Steps*. New York: HarperCollins.

Kasl, C. (1989). *Women, sex and addiction: A search for love and power.* New York: Ticknor and Fields.

Keyes, K. (1975). *Handbook to higher consciousness*. St. Mary, Ky.: Living Love Center.

Morgan, R. (1970). *Sisterhood is powerful: An anthology of writings from the women's liberation movement*. New York: Vintage.

Part Three

Pastoral-Clinical and Recovery News

CHAPTER 7

Unconditional Surrender

Robert H. Albers

The complex circumstances which occasion the development of addiction to mood altering substances preclude proffering a simple solution. Historically, those who have worked in the field have characterized it as a *holistic disease* that affects the totality of the person, triggering adverse effects in the body, mind, and spirit as well as the social milieu or matrix in which the person lives. The narratives of the individuals who have been ensnared in the web of addiction are replete with data evidencing the downward spiraling lifestyle which, like a strong undercurrent, totally sweeps them away as persons.

It has been appropriately suggested that this is more than an illness that afflicts only the individual; it is a familial malady as well as a social disease. The complicity of the social structure is evident as rampant denial exists in all quarters of society. It is imperative that the systemic dimension of this phenomenon be identified and that appropriate action be implemented to address the larger picture. Already in 1961, the ad hoc committee of the surgeon general generated the following recommendation with regard to alcoholism: "A comprehensive treatment program of the alcoholic should include consideration of his [*sic*] family and his immediate social environment" (Blum, 1967, p. 275). The concern must reach beyond the 'immedate social environment' to an even wider angle of vision that encompasses society as a whole and addresses social attitudes.

The purpose and intent of this chapter is not to address that larger picture, but rather to keep it in mind as a critical backdrop upon which the portrait of addiction is painted. What will be set forth is one of many perspectives on this phenomenon which has been instructive in dealing with addiction whether one is speaking of its etiology, progression, intervention, treatment, or aftercare. Furthermore, as a pastoral theologian, the perspective will incorporate the biblical and theological contributions that arise out of my own tradition. Since the spirituality of the person who is afflicted with addiction is an integral part of its evolution and resolution, it seems judicious to focus on this dimension as being critical in the larger tapestry which is woven. Resources from a variety of sources will be utilized in describing this particular perspective addressed under the general title of "Unconditional Surrender" with the hope and the prayer that it may provide a helpful addition both to the literature as well as to the ongoing development of theory and theology as it relates to addiction.

The Character of Spirituality

Those of us who represent the Judeo-Christian tradition wholeheartedly concur with the founders of Alcoholics Anonymous and other Twelve Step groups in stating that as a holistic disease, the life of the spirit is critical in the diagnosis, treatment and aftercare of those who are afflicted and affected by addiction. Extant literature in recovery points to the centrality of spirituality in most schemas of recovery. The difficulty in the utilization of the word spirituality is that it has not only multiple meanings, but is nuanced differently by different people in varying circumstances and cultures. It is an elusive term that begs for definition. It is not that one can offer a definitive definition that will suffice for all situations and occasions, but it is imperative to be clear conceptually as to what is intended and involved when one uses the term.

In treatment circles, spirituality is often held in sharp contrast and even antithesis to religion. The impression given is that religion is relegated to the realm of antiquated ritual, stultifying forms, and stolid belief systems. Spirituality, on the other hand, is dynamic, energetic, unencumbered by dogma and the trappings of structure and form. Historically, institutionalized religion of most every stripe has not had a glowing track record in dealing with those who are afflicted and affected by addiction which may, at least in part, explain the existence of such dichotomous thinking. Setting up religion and spirituality as two unrelated and dissimilar entities has resulted in a disservice to both. Alcoholics Anonymous in its literature suggests and encourages those in recovery to once again find their religious roots and utilize both that tradition and the AA program for the total healing of the whole person rather than viewing them as antithetical to one another.

Spirituality, in the opinion of others, has to do with a particular piety or even devotional discipline whereby one is drawn closer to God. The initiative resides with the seeker, and in the process of seeking one discovers the joys of being in relationship with God. At first blush this seems to hold true to form, but for many people, haunting questions remain: When have I done enough? Is my spirituality all that it could be? Is there something more or something that I am missing? The onus of responsibility falls completely on the individual. There is no standard set of criteria whereby the person can ultimately gauge whether or not a true or complete spirituality has been attained.

For others, spirituality seems to be defined as a 'good feeling' about oneself, that is, one's position or disposition in life in relationship to others and the world. In other words, it rests in large part upon an emotionally subjective experience of well-being. Spirituality then becomes a privatized and individualized enterprise predicated solely upon the individual herself or himself. As human beings, we are subject to the ebb and flow of our emotions, experiencing highs and lows as dictated by the circumstances in which we find ourselves. While the totality of who we are, including our emotions, is an integral part of our spirituality, the fluctuations characteristic of our affective nature can leave us wanting when the chips are down.

Because of its multidimensional character, the word spirituality may lend itself more to a descriptive analysis than to a definitive definition. The following paragraph penned by Dr. Brad Holt (1993, p. 5) has served well in articulating the nature of spirituality.

> From a Christian perspective, *spirituality* calls us to recognize the importance of its root term, *spirit*, an important biblical word. In both Hebrew and Greek, the same word (*ruach* and *pneuma*, respectively) is used for breath, wind, and spirit. The Bible refers both to human spirit and to divine Spirit. How one understands spirit will determine how one understands spirituality. For example, if *spirit* is separated from physical reality, in a realm of its own, apart from the daily life of human experience, the resulting spirituality will become an escape into another world. But if God created the world good, and later became flesh, as the Gospel of John asserts, then spirit is a dimension of reality compatible with physical existence. Humans are not divided but, rather, are unities of body, mind, and spirit. The result is that spirituality has a much more wholistic and down-to-earth meaning. It encompasses the whole of human life and will develop in a variety of styles, depending on cultures, denominations, personalities, and gifts.

My own understanding of spirituality rests with the holistic idea of the total person in relationship to God, others, nature, and oneself. Several implications of significant consequence for addressing the issues of addiction and recovery stem from this understanding. The salient characteristics of spirituality, as understood from this author's perspective, will be proffered and their significance and applicability to the holistic understanding of the disease and process of recovery will be indicated.

1. Spirituality is anchored in the reality and initiative of God.

The biblical tradition is replete with evidence not only that God exists, but that God is relational and exercises initiative in relationship to creation.

The unilateral covenant that God established in the election of Israel is beautifully articulated, for example, in Deutero-Isaiah, where we read:

> But you, Israel, my servant, Jacob, whom I have chosen, the offspring of Abraham, my friend; you whom I took from the ends of the earth, and called from its farthest corners, saying to you, 'You are my servant, I have chosen you and not cast you off'; do not fear, for I am with you, do not be afraid, for I am your God; I will strengthen you, I will help you, I will uphold you with my victorious right hand. (Isaiah 41:8–10 NRSV)

The repeated utilization of the personal pronoun "I" leaves no doubt in the mind of the reader that the initiative in this relationship rests with God. The Johannine tradition leaves a clear message for the readers regarding the initiative of Jesus in the selection of his disciples: "You did not choose me, but I chose you. And I appointed you to go and bear fruit, fruit that will last, so that the Father will give you whatever you ask him in my name." (John 15:16 NRSV). The post-Easter narrative in John's Gospel likewise emphatically states that the spirituality of the disciples has its origin in the risen Christ: "Jesus said to them again, 'Peace be with you. As the Father has sent me so I send you.' When he had said this, he breathed, *(emphusao*, used as a means of transmitting the Spirit) on them and said to them, 'Receive the Holy Spirit'" (John 20:21–22 NRSV). As will be noted later, the anchoring of spirituality for the Judeo-Christian tradition in God alone has significant implications for the recovery process. From the Christian perspective, it is not just "any god," but the God of grace and love, revealed in creation, and most specifically manifested in Christ and in the activity of the Holy Spirit.

2. Spirituality is centered in relationships.

To utilize an oft-cited metaphor, relationships have both a vertical as well as a horizontal dimension to them. In attending initially to the vertical dimension, God exercises the initiative in establishing this relationship of love and acceptance with human beings, and human beings in turn respond with gratitude. The biblical story is a saga spanning several centuries that records the efforts of a gracious God to establish and maintain a relationship with all creatures. The scriptural narratives portray the divine-human encounter as a stormy relationship of election, apostasy, forgiveness, estrangement, and reconciliation undulating through history. While human beings have exhibited frequent faithlessness, God has always been faithful, providing an unfailing promise. This promise of God's fidelity is articulated frequently throughout the checkered history of God's relationship with people. The psalmist writes without equivocation, "For the LORD will not forsake his people; he will not abandon his heritage" (Psalm 94:14 NRSV). The Pauline certainty rises to an unparalleled crescendo when, after enumerating all of the vicissitudes that human beings can suffer, these words are written:

> No, in all these things we are more than conquerors through him who loved us. For I am convinced that neither death, nor life, nor angels, nor rulers, nor things present, nor things to come, nor powers, nor height, nor depth, nor anything else in all creation, will be able to separate us from the love of God in Christ Jesus our Lord. (Romans 8:37–39 NRSV)

For people caught in the throes of addiction, these promises of a God who both desires and is determined to be in relationship with all human beings irrespective of who they are, what they have done, or where they have been is a critical part of the acceptance so necessary in the recovery process. Spirituality is deeply relational with its focus upon God who can do, and does, for human beings what they cannot do for themselves.

The human response to the Divine overture is one of gratitude and praise. The relationship with God or a Higher Power is cultivated in prayer and meditation. The directive for this exists in the eleventh step of the Twelve Step program which enjoins members to seek through prayer and meditation to increase their conscious contact with God. The nurturing of the spiritual/relational life with God is found in thanksgiving, meditation, prayer, and praise. These are "spiritual tools," provided as avenues of enrichment for cultivating this gift of God's relationship with humankind. Gratitude is the safeguard against lassitude; prayer is the antidote to the poisonous idea that recovery is solely a human enterprise; and meditation provides the matrix in which one can contemplate about all that God has done and given. Spirituality finds its expressive response to the Divine relationship in prayer and meditation. Spirituality also has a horizontal dimension.

3. Spirituality is experienced in community.

While the essence of spirituality is grounded in a relationship with God, the expression of spirituality is experienced in community. While individuals may and certainly do practice a particular piety or have spiritual exercises which they find meaningful in terms of their own growth, the witness of the Judeo-Christian tradition is that spiritual living is found in community. While there are stories about individuals in scripture, they are not thought of apart from the communal settings in which they live and move and have their being. The concept of corporate personality in the Hebrew Scriptures is alien to the individualistic orientation of the western world. The importance of communal life for the early Christians is succinctly summarized in the book of Acts, which describes the community's activities as devoting themselves to the apostles' teaching, fellowship, the breaking of bread and prayers. (Acts 2:42)

The solidarity of these communal relationships, which gave rise to a sense of security, acceptance, participation, worth, and value, was central to the lives of the primitive Christian community. The communal structure did not preclude conflict or difficulties, but there was a sense in which 'belonging' to something greater than oneself was paramount to understanding one's identity. The primacy of relationships with an abstinent peer group is likewise vital to the sustained recovery process of those who suffer from addiction. By the same token, all of those significant other persons who are adversely affected by the addictive process also find their refuge and support in the communal setting. Thus, any spirituality which is to functionally serve the recovery process has this important component.

4. Spirituality is rooted in reconciliation.

The universal human condition might be characterized as that of alienation, estrangement, and brokenness. There is deeply experienced desire in the hearts of most people for binding up, healing, and repairing the damage that lays strewn in the path of life. Once again, the reconciliation process is made available by the action of God. The sacrificial *cultus* of the Hebrew Scriptures which culminated in *Yom Kippur* (the Day of Atonement) is evidence of God's desire for reconciliation with God's people as well as a ritual for bringing that about. The Exodus and Levitical traditions of the scriptures are instructive regarding the manner by which reconciliation or atonement (at-one-ment) with God is accomplished. The misdeeds of the people are covered *(kaphar)* through this prescribed ritual or are symbolically removed from the community via the 'scapegoat' (*azazel*, a goat for going away) as stipulated in Leviticus 16. There is the recognition that estrangement and alienation from the Creator is occasioned by disobedient creatures, and that reconciliation through prescribed rituals of atonement are necessary. Being separated from God is the anxiety and horror that most threatens the existence of God's people.

That same theme emerges in the New Testament, particularly in the Pauline and deutero-Pauline corpus. Since all have sinned and fallen short of the glory of God (Romans 6:23), divine initiative is exercised in once again effecting the reconciliation process in the person of Christ (Romans 5:10). The recognition of the centrality of this truth is most poignantly stated by the apostle Paul in 2 Corinthians 5:18–19 (NRSV): "All this is from God, who reconciled us to himself through Christ, and has given us the ministry of reconciliation; that is, in Christ God was reconciling the world to himself, not counting their trespasses against them, and entrusting the message of reconciliation to us." The theme of the Hebrew Scriptures is picked up in Ephesians 2:16 and Colossians 1:20–21, where reconciliation, or atonement, is accomplished not through the ritual of animal sacrifice, but through the sacrifice of the cross.

Because of sin, a gulf or chasm is created between the Creator and the creature that must be bridged in order for relationships to be restored and for peace to prevail. The Good News (*euaggelion)* of Christian proclamation is that God has exercised the initiative in bridging the gap, spanning the chasm that separates humankind from God. By the miracle of God's grace, a restored relationship of forgiveness and the promise of "new life" is made possible. The forgiven person is the person who is reconciled or who again experiences *at-one-ment* with God, others, nature, and self.

To utilize another image, the restlessness that plagues the human heart is not ameliorated, as Saint Augustine so emphatically stated, until the human heart rests in God. The vacuity of human life needs filling and the emptiness is not satisfied by satiation. Paul Tillich characterized our age as one of anxiety and meaninglessness in his work, *The courage to be* (1952). That existential anxiety, which issues in restlessness, uneasiness, and emptiness is assuaged only by a divine "filling up," an indwelling of God's Spirit in the human spirit so that the aridity of the human spirit can be drenched in the springs of living water that gush up to eternal life (John 4:13–14). Having a "hole in the gut" is the metaphor that is utilized by many addicts to describe the experience of addiction. There is an emptiness occasioned by being drained of all significant relationships, except the relationship with the drug of choice. The isolation which ensues is comparable to solitary confinement, cut off from the mainstream of life and condemned to an existence of isolation and darkness. A spirituality that offers reconciliation with God, others, nature, and self is a necessary antidote to the insular existence experienced while addicted.

Spiritual Considerations in the Diagnostic Process

Given the fact that addiction is a holistic phenomenon and that the spiritual condition of the one addicted is a critical reality, a "spiritual assessment" of those who are addicted is a key factor in understanding the disease. For the purpose of expediency, alcoholism will serve as the paradigm of addiction in this essay. There are many general characteristics which are applicable to addiction in general, but each has its idiosyncratic expression. Since alcoholism is seemingly the most pervasive addictive phenomenon in the United States, it will serve well as the representative addiction in this presentation.

Many treatment centers will use some form of a spiritual assessment to determine the person's understanding of God, a faith community, meaning and purpose in life, as well as salient spiritual issues involving grief, abuse, guilt, pain, shame, and broken relationships. It is impossible to create a description of a typical alcoholic, because the manifestation of the disease, according to E.M. Jellenik (1960), is in and of itself multiple. The profile of an alcoholic is contingent upon a multiplicity of factors such as gender, age, culture, ethnic background, gender orientation, religion, and race, as well as economic, social, and even political considerations. Dysfunctionality is evident in all quarters of the alcoholic's life, including her or his spirituality. A common thread that seems to run through most of the narratives of addicts is that of estrangement and alienation. This is experienced in relationship to God, others, and the self as well as the whole of creation. Paul Tillich suggests that this is the basic condition of humankind.

> The state of existence is the state of estrangement. Man [*sic*] is estranged from the ground of his being, from other beings, and from himself. (Tillich, 1957, p. 60)

John Keller (1966) says that this may not be the most conscious anxiety that human beings experience, but that theologically it is most basic. Alienation is a universal human condition and therefore not unique to one who becomes addicted. Spiritually for the addict, this condition prompts "dis-ease" in the person, and resolution of the basic state of estrangement and anxiety is accomplished by anesthetizing one's self to this frightening reality. As has frequently been postulated, alcohol is not the problem, it is the solution to the challenge of living. This antidote is both illusory and ephemeral, however. Reality becomes doubly difficult to deal with when the person becomes sober because the existential anxiety and estrangement remain, and now the condition is complicated and exacerbated by feelings of remorse, guilt, and shame. In terms of a spiritual diagnosis, the phenomenon of estrangement and alienation, which prompts anxiety about the meaning and purpose of life, is a critical issue to be addressed in the diagnosis, treatment, and aftercare of recovering persons.

In my own experience as a clinical chaplain in a treatment center and in conversation with people in recovery, the issue of estrangement is a recurring theme with all the concomitant problems attendant to this condition. A spiritual assessment serves well to determine the multiplicity of relationships that are in a state of estrangement and alienation.

Cognizant of this reality at some level of consciousness, the alcoholic makes a vain attempt to rectify the situation by denying her or his finitude and engaging in self-deification. Tillich states that,"All men [*sic*] have the hidden desire to be like God, and they act accordingly in their self-evaluation and self-affirmation"(1957, p. 51). In clinical terms, this is often referred to as the phenomenon of grandiosity. Psychologically, it is viewed as a defense mechanism of profound proportions. Theologically, it is an attempt to become like God. "The effect of alcohol appears to make divinity attainable. When drinking the person may posit the ability to accomplish feats which are superhuman in nature, there is created a pseudo-transcendent sensation of having risen above the exigencies of life and being omnipotent in one's actions and omniscient in one's knowledge" (Albers, 1982, p. 304). The age-old temptation of Genesis 3 in desiring to be "like God" is a vain attempt at finding meaning, but it is doomed to failure from the outset. The creature is not to be confused with the Creator!

Failing miserably to attain the level of divinity with all of the supposed rights, privileges, and control which that affords, a further spiritual analysis may reveal the phenomenon of deep defiance. Dr. L. S. Sillman, an early medical pioneer in the treatment of alcoholism, distilled his characterological analysis of the alcoholic into two categories: grandiosity and defiant individuality (see Tiebout, 1944a, p. 469). Defiance is often the overt expression of covert anger that eats away like a cancer in the whole being of the alcoholic. It may be anger at God, who is held responsible for the miserable condition of the alcoholic; it may be anger at others who let them down, abandoned them, or ignored them. But often, it is anger at the self, despising what the person has become, feeling powerless to do anything about it; lashing out in defiant rebellion against everyone and everything becomes the *modus operandi* of the individual. Narcissism runs rampant, egocentricity becomes a lifestyle, and rebellion against all real or imagined forms of authority prevails.

At the core of all these spiritual manifestations associated with the disease of alcoholism is the issue of estrangement and alienation and the futile attempts to overcome this condition by one's own efforts. Howard Clinebell nicely summarizes the issue in this manner:

> The alcoholic handles his [*sic*] existential anxiety by either religious or pseudo-religious means. His religious needs include a need for experiences of the transcendent, for a sense of meaning and value in one's existence, and for a feeling of deep trust and relatedness to life. As the alcoholic's illness progresses, he tends increasingly to handle all three aspects of his religious need by means of alcohol. It provides a kind of mystical life, a *summum bonum* to fill his value-vacuum (Frankl), and temporary feelings of trust and closeness to people. Alcohol is, a Janus-faced god; its hidden face is that of a demon. (Clinebell, 1962, p. 44)

As has already been indicated, addiction is a multifaceted and complex phenomenon, defying reduction to any singular cause or manifestation. If one is to take seriously the spiritual dimension as an integral factor in its etiology, development, and treatment, then the nature of the human condition in relationship to God is a central consideration. The spiritual assessment may indeed reveal that the components of a healthy spirituality, as outlined in the initial part of this essay, may either be missing or severely distorted. The "spiritual diagnosis" is as critical as the medical, psychological, and social aspects of the disease. Addiction creates a pseudo-spirituality which is anchored not in God, but in the self. Relationships, which are essential in a healthy spirituality, are missing, as is the communal experience of solidarity with others. Estrangement and alienation have supplanted any sense of reconciliation or at-one-ment with God, others, the self, or creation. Howard Clinebell astutely asserts that, since addiction takes on a life of its own and becomes the all-consuming passion of the one addicted, it is most accurately described theologically as *idolatry*.

> The alienation from God which results from this idolatry is at the very root of man's [*sic*] aloneness and anxiety. By making himself

> the center of the universe, man cuts himself off from his own fulfillment which can take place only as he establishes a genuine relatedness to the rest of creation and to the Creator. (Clinebell, 1968, p. 171)

Mired in the quagmire of addiction, the inexorable pull downward into the depths of despair and ultimately death seem inevitable unless there is a substantive change in what is occurring. A complete metamorphosis or transformation is imperative if life is to prevail.

Spiritual Considerations in the Transformative Process

The end result of the addictive process for the alcoholic is fourfold: (1) imprisonment because of legal entanglements, (2) psychiatric confinement as a result of alcoholic psychosis, (3) death resulting from accident or a disease related condition as a consequence of the alcoholism or (4) recovery. Given these "multiple choice" options, it would seem that the answer would be obvious. But, the actual choice is not so simple. Statistically, only about one in ten recover from the disease. A combination of factors can be cited as to the reason why the recovery rate is so small. The reasons range from the larger systemic or social realities, as the larger canvas upon which the portrait of addiction is painted, to the numerous smaller units of communities and families, to the individual her or himself. It seems judicious to focus on what works as opposed to fixating on what has not worked. It is my contention that the spiritual dimension is an important key in unlocking the shackles that hold the alcoholic in bondage.

It is a fundamental theological conviction that the transformative process that occasions recovery (whether named, acknowledged, or not) is the grace of God. The basic definition of grace is articulated simply in varying ways and places throughout the Big Book of Alcoholics Anonymous with the confession that "God has done for us what we could not do for ourselves." The description of the process whereby a person is even open to the operation of divine grace constitutes a subject of immense proportions. It has often been postulated that the key which may unlock the door to divine intervention is *pain.* The alcoholic system tends to remain intact until there is pain of such magnitude that something has to give! In a presentation that Father Joseph Martin once gave to a group of clergy, he unequivocally stated that God's greatest gift to the alcoholic and the alcoholic family is pain. It ultimately moves one to action. But one ought *never underestimate the human capacity for the toleration of pain!* The point is that the crisis that occasions such excruciating pain must be viewed as the window of opportunity for the grace of God to begin its work in the life of those afflicted with and affected by alcoholism. The management of such pain in the transformative process is a critical issue because, if handled improperly, it can lead to greater despair and darkness. When utilized properly, however, it can become the hammer which cracks open the recalcitrant system that previously seemed impervious and therefore beyond help. Paul Johnson says it well:

> Desperate need calls for greater resources than our customary defenses and feeble futilities. When the half-gods go, we turn to the ultimate Thou, realizing as never before that no other will be relevant to our ultimate concern. (Johnson, 1959, p. 108)

The pain or crisis itself does not occasion the transformation or change, rather the pain becomes the mechanism that opens the heart of a person to the grace of God.

A descriptive analysis of the transformative process has been cogently outlined by Dr. Harry A. Tiebout, a pioneer psychiatrist in the treatment of alcoholics. Tiebout left a modest legacy of essays for posterity, but in my opinion they exegete very well the addictive condition and the process of recovery .[1] He came to the conclusion that the ultimate source of help for the alcoholic was spiritual in nature, and that what was necessitated was a conversion experience whereby the person completely surrendered all illusions of power and control. The fundamental thrust of his approach might be most succinctly summarized with the words, "unconditional surrender." (See Morgan's chapter 1 for further explanation of Tiebout's role in the recovery moment.)

In observing his patients, he witnessed an inexplicable transformation of their attitude and approach to life. This mysterious conversion could not be empirically documented in any scientific way, rather it was a radical reversal in lifestyle attributed to an ontological change at the very core of a person's being. One of his descriptive paragraphs is quoted to give the reader a flavor of what Tiebout observed.

> When the wall suddenly melts as in a sweeping personality turnabout, there develops a peculiar phenomenon which people conversant with religion refer to as "a release of power"...Conflict, tension, doubt, anxiety, hostility, all dissolve as though they were nothing and the individual discovers himself [*sic*] on an exalted plane where he feels secure in communion with God, man and all the creative forces of the universe. (Tiebout, 1944b, p.1)

The process may take the form of an instant cataclysmic change of the person, as is described in chapter one of *Alcoholics Anonymous* (1955) entitled "Bill's Story". More often, it is a gradual re awakening, rebirth and restyling of life. Stated in another fashion, rather than one momentous conversion experience of unconditional surrender, the process may be a series of 'small surrenders' before the grace of God has effected an arrest of the disease and unconditional surrender is the result. Whatever the process may

[1] For a more complete treatment of the subject matter, refer to my dissertation (Albers, 1982). See also: Robert H. Albers, "Spirituality and surrender: A theological analysis of Tiebout's theory for ministry to the alcoholic," in *Journal of Ministry in Addiction and Recovery, 1*(2), 47–68.

be, Tiebout asserts that "the key to an understanding of that experience may be found in the act of surrender which, in my opinion, sets in motion the conversion switch"(Tiebout, n.d., p. 2).

Most significant is this perceptive insight regarding what he saw in the lives of those who experienced conversion through unconditional surrender:

> With respect to the act of surrender, let me emphasize this point—it is an unconscious event, not willed by the patient even if he [*sic*] should desire to do so. It can occur only when an individual with certain traits in his unconscious mind becomes involved in a certain set of circumstances. (Tiebout, n.d., p. 3)

From a spiritual perspective, one can discern the gracious hand of God effecting the conversion of the person from death to life, from bondage to freedom, from darkness to light. The critical factor for all of us who provide spiritual care is that *we cannot force the issue!* We cannot coerce the person into this experience, nor should we be so presumptuous as to believe that we can control God in the timing. Therein is often the frustration in providing spiritual care. We may be instrumental in helping to create an environment that we feel is conducive to conversion, but we cannot make it happen. Caregivers, as well as those being cared for, need to pray for, and rely upon, God's grace. It is a humbling experience for all parties involved not to be in control!

Linda Mercadante has an excellent discussion of the understanding of grace relative to the recovery process and provides a sound theological elaboration and explication, as well as implications for the spiritual caregiver in her work, *Victims and sinners* (1996). Spiritual considerations in the understanding of recovery provide rich soil into which the seeds for sustained sobriety may be planted.

The whole process is a venture of faith in a power greater than self. Paul Tillich (1963) characterizes three specific elements of faith that elucidate its character in life. Even though Tillich was not writing about chemical addiction and recovery, his words of explication fit well into the discussion of conversion and a transformed life for those afflicted and affected by alcoholism.

> The first element in faith is its receptive character, its mere passivity in relation to the divine Spirit. The second element is faith in its paradoxical character, its courageous standing in the Spiritual Presence. The third element characterizes faith as anticipatory, its quality as hope for the fulfilling creativity of the divine Spirit. (1963, p. 133)

Dealing with the spiritual blocks identified in the spiritual assessment will in all likelihood reveal the dynamics of grandiosity, defiance, egocentricity, and the rest of the laundry list of barriers that create significant resistance to the recovery process. Coming to terms with the reality that one is powerless and life has become unmanageable, necessitating a power greater than self, is a challenge to the entrenched idolatrous posture of the alcoholic. Acknowledgement of a "spiritual presence" that can restore one to sanity, opening up a quality of hope never before experienced, is a vital component in initiating recovery. Entering into a new lifestyle is a "leap of faith" to use a Kierkegaardian term. The one leaping comes to realize that it is a leap into the arms of a loving God who is able to provide the security of a sobriety with serenity.

It is critically important to take seriously the feminist critique of advocating *powerlessness* for those who are already rendered powerless by virtue of their gender. Powerlessness, as used in this context, is related singularly to powerlessness over the drug of choice. Irrespective of gender, sexual orientation, or other mitigating factors, the person cannot *not* use, and thus is truly powerless. It has also been helpful to conceptualize the acknowledgement of powerlessness as the avenue for empowerment! The truth in the paradoxical assertion that empowerment comes through acknowledgement of powerlessness is succinctly summarized by the apostle Paul when he writes: "For whenever I am weak, then I am strong" (2 Cor. 12:10b). In surrendering to the reality of powerlessness and commending one's self into the hands of a gracious and loving God, transformation occurs.

Spiritual Considerations in Sustained Sobriety

Interrupting the disease process and even experiencing a "turning point" or metamorphosis in one's life, constitute only the beginning of the process. Quality sustained sobriety with serenity is the gift coveted so deeply. In my opinion, Alcoholics Anonymous (and Twelve Step groups for other addictive behaviors) provides a healthy blueprint for the building of an abundant life.

The rubrics governing the members of Alcoholics Anonymous simply state this reality concerning their recovery: "Our stories disclose in a general way what we used to be like, what happened, and what we are like now" (AA, 1955, p. 58). The spiritual life in recovery is constituted first of all by **memory**. Recovery is not a matter of forgetting the past, it is a matter of being forgiven for the past, but always recalling it in memory lest the recovering person forget what s/he used to be like and become doomed to repeat that personal history. The story is kept alive so that the recovering person might remain alive. There is also the element of **gratitude** for what happened by way of the person's own experience of conversion or transformation. Remembering "what happened" and who it was that effected this change is likewise a critical component in the ongoing process of recovery. The epitome of the process comes in the recitation of "what we are like now."

Members of the recovering community are cognizant of the fact that "what we are like now" is a result of having worked all of the steps of the program. It is in acknowledging the reality that I could not do it alone, that I came to believe that God could, and now I will allow God to do it for me (Steps 1–3).

The road to recovery, to borrow a biblical image, was difficult and narrow in leading the person to true life. It involved the painful process of recalling and rehearsing the rubble and ruin left in the wake of a destructive lifestyle (Steps 4 and 5). A complete "house cleaning" of attitudes, dispositions and other "defects of character" was imperative (Steps 6 and 7). The painful process of making amends where appropriate becomes a fitting response to the devastation of a life filled with remorse and regret (Steps 8 and 9). The watchful vigilance of a life lived a day at a time, dealing with the exigencies as well as the ecstasies of life, constitutes the new framework for living (Step 10). Utilizing the gifts of prayer and meditation to strengthen the relationship of grace is the essence of life (Step 11). Sharing this "good news" with others was the surprising discovery that dawned upon the cofounders of Alcoholics Anonymous (Step 12). They learned that even if others were not in recovery, reaching out to serve others could insure one's own sobriety because the focus of attention was shifted from the self to others.

Spirituality in the ongoing process of recovery might be imaged as a journey. As already noted, the most reliable road map for the journey are the Twelve Steps that suggest a way of living that insures sobriety with serenity (Albers, 1982, p. 417). The fact that this is a "suggested" way of living leaves room for alternative methodologies and strategies, but the Twelve Step program seems to fit so appropriately with the basic tenets of a healthy spirituality.[2] Spiritual caregivers would do well to support, encourage, nurture and advocate for Alcoholics Anonymous and other Twelve Step groups that have been the life link for so many people.

The radical reversal in lifestyle that comes about as a result of a spiritual awakening incorporates the characteristics of spirituality as proffered earlier in this essay. It is a spirituality that is anchored in God, who is a power of grace, love, and acceptance far greater than is humanly imaginable. Imaging God as Lord of the universe precludes the ludicrous suggestions that have sometimes been made that "anything" will suffice as a Higher Power. Spiritual caregivers would do well to challenge those who might suggest that a doorknob, a fence post, or a coffee cup can serve the purpose, as is sometimes suggested even in some AA groups. Such suggestions are an insult to the God who has created us. While some may initially adopt the power of the group as a power greater than self, ultimately they will encounter the fallibility of the group and its members as well. A healthy spirituality must be anchored in the reality of a gracious God who unconditionally and faithfully loves all of humankind and all of creation.

[2] Other chapters in this book, particularly those by Rev. Howard Gray, S.J., and Rabbi Carol Glass, give some further food for thought in this area.

In discussion and conversation about God, it is critically important to distinguish between theology, which may defined as faith seeking understanding, and spirituality, which is the word used to describe the dynamic relationship with the living God. Theology attempts to speak of the reality of God, utilizing human terminology and philosophical ideas. Even at best, all language about God must of necessity be metaphorical, lest some tradition claim to have encapsulated God in a theological system. One cannot reduce the understanding of who God is by intellectually assenting to a given set of dogmatic propositions. The God who is a power greater than self is not defined by human beings, but is the God above all other gods, real or imagined. Consequently, varying religious or spiritual traditions utilize different names for God, image God in a variety of ways and will offer their worship of God in a multiplicity of diverse rituals. While not defining who God is except in utilizing tentative metaphorical images, it seems critically important that spiritual caregivers heed the first statement of the Decalogue, namely that God not be equated with some graven image created by human ingenuity. A healthy spirituality needs to be fostered that allows God to be God.

A healthy spirituality in recovery is centered in this relationship of love and acceptance. Spiritual caregivers, who are symbolic representatives of God on this level of existence, model this relationship even though of necessity it will be in an imperfect way. Spirituality is about a healthy relationship with a God who is not characterized as one who elicits abject fear of punishment nor a God who is preeminently preoccupied with acts of retribution. These images of God are pervasive among many people who are addicted, and consequently many of them have understandably and rightfully rejected this conceptualization of God. Many have opted for agnosticism or atheism. The empathic and compassionate penning of chapter four in *Alcoholics Anonymous,* entitled "We Agnostics," is a persuasive argument for a relationship with a Higher Power which is *not* predicated on the ideas, images, or impressions of others. The spiritual caregiver needs to walk slowly and move gently through the labyrinth of concerns, doubts, and pain of those who are seeking a reliable and trustworthy relationship with a gracious God. Questions should be honored, inquiries taken seriously, and hesitation and skepticism treated with patience.

Healthy spirituality is communal in nature and finds its expression in a loving, accepting, and caring community. As has already been suggested, Twelve Step groups seem to fill the bill because of their solidarity of purpose and resolve to maintain sobriety as the number one priority. Hopefully, varying spiritual and religious traditions can emulate this environment in their own supportive way. There is no blueprint available except to assert that it must be a community not of pretense but of honesty, not given to arrogance but humility, and perhaps most importantly of all, one that is governed by love rather than judgment.

It needs to be a community that is ready both to share and to listen to stories. The strength of the community is directly proportionate to its ability to embrace a fellow human being whose story of struggle and pain will be heard. It is a community of commiseration bound together in the solidarity of a common humanity. Mutual disclosure is facilitated by implicit trust, mutual acceptance is accomplished by unqualified acceptance, and mutual recovery is experienced in the solidarity of purpose and mission.

Finally, a healthy spirituality embraces the necessity of reconciliation with God, others, nature, and one's self. Spiritual caregivers are in a unique position to offer this as a gift to others. God offers the gift of reconciliation as a way of binding up an estranged and alienated creature who has drifted from the purpose and intent for which s/he was created. The promise and the invitation are never withdrawn.

But reconciliation with others, particularly those most closely associated with the addict, is also important. Once again, spiritual caregivers are in a strategic position to facilitate this process as well. While reconciliation with others is the ideal, spiritual caregiving also needs to recognize that sometimes the wounds that were inflicted were so deep that forgiveness and reconciliation with others may not occur. It is particularly important then to walk with the person through that agonizing reality. While it is appropriate for the addict to offer amends, there is no guarantee that those amends will be honored or accepted.

However, there is no more gratifying spiritual experience than to participate in the process of forgiveness and reconciliation that is inspired by the Spirit of God, as it touches the spirit of human beings and dissipates the walls of anger, hostility, hatred, and indifference. These are some of the most amazing miracles of grace.

Learning Further about Spirituality and Addiction

Given the complexity of spirituality as already noted in this essay and its varying roles in the process of recovery, what further illumination might result from relevant research in this arena? A variety of questions might be posed to both research and reflect upon in greater detail. Is the spirituality of a person in recovery substantively different from the spirituality of someone who is not in recovery? Or to frame the same question in another way, is there anything particularly unique in the spirituality of recovering people? What accounts for the differences in spirituality among those who are in recovery? Are there unique features to the spirituality of a recovering person contingent upon her or his particular addiction? Should efforts even be made to codify or systematize the nature, experience, or expression of spirituality?

Research and reflection are to be encouraged, if the purpose is to enlighten or further elucidate the dynamics which are operative in assisting the recovery process. In that process, the issue of discretion needs to be exercised, lest the research become a kind of voyeurism and violate boundaries of propriety.[3]

Methodologically, it seems that listening attentively to the narratives of those in recovery, as they integrate their stories of recovery with their understandings, perceptions, and experiences of spirituality, would provide the most cogent information. It may be possible to extrapolate from such narratives common themes that are characteristic core spiritual issues for those in recovery. Another fruitful avenue of exploration might be to correlate the "spiritual blocks" which are identified in spiritual assessments with the spiritual resources utilized by recovering persons in being liberated from bondage.

The observations of "significant others" might likewise prove to be a valuable source of insight. The recovering person may not always be cognizant of what is happening, but another person in the circle of significant others may be more articulate about the process of spirituality in their loved one. Clergy who work extensively or exclusively with recovering persons might also be more objective observers and provide a theological interpretation of what is seen in the spiritual evolution of a recovering person.

We may also need to admit that in many instances the mystery of the working of God's Spirit in the hearts and lives of recovering people may defy any kind of analytical explication. The transformative process is to be celebrated, and praise is to be rendered to the One who effected the transformation. God continues to move in mysterious ways, performing miracles of change that remain incomprehensible to the human mind but are nevertheless experienced fully in the human heart.

Conclusion

This essay claims to be nothing more than one perspective or angle of vision on the topic of spirituality as it relates to addiction and recovery. It has been an attempt to consciously integrate some of the tenets of the Judeo-Christian tradition into an understanding of addiction and recovery, with particular attention given to the role of the spiritual caregiver in the process. Its principal contribution is focusing on the idea of "unconditional surrender" which paradoxically becomes the occasion for an "unconditional victory" over addiction. Some may see it as eclectic and syncretistic in nature, others may read it as too parochial or limited in scope. As has been heard at so many Twelve Step meetings over the years, take what is useful and discard the rest!

Our primary commitment as spiritual caregivers is that we be open to continued learning, refinement, revision, and new revelations that may

---

[3] For example, for a description of "discretionary" shame as well as "disgrace" shame, see Robert H. Albers (1995). *Shame: A faith perspective.* Binghamton, N. Y. : Haworth Press, pp. 7–14, 29–65.

appear as the task of addressing addiction and recovery continues not only in the U.S., but throughout the world. In so doing, may God grant us the serenity to accept the things we cannot change, the courage to change the things we can, and the wisdom to know the difference.

References

Albers, R. H. (1994). Spirituality and surrender: A theological analysis of Tiebout's theory for ministry to the alcoholic, *Journal of Ministry in Addiction and Recovery, 1*(2), 47–68.

Albers, R. H. (1982). *The theological and psychological dynamics of transformation in the recovery from the disease of alcoholism.* Ann Arbor: University Microfilms International.

Alcoholics Anonymous World Services (1955). *Alcoholics Anonymous.* New York: Author.

Blum, E. M. and R. H. (1967). *Alcoholism.* San Francisco: Jossey-Bass.

Clinebell, H. J., Jr. (1968). *Understanding and counseling the alcoholic.* Nashville: Abingdon.

Clinebell, H. J., Jr. (1962). Alcoholism and ethical issues. In *The pastoral care function of the congregation to the alcoholic and his family.* New York: National Council of Churches.

Holt, B. P. (1993). *Thirsty for God: A brief history of Christian spirituality.* Minneapolis: Augsburg.

Jellinek, E. M. (1960). *The disease concept of alcoholism.* New Haven: College and University Press.

Johnson, P. (1959). *The psychology of religion.* Nashville: Abingdon.

Keller, J. (1966). *Ministering to the alcoholic.* Minneapolis: Augsburg.

Mercadante, L. (1996). *Victims and sinners: Spiritual roots of addiction and recovery.* Louisville: Westminster John Knox.

Tiebout, H. A. (1944a). Therapeutic mechanisms of Alcoholics Anonymous. *American Journal of Psychology, 100,* 469.

Tiebout, H. A. (1944b). Conversion as a psychological phenomenon. New York: National Council on Alcoholism.

Tiebout, H. A. (n.d.). The act of surrender in the therapeutic process. New York: National Council on Alcoholism. [Reprinted in *Quarterly Journal of Studies on Alcohol, 10,* 48-58].

Tillich, P. (1963). *Systematic theology, Volume III.* Chicago: Chicago University Press.

Tillich, P. (1957). *Systematic theology, Volume II.* Chicago: University of Chicago Press.

Tillich, P. (1952). *The courage to be.* New Haven: Yale University Press.

CHAPTER 8

The Spirituality of Recovery: Recovery Is Learning to Love

Earnie Larsen

"Chemicals medicate pain" was the main point of a lecture given in the early 1970s by a front line counselor at a hospital-based treatment center. For some reason that I did not understand at the time, the sentence set off a jangle of bells. On some level I knew there was a mighty truth here beneath the easily said words. It is now some twenty years later and I am still attempting to understand more fully the implications of that truth.

Whatever else addictions are (and here I am speaking mostly of the addiction to alcohol), in the addictive stage the chemical is used to escape pain. However short term or ultimately self-deceptive that attempt might be, the intention of use is to escape. If that be true, then clearly once the "medication" is removed, what remains is the pain. If the medication is taken to escape the pain involved in day-in and day-out living, then it stands to reason that pain must also be addressed and dealt with in a more creative manner. There are but three alternatives to sobriety, understood as the absence of the mood-altering chemical:

(1) Relapse
(2) Switched addictions
(3) White-knuckle sobriety, or at least a far diminished capacity for joy and serenity.

The point, then, of addressing underlying living issues became not only increasingly clear but important. It became, in fact, the condition upon which the quality of recovery would depend. If chemicals medicate pain, then somewhere in the recovery process attention must be paid to the source of pain involved in living. Even a little experience in recovery clearly shows that pain was part of the person's life *before* s/he became addicted, *worsened* during the use stage, and certainly remain *after* sobriety had been achieved. Variously, this pain was identified as living problems such as low self-esteem, repressed anger, emotional dysfunction, lack of intimacy skills, an abiding sense of victimization, post-traumatic stress disorder, guilt, shame, untreated grief, or a host of others. The point was that, if these issues were not part of the primary modality of recovery, much would be lost.

Being a hospital-based unit we often made this point: "The cancer ward is on the fifth floor. Imagine some poor soul up there suffering bone cancer, in terrible pain. The staff gives him medication for the sake of relief. Then, they take the medications away. What does he have left?" The answer, of course, is "pain." The analogy was easily made: "Take the chemical away from the chemically dependent, what do they have?" Again the answer is self-evident: pain.

What has taken more than twenty years is pursuing the implications. It is one thing to state a truth. It is another to create modalities that allow that truth to be implemented. In my own recovery, as well as with the multitude of gallant souls I've had the privilege to work with over the years, what became abundantly clear was that there is no clearly defined or easily utilized method to deal with life once the addiction has been arrested. Creating that model and making it available has been my focus for close to three decades now.

Recovering Is Learning to Love

There is all the difference in the world between discussing addictions and the *people* who suffer addictions. It is easy to sanctify the tool at the expense of the art the tool is created to serve. People are not defined by addictions. It is addictions that must be seen in the light of the human condition. When one starts with the premise, it is the *person* in recovery; it is *people* who recover, then the damage addictions do is done to the care of one's humanity. Recover what? What was lost? What needs healing?

I believe it is only from the standpoint of a clear understanding of these questions and answers that a true model of recovery can be drawn. Whatever the pharmacology of addictions and recovery, whatever the psychology or epidemiology of addictions and recovery, it is still the *person* who is addicted, and the *person* who must recover.

Any number of starting places can be chosen, of course, as to "what it means to be human" or "what is the deepest wound addictions cause to one's humanity." Whatever starting place one chooses, however, a choice must be made or the focus of recovery becomes blurred.

Our starting point is simple: In human well-being all there is, is love and love denied. Where love has been denied, there is a wound. Whatever genetic predispositions may exist for addictions, it is primarily along the line of the vulnerability resulting from the damaged core of love denied that the progression to addictions happens. And, it is the psychic and spiritual healing of these wounds that ultimately must happen if there is to be quality recovery.

My starting point with every addict, whether it be a convicted felon in prison or an unsuspecting grandmother who became addicted to prescription pain killers, is this: The two greatest needs of every human being who ever lived is the need to love and be loved and the need for acceptance and belonging. The fact is that, even though we are born with these needs, we are not born with the skills to meet these needs. How we learn to meet these needs depends on a great many factors. The family system we are born into is among the most important, however. Early on, every human being learns what it takes to get "the good stuff." We learn our rules. Where these rules represent self-defeating values and behaviors such as "I am only as good as I work," "safe is to be invisible", or "They will only love me if I do for them," or a host of other paradigm beliefs, there will be a lack of development of the foundation for the *ability* for sharing in intimate relationships. Not the *want* for them, but the ability to participate. Substitute compensations are learned, habits from around these early, deep lessons. Those habits dictate reality. Being incapable of forming the kind of relationships that satisfy those deepest needs both with self and others, a worsening cycle of life-as-painful develops. The forms of trying to deal with the pain of unmet needs are many but the cause is universal. Riding along this line of vulnerability—in conjunction with whatever precursors to addiction may exist—come, the increased susceptibility to addictions as "medication for pain."(Further explication of these issues can be seen in Doweiko's chapter 2, Jampolsky's chapter 3, and Albers' chapter 7).

Thus, the second sentence at the opening of this article emerged: If chemicals medicate pain, then ultimately the progression of recovery has to address the cause of that pain. Ultimately, then, recovery is learning to love.

Stage I and Stage II

Expanding this line of thinking, along with the fieldtesting that validated each step, came the evolution of the concept of Stage I and Stage II in recovery (Larsen, 1985). Anyone with much experience in the recovery field soon understands from witnessing the obvious, that there is a stage of recovery where all the individual's energy and effort must be focused solely on arresting the addiction: sobriety. Considerations such as one's impediment to connectedness with self and others are beyond the scope or ability of a person at this stage. This first stage of recovery is addressed with well-known modalities such as assessment, intervention, detoxification programs, basic treatment programs of whatever style and duration. The goal of all these technologies is primary sobriety. As well it should be. Until there is sobriety, no other good can follow. This stage we designate as Stage I.

However, experience also dictates that at some point in the recovery process, if the statement "chemicals medicate pain" be true, attention must be paid to the underlying causes of the pain of life. Addressing these issues is what I term Stage II. The program for addressing these issues we call the life management program.

The life management program is our methodology for achieving Stage II recovery. A way to illustrate the difference between Stage I and Stage II can be seen in the following chart:

Stage I	Stage II
Goal: Establish stability. Intervene if necessary in order to successfully deal with the crisis situation.	**Goal:** Discover the underlying patterns that cause recurring crises.
Focus: Arrest addiction to substance or behavior.	**Focus:** Create new patterns and develop new skills for dealing with ongoing situations.
Program: Sobriety; information and support for abstinence such as Twelve Step programs.	**Program:** Family of origin work; affirmations; start/stop behaviors.

Discovery

Things get fixed; people heal. Though different, where the lines cross is that both fixing and healing demand understanding. No one can consistently, positively affect what they do not thoroughly understand. We can hire experts to fix our things. Mechanics can fix the car whose workings we don't understand, but we cannot hire someone to heal ourselves. Others can be of enormous help, yet no one can heal us but ourselves, nor can anyone help us without our permission. We must become our own experts.

It has long been our belief that the journey to freedom (whether called self-help, recovery or spiritual growth) has at least two fundamental segments: discovery and recovery. Discovery is understanding. Recovery is doing something positive about what is understood. It has further been our belief, especially in this past decade of label profusion, that there are countless goodwilled, committed people working hard at recovery without adequate discovery. They are trying to heal what they do not understand. Knowing *that* I hurt is one thing. Knowing *what* hurts is a step further down the road. But, knowing *why* I hurt is a step further yet, and essential if any lasting healing is possible.

It is common that people are not at all certain about even *what* hurts. One of the first orders of business for those starting Stage II Recovery is to focus on a specific issue that is causing pain in their lives. What hurts, we ask them? Usually much is hurting with overlapping boundaries and hidden causes. With so many easy labels attached to the discomfort, many people in recovery have no idea where to start or, more precisely, they begin to panic over "where is the right place to start."

Notice the symptomology most often listed describing various labels:

Dry Drunk: difficulty trusting, repressed anger, intimacy issues, mood swings, overly aggressive or passive in stating needs or wants, out of touch with feelings.

Codependent: trouble trusting others, intimacy issues, passive/aggressive tendencies, unresolved anger, emotional chaos.

Adult Child: bad boundaries around trust, difficulty with love relationships, enormous repressed anger, inability to ask for what they need, inability to establish their own feelings.

Shame Based: confusion over trust boundaries; sabotage relationships; unable to ask for needs, wants, and feelings; anger dealt with in unfocused manner; consistent feeling of dread and apprehension.

Inner Child: unable to trust in healthy manner, confusion over needs and how to fulfill needs, inability to break cycle of destructive behavior and feelings, terribly confused emotional life.

Spiritual Immaturity: inability to trust or trusting without foundation, intimacy issues, misplaced anger, confusion around feelings, feeling inadequate, defer to others, avoid success.

Low Self-Esteem: expect failure, distances oneself from intimacy, passive about rights, fears conflict, feels insecure, hides anger.

If all of these issues look like a duck, walk like a duck and sound like a duck, then they must be a duck. The insight suggests that, if all these labels create the same basic symptoms or pain, then there must be a *common process* causing them. It was this process, we reasoned, that must be understood if genuine change or healing was to be experienced. This is discovery. Getting relief from symptoms is one thing, understanding and then altering the process at the cause of those symptoms is quite something else. This very real change is the goal of Stage II Recovery.

This is not to say that the various labels all name exactly the same reality. They do not. It is to say that there is a common process at work behind all of the labels. Once that process or model is understood, the labels clearly reveal themselves as being different focuses on the same process, as we will shortly see.

Principles

Models are theories carried to the next step. If a theory does not condense into a working model, it remains just a thought, a more or less good idea. All theories and their evolved models are based on principles. Principles are the spine of the theory-turned-model. If the principles are true and simple, the model will be true and simple. True, because it can be validated; simple, because it can be understood and replicated. The (surely) simple and (we believe) true principles on which our model is based are these:

1. No one can outperform our own self-definition.
2. We do not see the world the way it is; we see the world the way we are.
3. Our self-definition creates consequences.

1. We cannot outperform our own self-definition.

Self-definition is the same as self-image. Definitions about who we are came from lessons that ranged from verbal instructions, physical handling, and other forms of overt behavior to more subtle messages like body language, tone of voice, and the look in someone's eye.

Early in our life, messages and lessons came from people of importance and power, namely, our parents, siblings, coaches, teachers, and clergy. As a child, we wanted these people to accept us and tell us that we were safe and wonderful, since that fed the basic needs we spoke of previously. We would do anything to gain approval.

These messages and lessons had power. Lessons about acceptance and self-worth are not static sentences written in a book. They are woven into the very fabric of life. These lessons soon become imperatives: *musts*. If the "must" was broken, punishment followed. Punishment came not only from those whose rules were broken, but from the inner sanctum of our sense of self. As we grew into adulthood, the lessons sorted themselves out. Some lessons were positive and conducive to a healthy life; others were negative and led us to confusing, discouraging, and hurtful consequences. In any case, these messages were imprinted in our psyche, and we learned to act them out without so much as a second thought.

As with most messages, positive or negative, we are scarcely aware of their existence. We are unaware that these messages are the driving force of our life. It is these messages we use to interpret and organize our lives. These definitions tell us what is appropriate and what is not, what is to be expected and deserved, and what is beyond our grasp. If we've been taught that we can't succeed, can't be loved, can't state our opinion, can't have a loving relationship with God, can't do anything, then we cannot. We cannot outperform our self-definition.

Those of us who become workaholics do so because our self-definition is that we are only as good as our work. If, in our own eyes, we are not being productive, then we are failing. If our work is judged by another person as mediocre, then we feel mediocre. If we are playing (i.e., not working), then we are "bad." We cannot outperform our self-definition.

Some of us were taught success meant wealth and that it was impossible to have enough of either. Others of us learn that wealth requires a special brand of intelligence that we don't have. Still others of us learn that we must be poor because good people always are poor. Financial success will never happen for any of these people. It cannot happen; we cannot outperform our own self-definition. The behaviors that lead to financial success are not allowed within the context of our self-definitions.

Some of us act as if food is our best friend, because food never asks how well we have performed. When food is the primary way one expresses love for oneself and others, then more than likely an addiction around food will appear. The problem is not the food but the reason for the food. At the core of our obsession is a self-definition that states: I eat to relieve pain; I give myself a hug with food. Regardless of our intentions and willpower, as long as the self-definition about food as love remains, we will be unable to use food in a healthy manner.

The power of the deeply ingrained self-definition demands obedience! Definitions have fangs. There is nothing more fundamental in a human being then one's definitions of self, others, and life in general. (This viewpoint is similar to the Addictive Belief System described by Jampolsky in chapter 3.)

2. We do not see the world the way it is. We see the world the way we are.

How we define ourselves is how we define the world. People with positive self-images usually live in a nurturing, humane environment. Those of us with negative views of ourselves find the world around us harsh, abusive, and uncaring. When we have learned to see ourselves as hammers, then the whole world becomes a nail and we will pound away with a vengeance.

Those of us who see ourselves as victims find ourselves in a world populated with abusers. Victims always seem to find and get involved with abusers. For some people, taking a risk means finding an opportunity for gain; for victims, however, risk is simply another opportunity to be devastated.

Caretakers see the world as a broken pile of wreckage that only our personal attention can set right. Our purpose in life becomes an obsession to ease the burden of others' afflictions whether they want the help or not. We let no catastrophe go unaided.

Workaholics view the world as a series of unfinished tasks demanding immediate attention. We are seduced by guilt and surrounded by endless projects. Nothing is more unsettling than leisure time.

People-pleasers see the world and everyone in it as potentially angry with them. Their worst fear is that they will upset someone. Their lives are devoted to second-guessing other people's reactions because they feel compelled to protect themselves from disagreeable situations at all costs.

Emotional tap-dancers see every commitment as a potential prison. No matter how desperately they long for intimacy, every possible partner they encounter is a potential jailer. They dance around commitments and relationships like moths around a flame.

We all live in the same world, but each of us sees it through a different set of glasses, a different set of perceptions dictated by definitions. There is an old story about five men who walked past a stand of cherry trees. The first man was a farmer who saw in the cherry trees the condition of the fruit. The next man was a cabinetmaker who saw in the trees wood from which he could craft beautiful furniture. The third man was a tired, hungry traveler. He saw the stand as a place to rest in the shade and get energy from the fruit. The fourth man was a developer who saw the advantages of building his homes near the trees in order to increase the value of each property. The last man was a conservationist who saw that the cherry trees needed to be protected from encroaching civilization. One stand of trees evoked five different responses. But each man's response was predictable, based on the definition of who he was.

3. Our self-definitions create consequences.

Our definition of ourself is at our core. As these definitions are acted out, life's consequences fall into place. If we see the definitions clearly enough, the results are predictable. Once we understand our self-definitions, we will realize that very little in life is accidental or mysterious. It is not magic or God's will that the same things keep happening to us. These repetitive events, healthy or not, happen because at our core is a definition of who we are, seated squarely upon its throne, demanding obedience.

There is enormous power in our self-definition. We become the learned messages we have acquired. Self-definitions are buried in our subconscious. They cannot be challenged until we first become aware of them, and then act with considerable effort and courage.

Imagine an underground electrical cable that carries current to a large shopping center. The lights turn on and off, there is heat in the winter and air conditioning in the summer, neon signs blaze away. People come and go, unaware of the presence or function of the buried cable. But, suppose there is a malfunction in the cable. When the lights go off or the heat fails, repairmen may be able to rig temporary solutions, but if repairs are to be permanent, the cable must be dug up and fixed.

When our self-definition is positive, we create positive results, and positive results mean healthy, fulfilling lives. People with positive self-definition, may not have perfect lives—no one does—but they do have the "machinery" to live positively and deal appropriately with whatever comes their way.

In the same way, a negative self-definition creates negative results. To be surrounded with negativity is to be paddling against the current. With negative definition, people feel their only choice is to endure problems and hope life doesn't get worse. Those with negative self-definitions may try on a few labels and programs for help, and they may find temporary relief. But, when ready and willing to make permanent repairs to their self-image, they have to address the real issue: self-definition.

Self-definitions

Definitions are not sterile, impotent statements. Self-definitions are the basic flesh and blood, the emotional directives of our life. Our self-definitions dictate the quality of our lives.

If there is to be consistent success on the job, or permanency in our relationships, or a newfound ability to tell the truth, then it is essential that our self-definitions be changed from negative to positive.

Self-definitions include thoughts, feelings, and actions. Self-definitions are generated from all the systems and experiences that make up our reality, our truth. When we encounter a situation where the definitions are challenged, or when we consciously consider making attempts at behavior contradicting the old definitions, we find a veritable army of fearsome obstacles. Our minds may be stampeded with old thoughts demanding that the old belief not be violated: "They are only trying to trick me." "I'll be hurt once again." "They are all liars." Justifications for remaining loyal to all old definitions slam into place, as if thrown from heaven by an angry god. Emotions become a roller coaster of confusion, ranging from guilt to fear to betrayal. And the most powerful emotion of all is the one that says: "Stop or disaster will happen again!"

Under the barrage of thoughts and emotions, we react. Our heart rate increases, our stomach tightens, adrenaline floods our blood system. We are stressed. Now the old coping mechanisms for relieving emotional pain spring into action: binge eating, extra hours sleeping or working, or shopping. Addictions are triggered.

But what has really happened is that we have challenged a negative definition. The old voices in our head begin the old chants: "Stop thinking about sharing feelings; stop trying to trust others; stop the diet; no one cares; I will always be alone; others will deceive me; I'll be just as miserable thin as fat, so have another chocolate bar." When we pulled out our old coping mechanisms of destructive, unhealthy, and addictive behaviors, our negative self-talk increased, and we were back to the comfort of "normal" once again, even if "normal" was full of pain.

Labels and self-definitions

Labels are names that we use to define behavior and feelings. Self-definitions are the images we have of ourselves. In Stage II recovery, if a self-definition is "I don't deserve to be loved," it makes no difference whether we call ourselves "adult children" or persons with low self-esteem, the results will be the same. Labels blur into meaninglessness. Labels are different names for different starting points, but all lend themselves to the same program of Stage II recovery.

The distinction here between Stage I and Stage II is critical. Though both are segments of the one journey of personal growth or recovery, they are vastly different realities calling for vastly different programs for forward movement. A Stage I program does not provide Stage II healing.

True and simple

If the principle is true that no one can outperform his or her own self-definition—that in fact we always live up to or down to the definition, we have of ourselves—then regardless of whatever label we prefer, it does not take a rocket scientist to see the connections in the following sample chart:

NEGATIVE DEFINITION	IMPERATIVE BEHAVIOR OR AVOIDANCE OR BEHAVIOR	CONSEQUENCE
1. I am only as good as my work	non-stop work; over volunteer; resistant leisure; sabotage time off	WORKAHOLIC: stress, anxiety over too much to do with too little time; rushed life; loved ones not given adequate time
2. I must do better	endless" fixing"; critical of self and others; over committed	PERFECTIONIST: never satisfied; critical of others; no joy in accomplishments; live with abiding sense of disapproval from self and expected disapproval from others
3. I will never amount to anything	avoid legitimate risk; sabotage success; settle for less	SHAME BASES: frustration; feel a failure; repeated cycle of hope and bitter disappointment; give up on life
4. I'll never be loved	enter abusive relationships; avoid intimacy; sabotage working relationships	INTIMACY ISSUES: abiding fear of losing out on life: deep loneliness; anger at self and others for "failing to come through"
5. "They" will always leave me	join with untrustworthy people; drive others away; repress feelings; avoid conflict	ABANDONMENT ISSUES: ever-present sense of fear; expect the worst; outburst of anger
6. I must never make waves	pretend agreement; agree to what I do not believe; sacrifice integrity; repress feelings; lie	PEOPLE PLEASER: live under a cloud of fear; emotional exhaustion; life seems too hard; never experience inner peace or freedom
7. Don't expect too much	do without what I may need or want; sacrifice for others; avoid goal setting; sabotage success	MARTYR: feel cheated; joy is a stranger; angry; unhappy, frustrated
8. Feelings are dangerous	hide feelings from self and others; verbalize only what seems "safe"; pretend feelings to fit in	EMOTIONAL RIGOR MORTIS: lose touch with feelings; feel nothing; life becomes flat; much fear; sense of missing out on life

This is a sample chart because obviously the possibilities are endless. A staggering number of different nuances generated from the same definition can fluctuate wildly. How the definition is acted out may depend on who is involved in the situation. A definition may be acted out differently if a man or woman is involved, or if the individual perceives s/he has power in this situation, or needs to "hide." No chart, or any number of charts, can exhaust the possibilities. The point is not to illustrate every possible situation but to make the point that, if the principle is true that "no one can outperform his or her own self-definition," then, given the definition, the consequences become not only predictable but mandatory. The *cause* of the consequences that are beneath whatever label you may prefer to call it begins to present itself as an understandable, manageable process. Given the definition and the situation, the consequences will surely appear.

In this context we are, of course, talking about individuals. Institutions, societies, and nations also exhibit self-definitions, negative or positive, that become acted out with equally clear and predictable consequences. An institution that has buried in its collective consciousness a definition that it is above the law or possesses ultimate wisdom will inevitably be an institution or corporation that flaunts the law and treats others with arrogant disregard. Consequences cannot be different than definitions. A society that has internalized a definition that "might is right" will tolerate and encourage an astounding amount of violence and abuse toward the weak and powerless. On the other hand, a nation that shifts basic definitions from "nature exists for our use and abuse; it is ours to do with as we will" to "we are one; we must nurture the environment as it nurtures us," will treat the environment totally different. Obviously, when dealing with institutions, societies, or nations, the acting out is much more complex due to the increased number of people involved. But, the patterns are there to be seen for anyone who cares to look, written into their history, showing its face in multiple ways in the present, invariably acting out the imperatives buried in the heart.

The Model

The model that incorporates this theory and principle into a view of individuals looks like this: First, pick an issue; the more personal, the better. The point is not to pick "the right" issue but any issue that is presently causing discomfort. We are not after bandaging symptoms (the issue), but we use the issue as a "door" through which the process (the cause) can be understood and altered.

Secondly, we begin working with the client to identify the negative self-definition at the core. The issue cannot exist if the definition does not exist. One is the reality, the other is the reflection, mirror-like, of that reality. At the outset, few are clear about their negative self-definitions. Definitions are hidden, undetected, residing on the subconscious level. But if the issue or consequence is there, you can bet the farm that the definition is hidden away at its core. Understanding the causal relationship between definition and issue becomes tremendously empowering.

Thirdly, we point out that issues are generalities. Where the rubber hits the highway is when these issues get triggered in a concrete, here and now situation. Many a person has been fooled into thinking that an issue has been healed, simply by avoiding the situation. But when a person with a history of repeating toxic relationships refuses to go on a date, there is no healing of the dysfunction that caused the choice of those repetitive toxic relationships in the first place.

What also becomes abundantly clear very quickly is that the Stage II work and understanding, unlike a Stage I situation which is focused on arresting an addiction or obsessive behavior, usually requires direct assistance. Not many people, we have found, can simply look at this model and progress by themselves to a clear understanding of the process propelling them into their pain. Some knowledgeable outside direction is usually necessary.

The definition, once triggered by a concrete situation, always manifests itself in thought (self-talk), feelings, and actions, resulting inevitably in predictable consequences or issues. The more one clearly and thoroughly understands exactly how *for oneself* this rational, emotional, and behavioral response is acted out in a given situation, and the basic belief system behind

Thought →	**Feeling →**	Action →	Consequence
1.	1.	1.	1.
2.	2.	2.	2.
3.	3.	3.	3.

that response (the self-definition), the more s/he is empowered to effect positive change. Understanding empowers; ignorance imprisons. In graph form, the model takes on this shape:

An example we often use at seminars explaining this model is "Mary." Mary happens to be an adult child of an alcoholic family system. This means, of course, that she is codependent, shame-based, probably houses a covey of wounded inner children, and no doubt suffers from low self-esteem. All of which means, we believe, that she has internalized a number of negative self-definitions, totally beyond her awareness, that drive her crazy.

At this time, let's say she is focusing on her desperate desire for a loving, close relationship and her apparent inability to "find" or share in such a relationship. She knows about toxic, abusive, emotionally distant relationships. Here she is an expert. About being loved, feeling safe, enjoying trust, however, she is totally in the dark. Mary has decided she has an intimacy issue.

She writes "afraid I'll never be loved" in the line for issue. But about her negative self-definition she has not a clue. She agrees it feels right to say something like, "I'll never be loved" or "good things never happen to me." She really perks up when it is suggested that she might be harboring a definition like "men hurt," or "when I trust I lose," or "men never treat women fairly." (It does not take much family-of-origin work for Mary to understand where those definitions came from in her violent, dysfunctional, alcoholic background). With understanding, the whole process becomes achingly clear. On the second line, Mary writes, "Men always abuse me. I'll never be loved. I do not trust men."

Now as to the situation: Here she is at a dance with a loaded double-barreled shotgun of destruction. On the one hand, there is nothing in the whole world she wants or needs more than a trusting, loving relationship with a man. This is the relationship she never had, the love forever denied. On the other hand, she has a tyrannical, hidden, negative imperative that says all men are treacherous and not to be trusted. While all these needs gnaw at Mary's heart, an attractive man approaches and asks her to dance (Little does Mary know he also is working through his problems. From his background, he has a terrible fear of intimacy and women imprinted in him. He is taking a *terrible* risk approaching her! Little does he know the network of destruction he is walking into!)

Because he is not drunk, unappealing, or obnoxious (all conditions that Mary's definition would welcome), as soon as he asks Mary to dance, her definition is triggered like adrenaline hitting the blood stream, setting off furious activity. Totally unaware as to cause, Mary experiences the all too familiar, thunderous thought patterns as she is asked to dance:

> THOUGHT: "Here it goes again! You'll get hurt again. Who does he think he is, pulling this stuff." Generated by the negative self-definition and fueled by the onslaught of negative thoughts that bolstered that definition, there arise:
>
> FEELINGS: Standing there facing that attractive man, with a heart full of want, Mary—for reasons she cannot name—feels panic, anxiety, and, strangest of all, mounting anger at the gentleman before her. All of this emotional eruption is in a nanosecond. The gentleman is looking at an attractive, pleasant-looking woman on the outside. He has no idea that under the outer appearance there is a process in motion that spells disaster. Thoughts and feelings always translate into:
>
> ACTION: Mary tells that man to get lost. She turns her back, and with regal disdain walks away, leaving a masculine tower of confused hurt in her wake. A lovely "could have been" lies murdered on the altar of negative self-definition. Definitions translated into thought, feelings, and actions, of course, always generate:
>
> CONSEQUENCES: They are multiple: Mary has ruined any chance for fun she might have had at the dance. She has further convinced herself that she is basically insane, an emotional wreck, and not worthy of the attention of any semi-attractive man. Her shame deepens. Her codependency grows yet another layer. Her inner child has another spike driven through its heart. All of this, of course, says nothing about the damage done to the brave man taking a risk and asking her to dance. He received a stone anchor, rather than being thrown a lifeline.

As people familiarize themselves with the model, it becomes as clear as the gloom on Mary's face that "things" could not have turned out any other way. If the principle is true, there is no other consequence possible, given the negative belief system. If the train tracks go to Milwaukee and the train is on the tracks, it doesn't take a Ph.D. in psychology to figure out where that train is going to end up.

Take time to play with the model. Change Mary's negative self-definition from "I'll never be loved" to "I don't have a right to tell a man no" and see what happens. Substitute a basically nice guy approaching her to some totally obnoxious, abusive individual. Mary no more wants to dance with him than she wants to eat glass. But given the situation of a man asking and her definition that prohibits saying "no," the consequences are predictable. In a later situation, throw in the man saying, "Let's get out of here and go someplace more private" and the tragic results are equally predictable.

Make the scenario a man with a food issue. The definition, learned early and deep, might be: "Food is my only friend; food is my basic hug." Put that man, desperate to control his eating by attending every calorie-counting, food maintenance program in existence, in a situation where he feels rejected, insecure, or lonely, and watch what happens. If the prime principle is true, what else could possibly happen?

Draw a situation with a young person, male or female, who has internalized a perception and attitude causing a definition that says: "You are dumb. No one cares about your rights or feelings. Never speak up or you will be punished." Put that person in a situation where it is important to speak up, to stand one's ground, to take affirmative action, and see where the train of life will and *must* end up. Given any number of subtle variations, this young person may become terminally passive. He or she may also simply boil over into violent, enraged behavior in an attempt to get back at what is being "done" to them. However, if the individual acts out this perceived powerlessness or reacts to situations where his or her rights are abused, you can bet there will be tragedy with a good dose of self-damage inflicted. The more time is taken to role play various possibilities within the presented model, the more obvious the process becomes regardless of what label is attached. The more obvious the process built on those guiding principles, the more obvious the results. And, of course, it is those results that dictate the quality of each of our lives.

Recovery

Once a recovering person has integrated these models (discovery), effective Stage II recovery can happen. Focused practice based on understanding is the key, not just behavior modification or "fake it till you make it," but truly effective action taken with a conscious connection to the self-definition in question.

- Sharing a feeling a day is not just positive action but a direct, coscious program to attack a negative self-definition that "my rights don't count."

The same can be said for behaviors such as:

- asking for help every day
- asking a question every day
- scheduling twenty minutes every day that is just for you
- consciously listening to two people every day
- waving two people ahead of you in traffic every day

and so on.

It is strongly recommended that all recovery efforts take place in the context of an accountability/support group. That is, each person in the accountability group makes a commitment to the daily practice of the behaviors that their "discovery" told them was necessary for a changed self-definition. Each day the complete behavior is logged. The business of the accountability group is to open one's log and "be held accountable" for the specific behaviors to which one is committed.

An accountable program is always effective, whether in bringing a person to an acceptable level of change or bringing one to the awareness of the need for a deeper level of recovery.

CHAPTER 9

Spirituality for High and Low Rollers: The Paradox of Self-esteem in Gambling Recovery

Joseph W. Ciarrocchi

In comparison to other addictions, writers have paid little attention to spiritual issues in recovery from pathological gambling. As in so many other ways, the field of gambling treatment remains far behind substance abuse. Despite the enormous social costs of problem gambling, few government bodies have apportioned money for prevention, treatment, or research. The United States, for example, which has government-funded national institutes for alcohol and drug problems, has given less than the proverbial "drop in the bucket" for research into problem gambling. Indeed, many major health insurance companies do not even recognize pathological gambling as a disorder eligible for reimbursement for psychotherapy. These companies reimburse only when an additional "eligible" disorder exists.

Nevertheless, the costs of problem gambling are enormous. Reliable data conclude that 1 to 3 percent of the general population fall into the categories of problem or pathological gambling (Volberg and Steadman, 1989). Studies of gamblers entering treatment have found the average indebtedness to be ninety two thousand dollars (Politzer, Morrow and Leavey, 1985). Nor should we expect the problems to decrease. Approximately 80 percent of Americans gamble, spending more than 200 billion dollars annually in legalized gambling, with estimates of an equal amount illegally. This represents more than a 1,000 percent increase in less than two decades. Forty-eight of fifty states in the United States have legalized gambling and new forms continue to proliferate. Casinos arise regularly, either on Native American reservations or on riverboats docked on shores. Effective opposition to legalization of gambling has largely ended, with state governments now relying on gambling revenues for essential social services. In some states, gambling taxes exceed revenues from traditional sources such as sales taxes.

This chapter will focus on spiritual issues related to recovery from gambling problems. It is not intended as a general clinical overview. A discussion of problem gambling and its implications for pastoral counseling may be found elsewhere (Ciarrocchi, 1992, 1993).

As a framework for understanding spirituality in gambling recovery, I have chosen self-esteem as the lens from which to view that process. Decades of clinical wisdom, whether directed toward addictive behavior or other mental disorders, point to the important influence of low self-esteem in the origins of these conditions. Indeed, it is almost a truism in the field to observe that depressed, traumatized, abused, or otherwise stressed persons might drink or use drugs to escape the emotional pain from poor self-images.

Clinicians in the gambling treatment field have often accepted this wisdom, as we shall note below. However, as we tried to apply these notions to our everyday clinical situations, we realized that our patients often looked dramatically different from the low self-esteem portrait observed in alcoholics or drug addicts. Consider the following case example.

> George was a 45-year-old married man, twice divorced, whose father was a wealthy West Coast financier and his mother a homemaker. The family was of Italian descent and tight-knit. In his younger days George had gone to medical school, graduated, but failed his licensing exams multiple times because of distractions related to his gambling disorder. Abandoning medicine, and with his father's business connections, George used his interpersonal charms to achieve minor success in the entertainment industry by organizing small groups of investors to finance movie scripts. Because George continued to lose money gambling, however, he often played fast and loose with his investors' money. Repeatedly he would dip into these funds and end up owing anything from ten to sixty thousand dollars. Each time his father and mother would bail him out.
>
> With enormous pressure from his wife and parents to give up sports betting, George turned to the stock market, and in particular to options. The options market is a challenge to even the most astute investor, but for George it quickly proved too much. When he entered treatment, his parents estimated that they had paid out over $300,000 to cover George's losses from gambling over the years.

> What impressed his therapist was George's near total indifference to others' needs. Once, to pay off gambling debts, he persuaded his sister to loan him inherited family silverware to take to a pawnshop. Eventually, when she asked him to return it to her, he "allowed" her to buy it back for several thousand dollars. He continued to blame his mother (who provided him with most of his lump-sum bailouts from her sizeable accounts) for not giving him sufficient start-up funds for his options deals. In his mind his losses were not truly gambling losses but due rather to his parents' "undercapitalizing" him. His attitude toward his wife was one of managing her. He was not averse to periodic one-night affairs, but he avoided women who might want a sustained relationship.
>
> A prototypical example of his lack of empathy occurred when his parents, returning from a vacation in Hawaii, asked him to pick them up at the airport and he refused. Without guilt he explained to his therapist that his parents could certainly afford the cab ride to their home and, besides, it would entail his having to carry bags for them. These same parents, who were not worth the inconvenience of a trip to the airport, paid the full private school tuition annually for his three children. In addition they gave his spouse $3000 a month to compensate for their son's unemployment. When the therapist suggested that the patient agree to "accept" employment in one of his father's businesses for an annual salary between thirty and forty thousand dollars, he replied that such a sum was much too low for his talents.

Although this represents an extreme case, the interpersonal arrogance and unwarranted belief in his own skills is representative of many problem gamblers. The traditional understanding of such behavior is that such behavior actually implies low self-esteem. Thus, experts such as Robert Custer (Custer and Milt, 1985), the psychiatrist responsible for having pathological gambling recognized as a mental disorder, view arrogant behavior in gamblers as covering up negative self-worth.

I find this analysis unconvincing. The sense of entitlement in these acts of social indifference suggests a belief that one is actually above the rules. A continual belief in "a system" for betting in the face of constant disconfirmation suggests a powerful belief that one has unusual gifts or powers. The low self-esteem analysis requires a conceptual pirouette to hold that it drives *both* interpersonal submission and aggression, a belief *both* in one's powerlessness *or* in one's exalted powers.

Is there a cogent alternative to the low self-esteem hypothesis? Recently a body of work in social psychology has emerged to provide an alternative. Summarized by Roy Baumeister and his colleagues (Baumeister, 1991a, 1991b, 1993; Baumeister, Heatherton, & Tice, 1994) in several literature reviews and books, this research indicates that *exaggerated self-esteem* may be problematic as well. For example, in their review of the literature on violence, Baumeister and his colleagues (Baumeister, Boden and Smart, 1996) found that high self-esteem is more likely to be associated with violence under threat conditions than is low self-esteem. Similarly, laboratory studies found that high self-esteem persons make riskier bets after their abilities are called into question. This led to the conjecture that "in contrast to alcohol and eating (in which excess is linked to low self-esteem), it might be the case that compulsive gambling is linked to high self-esteem" (Baumeister, Heatherton, and Tice, 1994, p. 222). This implies that to provide a comprehensive framework for understanding gambling recovery, adaptive strategies for both high- and low self-esteem persons are required. For, although the prototypical pathological gambler represented in the clinical literature is a competitive, energetic, Type A, walk-on-the-edge personality, wagering on sports or fast-action casino games, there is probably an equal number of fearful, passive-dependent and avoidant types who wager on low-stake games such as bingo, lottery, and slot machines. This chapter rests on the assumption that self-esteem differences provide a useful typology for framing spiritual issues in recovery.

Self-esteem Versus Egotism

Our use of the popular term self-esteem may mislead us when discussing the pitfalls of exaggerated self-esteem. Most consider self-esteem a feature of healthy psychological functioning. Indeed, such is usually the case. Throughout this chapter, therefore, I will use the word "egotism" to describe *exaggerated* beliefs in one's self worth. Most people's self-esteem is positive when measured by reliable tests, with about 25 percent of the population falling in the low range. This chapter focuses on adapting spiritual strategies for the individual differences of unhealthy low self-esteem and unhealthy egotism. The position taken in this chapter, however, rejects the psychodynamic notion that egotism is "really" a reaction formation to poor self-esteem. (A technical discussion of this point can be found in Baumeister, 1996, chapter 5). To tie this once again into our discussion of gambling recovery, egotism and poor self-esteem present different clinical pictures. As presented earlier, the behavioral expressions in pathological gambling require separate clinical and spiritual approaches. The ultimate goal for either pattern is mature self-esteem.

Self as a burden

Addiction treatment commonly views compulsive behavior as an escape. Whether persons are escaping stressful jobs, failed relationships, or poverty, escape in the form of cocaine, several beers, or a game of poker provides a powerful distraction. Baumeister points out that escape patterns have different motivational paths. For low self-esteem individuals, forgetting the defeated self drives the escape. With egotism, forgetting the challenged self drives the escape. The challenged self requires always evaluating, "How am I doing?" It requires hypervigilance to anticipated threats to one's status or achievements. Each of these selves generates different compulsive gambling styles.

Escape patterns for the defeated self

> Sara was a 67-year-old widow who entered residential treatment for depression two years after her spouse died. They had been married for forty years, and he had been a successful businessman leaving her an estate worth nearly a million dollars. Her sons and daughters who accompanied her to the hospital had urged her to seek treatment after she had spent over half the estate in the past two years at bingo parlors. Nothing in her life led anyone to believe that she would lose control over gambling so quickly. She had been an exemplary homemaker and mother, and was quite frugal with the family finances. In fact, her children suggested, she was so resilient that few friends and acquaintances even knew that their mother had survived two years in a Nazi concentration camp where her parents and siblings were executed.

Similar clinical examples include a 28-year-old depressed man, recovering from alcoholism and drug addiction, who found that going to the race track distracted him from his suicidal feelings; or a 62-year-old divorced Methodist minister, who embezzled funds from his congregation to gamble at the slot machines in the riverboat casinos. Gradually, he revealed to his therapist that he went to the casinos to forget his bothersome homosexual feelings.

Each of these examples indicates the relationship between gambling and a self burdened with a sense of defeat. The emotional pain in each instance comes from failure, despair, or the threat of painful memories. Gambling leaves behind the beaten-down self in exchange for an adrenaline rush that captures the mind and senses.

Escape patterns for egotism

George, the options trader discussed above, represents the threatened ego. Unlike Sara, the bingo player, George was not running from trauma. Indeed, he was the proverbial poor little rich boy. Not that life went totally his way. However, when challenged, his strategy was to take risks. His gambling functioned more in the "I'll-show-them" mode than as a distraction from his pain and suffering. The same could be said of Bill, an energetic and creative real estate developer. With his brilliant knowledge of the market and exceptional powers of persuasion, he put together investment packages for the wealthy. His need for large sums of money for his sports betting, however, resulted in devising investment deals that ran afoul of state and federal tax laws.

Both George and Bill, far from appearing downtrodden and defeated, always appeared optimistic. Talking to them invariably convinced the average person that success was just around the corner. Evidence for clinical depression was difficult to obtain unless you caught them right after a loss. Psychiatrists, for example, often find that antidepressants seldom seem to help persons with a threatened ego.

Similarly, the gambling culture provides an effective environment for escape. Casinos usually are devoid of clocks, windows, and mirrors. Clocks and windows would add a note of temporal reality and possibly interfere with the gambler's focus. Mirrors make people self-conscious, possibly alerting them to their foolish behavior.

Belief patterns for the defeated self

Much evidence indicates that persons with low self-esteem, the defeated self in our pathological gambling model, have personal beliefs quite different from those with high self-esteem, the challenged self in our model. These beliefs revolve around three main areas: (1) the sense of self; (2) personal control; and (3) the future. Persons with low self-esteem typically have negative self-views, by definition, in comparison to other people. Typically, they rate themselves less positively, but it is useful to point out that even persons low in self-esteem are not totally devoid of positive self-affirmation. Their self-esteem is low relative to the general population but not low in an absolute sense. Most people have a fairly high opinion of themselves, and persons with low self-esteem have at least one quality on which they rate themselves highly.

Second, persons with low self-esteem tend to underestimate the degree to which they have personal control over events. They give more weight to chance, luck, or environmental factors when judging how much influence they have over positive events in their lives, but they see themselves as the cause of negative outcomes. Third, they tend to view the future somewhat more pessimistically than those with high self-esteem. These perspectives both contribute to gambling problems and interfere with recovery. Reduced belief in one's ability to control positive events creates a fateful "all-or-nothing" approach to gambling that relies on fate over rationality. The net result of these beliefs is to jettison behavior likely to promote positive outcomes. Abandoning rationality, in turn, leads to passivity about outcomes that further worsens the situation.

Culture may influence these beliefs as well. For example, clinicians that work in the Chinese-American community note a pervasive belief in fate. In this mindset, it matters little what one does, because the outcome is predetermined. Clinicians report that gamblers take this to mean that, if fate is working for them on a particular day, they cannot lose. Naturally this impedes recovery in those who require abstinence.

Belief patterns for egotism

Egotism, on the contrary, has opposite beliefs regarding personal control, sense of self, and the future. Specifically, such persons tend to overestimate their degree of personal control over positive events, and view negative events as caused by others, bad luck, or environmental forces. (Interestingly, this is the tendency of most people in the general population; some researchers believe this outlook works as a buffer against depression for most of us in our day-to-day lives.) Similar to most people, egotism is optimistic about the future, and results in positive self-views. Ordinarily these qualities have benefits for personal functioning. People with such beliefs tend to be less depressed and have more successful lives when measured in such terms as occupational achievements or social status.

Egotism, however, has a downside in comparison to mature self-esteem. Two areas that Baumeister calls attention to are aggression and risk-taking. Threatened egotism, not low self-esteem, is a more established factor in aggressive and violent behavior (Baumeister, Boden, and Smart, 1996). This conclusion is counterintuitive and flies in the face of so many educational initiatives to "enhance self-esteem" in disadvantaged youth. The second area, which is pertinent to this chapter, revolves around risk-taking (Baumeister, 1997). Studies demonstrate that, following threat, people with high self-esteem are more likely to engage in risky behavior than their low self-esteem counterparts. Indeed, in one study high and low self-esteem participants were invited to wager either a small or large amount following an insult. Low self-esteem subjects wagered a small amount on a relatively sure bet, whereas high self-esteem persons wagered a larger amount on a risky bet.

All of these studies, taken together, lead to the important conclusion that egotism is not always adaptive. In situations where they are challenged, persons with high self-esteem may have overconfidence in themselves, and this may lead to misjudging their actual capacities. As Heatherton and Ambady (1993, p. 142) point out, "the notion that high self-esteem needs to be treated at all may seem radical." It takes little imagination to extrapolate this pattern to the maladaptive risk-taking inherent in pathological gambling.

In addition to providing conceptual clarity to gambling motivation, this research validates clinical observations. The cases noted above in the threatened-self section traditionally were understood as people covering up low self-esteem with an outward façade of arrogance and bravado. Baumeister's insights do not require us to make this explanatory reversal. Rather, we can accept the arrogance and bravado for just what they appear to be, the behavioral manifestations of people who think highly of themselves and who act boldly and confidently no matter what the circumstances.

We would suspect that such beliefs would interfere with recovery in several important ways. First, such individuals will see their personal worth as especially tied into their achievements. When threatened with failure, they are inclined to react rashly. Financial and status losses inherent in pathological gambling trigger overreaching. Second, clinicians have long noted that such persons have trouble sharing the affection of significant others. Gambling treatment clinical lore is replete with paying close attention to certain high-risk situations such as a wife's pregnancy or illness, or the birth of a child. Excessive self-esteem would see such events as an ego threat propelling escape via high-risk activities such as gambling.

In my opinion, therefore, self-esteem issues interfere with recovery differentially. Persons with low self-esteem require treatment approaches (including spirituality) that emphasize empowerment. Egotistic individuals require treatment approaches, (including spiritual ones), that emphasize monitoring their own egos and how they respond to threats. The rest of this chapter will outline these varied approaches.

A Theology and Spirituality for Self-esteem Issues

Role and Definition of Spirituality

Spirituality that is grounded in a theology of faith can unify the paradoxes we have described in the psychology of self-esteem. Essays in this book present various perspectives on spirituality. For our purposes, let us use Joann Wolski Conn's definition of general religious spirituality.

> General or universal religious spirituality refers to the actualization of human self-transcendence (i.e., the capacity for relating, knowing, committing ourselves) by whatever is acknowledged as the ultimate or Holy. (Conn, 1993, p. 38)

For Conn, and many contemporary writers, the essence of spirituality is the capacity for relating to the Holy, via knowing, loving, and commiting. As she also states, "relatedness to the ultimate qualifies relationships to persons and things" (p. 39).

Biblical and theological dimensions of faith

Theologically, however, the very capacity for spirituality is grounded in faith. Belief in a God who inspires trust, love, and commitment gives the spiritual enterprise its meaning. Faith, further, has the capacity to ground spirituality for addiction recovery and to avoid the self-defeating traps of both low self-esteem and egotism. Relying on the summary of theologian Avery Dulles (1994), both biblical and theological notions of faith point to this spiritual grounding. The synoptic gospels (Matthew, Mark, and Luke), building on the Jewish notion of faith, anchor our security in God's faithfulness to us. If we have even small amounts of faith, we could move mountains. Yet faith can coexist with uncertainty: "Lord, I do believe; help my unbelief." In John's Gospel, faith is a new way of knowing; belief in Jesus leads to knowing and seeing God differently. For Paul, faith is the source of God's justifying and saving us—but it is a faith that must prove itself through love.

Over the centuries theologians have developed these biblical reflections further. Except for some extreme positions, their views tend to be complementary rather than exclusionary. Two out of the many traditions seem relevant to our discussion about self-esteem. First, in the Protestant tradition, Martin Luther emphasizes faith as an act of trust. Similar to St. Paul, this trust must prove itself in action. "Where works and love do not break forth, there faith is not right" (cited in Dulles, 1994, p. 45).

A second tradition, set forth by twentieth century Roman Catholic theologians Karl Rahner and Bernard Lonergan, emphasizes faith as God's providing us with a new way of seeing. In this tradition faith is "a new cognitive horizon, a divinely given perspective" (Dulles, 1994, p. 172). This perspective means accepting the nearness of God as "absolute mystery," (according to Karl Rahner), or as Lonergan states, faith renders the world to us through "the eye of religious love" (Dulles, p. 173).

Faith and self-esteem

In Matthew's Gospel, Jesus tells the parable of servants who received money from their master, "each one according to his ability" (22:15, American Bible Society, 1967). Two servants doubled their money from wise investments. The third, "paralyzed by fear" (Karris, p. 711), buried the money, thereby incurring the wrath of the master, who points out that the servant could have earned interest in a bank. This ancient parable describes typical patterns that result from negative self-esteem, behavior that pastoral counselor William Oglesby calls, "the twisted notion that the hiding is essential to preserve life" (1980, p. 80).

Such persons are so concerned with their reduced worth (in their eyes), that they refuse to take growth-oriented risks for fear of losing what they have. With Adam and Eve the sounds of life, including God's life, scare them. "'I heard you in the garden; but I was afraid, because I was naked, so I hid myself'" (Genesis 3:10, Benziger, 1988). When they do act, it is more out of fear of offending, rather than the exhilaration of accomplishment.

How contrary is this style to biblical and theological understandings of faith. Nothing is safe where faith is concerned. Who is not with me is against me; develop your talents for the kingdom or be thrown out into the darkness. What could we not accomplish, if we had genuine "acceptance of the nearness of God as absolute mystery" (Dulles,1994)?

This approach speaks also to many women's issues in recovery. As Rebecca Propst (1988) points out, traditional religion viewed sin as failure to accept our creatureliness. Women, and some men, often have the opposite problem: failure to accept that they are made in the image and likeness of God. That belief, along with faith in God's nearness, could enable the low self-esteem individual to embrace the risks required to walk the painful path toward greater autonomy.

The eye of religious love casts a different perspective on egotism. Biblical and spiritual traditions see exaggerated belief in one's self-sufficiency to be a barrier to spiritual growth. "For all that is in the world, sensual lust, enticement for the eyes, and a pretentious life, is not from the Father but is from the world" (1 John 2:16, Benziger, 1988). Cain and Abel represent the tragic side of egotism. Two brothers make an offering to God. God favors Abel's offering for reasons not disclosed. Cain cannot accept this blow to his self-esteem and becomes "resentful and crestfallen," the typical reaction of threatened egotism. God notices Cain's mood and essentially says, "There's no need to be glum—my liking something of your brother's is no reflection on you, unless you let this mood get out of hand." Cain promptly allows this to happen by killing Abel. This represents the classic response to threatened egotism—reassert your sense of power and put the offending person in his or her place.

Biblical wisdom literature roundly castigates egotism. "Pride goes before disaster, and a haughty spirit before a fall" (Proverbs 16:18, Benziger, 1988). The psalms touch on Baumeister's link between egotism and violence: "So pride adorns them as a necklace; as a robe violence enwraps them" (Psalm 73:6). In the Christian tradition Paul cautions those with exaggerated self-esteem: "For if anyone thinks he is something when he is nothing, he is deluding himself" (Galatians 6:3, Benziger, 1988). An even more explicit counsel toward accuracy in self-esteem occurs in the Letter to the Romans: "I say to all of you: Do not think of yourself more highly than you should. Instead be modest in your thinking, and judge yourself according to the amount of faith God has given you" (12:3, American Bible Society, 1992).

In the eyes of faith, egotism is self-deceiving. It uses the wrong criterion to estimate self-worth. My worth derives not from my amazing qualities, but from "the amount of faith God has given." Without that gift my specialness is delusional. Cain did not have the faith perspective Paul calls us to. "You should each judge your own conduct. If it is good, then you can be proud of what you yourself have done, without having to compare it with what someone else has done" (Galatians 6:4, American Bible Society, 1992).

Faith, then, is the proper corrective to both low self-esteem and egotism. On the one hand, faith tells us to act boldly, for we are images of God. On the other hand, we cannot be the purpose of our own existence: "He died for all, so that those who live might no longer live for themselves" (2 Corinthians 5:15, American Bible Society, 1992).

Practical Spirituality and Meaning in Life

Positive escape from the self is a requirement for healthy living. No one can long sustain the burden of coping with either a continuously defeated or threatened self. Positive escape takes at least three main forms. Absorbing interests in the form of work, hobbies, entertainment, reading, etc. comprise the first form. Social and interpersonal activities represent both positive escape and a distraction from maladaptive ruminating that amplifies negative mood (Nolen-Hoeksema, 1987).

In this chapter our concern is with a third form of escape represented by *spiritual devotion*. Baumeister reminds us that ecstasy, the object of mystical striving, has as its root meaning in Greek "to stand outside the self" (Baumeister, 1991a, p. 35). When one stands outside the self, in this sense, one experiences transcendence. Unlike hobbies or other absorbing distractions, transcendence creates escape through experiencing One who is greater than the self. This experience absorbs one's attention but, more importantly, it orients the self within a true perspective. Rather than a temporary fleeing of the self, which any earthbound interest can provide, transcendence provides escape from the burden of self via discovery of the true self in relationship to the One.

Spirituality, therefore, represents an escape from the self, even as one seeks higher meaning. Spirituality, when combined with participation in formal religion, combines the other positive escapes noted above. Cultural and intellectual study of one's faith tradition can provide many hours of absorbing stimulation. Additionally, the social dimensions of religion are well known for their communal support around day-to-day social needs and during times of personal crisis or loss.

Baumeister's (1991b) work on life meanings provides a comprehensive model for situating spirituality in gambling recovery. His review of the research literature concluded that four major psychological constructs represent the bulk of what constitutes meaning for most people. *Purpose* represents a crucial form of meaning and takes two forms. One form is the goals people set that provide some type of extrinsic motivation. Working primarily to obtain a paycheck or changing a screaming infant's soiled diaper represent externally motivated goals that give purpose. Other goals are intrinsically satisfying, and these vary from person to person: a stamp collection, volunteer work, sky diving, or pursuing a scientific discovery. *Values* represent a second form of meaning. Values are acts that require no justification or explanation. We do them solely for the "ought" associated with their nature. Values, like intrinsic purpose, vary enormously among people, but we tend to associate with persons having similar values. *Efficacy*, or exercising personal control, represents a third source of meaning. Research demonstrates that multiple negative consequences occur when personal control is lacking (Bandura, 1997). Weak self-efficacy is linked to depression, anxiety, weak task persistence, and a variety of health problems. Exercising control over our environment is so motivating that people will automatically increase the level of difficulty in a task once they have mastered it. Bandura refers to this phenomenon as "efficacy redundancy," and its popular expression is "not resting on one's laurels." *Self-worth* represents the fourth quality that is a major component of meaning. People need to maintain a positive view of themselves, and they work hard to ensure that others think well of them also. In fact, the origin of self-esteem may be the social function essential to others' thinking well of us. Without that respect few of us would survive, so we monitor our social respect quotient continuously.

Spirituality for low rollers

Clinically, we probably know the most about helping persons with low self-worth. Most people who enter therapy are in emotional pain and have poor self-worth. Many counseling strategies revolve around helping such persons improve their self-worth. A consensus has emerged, at least in the clinical research field, that self-worth is not a characteristic to work on directly. Rather, self-esteem improvement occurs in concert with genuine accomplishments, and any effect from positive thinking or self-affirmations is quite weak unless these are anchored in accomplishments. Using Baumeister's model for the four qualities of meaning, let us examine what a systematic spiritual recovery program would encompass for pathological gambling motivated by low self-esteem.

Purpose would entail projects that have both extrinsic and intrinsic goals. Overall, *empowerment* is the main theme in recovery for low self-esteem individuals. As Rebecca Propst (1988) aptly describes women's sense of "sin" in therapy as failing to believe in their own power, the same can be said of persons with low self-esteem. Their search for purpose should focus on projects that are intrinsically satisfying to them. Projects that are absorbing and interesting, rather than what they are asked to do, need to increase. Alan Marlatt (1985) described one important part of relapse prevention as balancing a person's "wants/shoulds ratio." By this he means reducing the proportion of duties and obligations in favor of enjoyable activities. Persons in recovery can make a simple two column list headed "wants" and "shoulds," then keep track of these events on a daily basis. Monitoring this list, either by oneself or with a counselor or sponsor, will prevent a pileup of "shoulds" that trigger feelings of owing oneself a relapse.

In terms of *value* a shift from other-directedness to self-direction is the main emphasis. Persons with low self-esteem tend to seek meaning from others' needs. In terms of the great commandment they seek fulfillment in love of neighbor. Balance in recovery means shifting the emphasis on this commandment closer to the "as-thyself" part of the equation. Priorities, goals, and objectives are now evaluated in terms of one's own needs and interests as opposed to pleasing those around them. This new ethic often feels most uncomfortable to such persons and religious persons, in particular, require a good deal of persuasion before they will comply with such directives. I once encouraged a mother of several young children to use the meager private time she had daily to refresh herself in some quiet reading or meditation instead of the household tasks she chose. To support my position I suggested she read a single chapter of Mark's Gospel each day and pay attention to the number of times the gospel describes Jesus "going aside" and resting. When I saw her two weeks later, she opened the session by saying in astonishment, "He hardly did anything!" She further noted how often it seemed that he allowed people, especially women, to do things for him. This discovery led her to pursue more personal time with less guilt.

Developing *efficacy* and personal control entails increasing assertiveness. Spirituality that accentuates meekness and humility is improper for persons with low self-esteem. Their faults go in the opposite direction. Fear makes them like the servant in the gospel parable who takes the master's monetary gift and buries it, thereby angering the master for not at least putting it in a bank to earn interest. Their anxiety about taking risks means they fail to grow personally and simultaneously fail to contribute to the growth of the kingdom. Recovery involves increased assertiveness for such individuals, and counselors are usually adept at developing tasks to develop these skills. Individuals working alone can find any number of excellent self-help manuals on this topic. An easy start is to increase the number of "I like" and "I dislike" statements by dropping five of each daily into one's conversations. They might start with low-key phrases ("I like peanut butter") and work their way up to more personal statements ("I did not like the tone of voice you used in requesting that"). Developing assertiveness requires finding opportunities to voice one's opinions on group decisions, recreation, committee work, disciplining children, and work projects.

Many people developing assertiveness confuse it with aggression. I find it useful to educate clients briefly that assertiveness and aggression are negatively correlated. This means that people who cannot legitimately assert their needs are more likely to use aggressive tactics when their frustration builds. Most unassertive people have two buttons only: an off-switch and an explosion switch. Assertiveness is a mean between the extremes of punishing or being punished. For Christians, Jesus represents an excellent model of assertiveness. In the majority of interpersonal encounters described in the gospel, Jesus states his opinion directly, often boldly challenging authority figures; at the same time his words are not mean-spirited or cruel. Similarly, Jesus admonishes his followers for being afraid, and he instructs them to have great confidence when speaking in his name.

Self-worth enhancement demands that people attend to personal qualities that will increase their positive self-evaluations. This process needs to be differentiated from a mindless "power of positive thinking" approach. That approach often enjoins people to create positive self-worth through reciting lists of affirmations that may have no personal relevance, or are based on hope alone. This is much like the children's story *The little engine that could* in which the train conquers the mountain by continuously repeating, "I think I can, I think I can." Effective self-enhancement occurs when people focus on positive qualities or accomplishments that *already exist*. It is not the case that low self-esteem individuals are devoid of worth; they direct their attention on their failures. Reorienting their myopic gaze is the first task in increasing self-esteem. Here the strategies of cognitive therapy are quite useful and, again, self-help books are in abundance.

Recovering persons should not neglect the social dimensions of self-esteem development. I sometimes give clients the following task: "Go find up to ten friends or close acquaintances. Tell them you're working on increasing your awareness of your positive qualities and could they help you out by naming some?" We review this list together and add it to the person's list of positive qualities to be read when feeling anxious or depressed. Another aspect of social life that recovering persons often feel negative about is their family life or close relationships. Some of this negativity is based on reality. Gamblers' families are often devastated financially and emotionally (Ciarrocchi and Hohman, 1989; Ciarrocchi and Reinert, 1993). It would be phony to pretend that a jalopy is a Rolls-Royce.

However, one can redirect attention. For this purpose I recommend a device called "The Good Book." In this journal the person keeps track on a daily or weekly basis of the positive aspects of family life or close relationships. Unlike an ordinary diary that records a wide range of events, this journal is meant to record only what is positively memorable. I have seen parents whose families were in difficult times, such as separation or divorce, use this device to maintain some belief in themselves as adequate parents. Furthermore, focusing on positive aspects of family life achieves two other goals. First, it can engender an attitude of gratefulness that plays a key role in a well-rounded spirituality. Second, going through a day keeping track of positive events has a subtle but real influence on mood. Finally, such a task may even engender positive self-fulfilling prophecies. That is, if I am looking for positive events to occur, I may even find myself subtly arranging my environment to make them happen.

Spirituality for high rollers

A well respected physician who lost everything due to his addiction, spent one entire year sweeping floors for a hospital's janitorial service. When questioned about his notable change in status, he responded that it was important for his spirituality to focus on one activity, no matter how apparently menial, to regain a sense of rhythm and pacing around work. This was in marked contrast to the chaos of his gambling lifestyle. This vignette suggests how *purpose* for persons with high self-esteem can benefit from the recovery process. Gamblers with this personality style work very hard to achieve *public* acclaim. The persona required for some forms of gambling demands that the person create an exaggerated, positive impression. Henry Lesieur (1984) points out in his sociological description of the gambling life style that gamblers survive on obtaining credit from their bookmakers or borrowing from friends. Who is willing to lend money to a loser? Gamblers, therefore, go to enormous lengths to look good, even when life is falling tragically apart.

The personality style that emerges is one that cherishes appearance over reality, superficiality over depth, looking good versus being good. To counteract this effect, a recovering spirituality needs to highlight deeds that have *private* meaning over and above those that will win public honor. In discussing this with recovering gamblers, I use the example of the medieval sculptors whose magnificent works adorn the tops of European cathedrals. They are out of sight from the masses who come to worship, yet these masters, believing what they did was for God's glory, found that to be sufficient motivation for their artistic expression.

Good works, then, can be selected from a host of quiet endeavors: working with the homeless (*not* running the agency), being Big Brother/ Sister, volunteering behind-the-scenes for nonprofit groups, etc. Working on this aspect of their personality is a lifetime project. Wives of recovering persons report that, many years into recovery, their husbands retain this need to make a public splash. For example, it remains important to obtain the "best" table for their group. Even in a middle-class restaurant they will cajole the host or hostess into doing so.

From the aspect of *values* the contrast with the prerecovery self centers around using one's ego as the criterion for ethical worth. In short, prerecovery involves choosing the self over all other bases for ethical decisions. Recovery involves honoring norms and criteria that are external to the self. In religious tradition it would include activities such as fasting and abstinence, observing dietary laws, keeping kosher, or adhering to traditional yet seemingly out-of-date practices. In areas of conscience, promoting values for high self-esteem persons would include being honest when there is no payoff. For example, filling out one's tax return scrupulously even when there would be no chance of getting caught for a minor infraction.

Many recovering gamblers with this personality style work in sales. All have insisted to me that no salesperson can be completely honest with a prospective customer. Do so, they assure me, and you will promptly be out of business. Because it is impossible to insist on total honesty in such cases, I invite the recovering gambler to try the following experiment. Select one new or current customer more or less at random and *just with this one person* be totally honest about your product. Their task is simply to observe what happens and report back on it. One merchant, who reported that only 10 percent of his sales was from repeat business, was astonished how a valued customer *increased* her purchases, "when I treated her well by saving the best merchandise." Although it may be true that salespersons need to embellish the truth (and customers probably factor this in), problem gamblers project their antisocial gambling attitudes to every aspect of reality. Challenging the core of their ethical decisions is an important aspect of recovery.

Excessive self-esteem creates a burden in the domain of *self-efficacy*. One reason gamblers may lose control, as Baumeister noted above, is that following failure they work hard to preserve their self-image. They risk setting overly ambitious goals (e.g., recouping my losses) and falling victim to their own impossible standards. In many situations persistence pays off, but if the task is inherently impossible or statistically improbable, persistence is counterproductive. Heatherton and Ambady (1993) point out that correcting this tendency entails ego change. First, recovering persons must distance themselves from their performances. They need to learn that luck is not a personal sign of worth or election. Luck is just luck. The same is true of personal efforts. In both Zen and Christian monasticism, monks undertake simple chores during which they reflect on separating out their ego from the task. Whether chopping wood or pulling weeds, repeating the task teaches the monk that the self is separate from one's output.

Second, they must learn to distance themselves from failure experiences. Low self-esteem persons should learn that, following failure, preserving self-esteem does not require *avoiding* risk-taking. People with high self-esteem must learn that preserving self-esteem, following failure, does not require *embracing* risk-taking. To enhance this process, I review with clients three or four of their most impulsive acts ever. Invariably, we are able to connect these acts with some real or imagined threat to their ego immediately prior to the behavior. Following this insight, they monitor their impulsive urges daily, and we discuss them in our sessions. Gradually, they see how automatic is their tendency to lose control following an insult, a challenge, or a threat. Through this self-awareness we then discuss alternative ways to handle this imagined loss of self-esteem.

Tasks that foster this separation between ego and outcome include those that project results only in the future. Tutoring and mentoring are examples of this, as well as participating in large-scale charitable or political projects. Although having a sense of personal control is crucial to survival, much can be learned from participating in worthy endeavors whose outcomes are unknowable.

In recovery, a third approach for balancing self-efficacy relates to time urgency. Commented on by many in the stress reduction field is this well-known characteristic of Type A persons. They foster an exaggerated sense of personal responsibility for controlling outcomes through detailed time management. They cannot waste a minute in unproductive time.

Sam, a 72-year-old merchant had been abstinent from gambling about eighteen months. Now that he was no longer dealing with the daily struggle to control his gambling urges, he desired to look at deeper issues in recovery. For example, he wanted to work on his "character flaws," as he called them. He was deriving considerable benefit from his Gamblers Anonymous meeting in this regard and wanted therapy to support this.

When I asked him which "character flaw" he wanted to work on first, Sam mentioned impatience. He then described a host of time-urgency issues.

For example, in his gambling days he never observed rules about parking in the handicapped zone if it would save him a few minutes. He pointed out how he knew he was making some progress when this very morning, arriving at the therapy office before me, he did not park in the convenient space where I usually parked. Other time-urgency behavior included reading the newspaper when urinating in a public restroom. Currently he found it quite annoying to wait for his instant coffee to warm up in the microwave oven. Several times daily he would make coffee, timing it for precisely 135 seconds, the optimal period. He described literally not knowing what to do while he waited, having the feeling of wanting to jump out of his skin.

I told Sam the custom of my colleague in the Pastoral Counseling department, Dr. Joanne Greer, who, hearing the faculty complain at a meeting about how long it took for the computers to boot up, pointed out that she used the time to pray. I asked him if he might want to pray while his coffee heated up. He thought this was a good idea but, embarrassed, acknowledged he did not know any prayers by heart. Nor was he comfortable attempting a spontaneous prayer. I advised him to consult his rabbi to obtain a two-minute prayer suitable during microwaving. When we met again, Sam revealed he could not call his rabbi, in Sam's words, for fear of shocking the rabbi. He realized, however, that he had memorized the Lord's Prayer from his GA meetings. Thereby began a sustained practice of ritualistic prayer several times daily from one who formerly prayed only on high holy days.

Finally, focusing on *self-worth* for high self-esteem persons does not mean that they have to suffer humiliation or degradation in recovery. My belief is that life willingly provides us these experiences without our seeking them out. What needs to change is the gambler's *defensiveness* about his or her self-worth. Low self-esteem individuals see failure as confirming their negative views; high self-esteem individuals tend to blame external forces, including other people. Recovery for high self-esteem persons obliges them to accept personal responsibility for their actions. Acceptance is not oriented toward enhancing guilt but toward restoring a measure of objectivity in their world view. Continuing to believe that they are responsible only for their good outcomes and blaming everyone and everything else for the bad fosters arrogance and irresponsibility. Both traits impede recovery and threaten relapse by reinforcing overconfidence and risk taking.

Conclusion

This chapter summarized the major differences between high and low self-esteem issues in a spiritually based recovery program for problem gambling. I have found this model useful in helping to individualize the spiritual focus for differing personality patterns. Furthermore, in numerous workshops, addiction counselors have responded enthusiastically to the typology presented here with its implications for therapeutic interventions.

In almost every aspect of understanding pathological gambling we need empirical research to determine the usefulness of this or any other model in sustaining recovery from gambling. Clinicians and persons in recovery, however, cannot afford the luxury of waiting until research guides our path. This model draws its rationale from promising work on self-esteem that relates well, in my opinion, to the clinical dimensions of this most devastating condition. I offer this model, therefore, with the tentative hope that it has captured an important dynamic for recovering persons. Finally, it has the potential to integrate a neglected but powerful resource in recovery, namely, the individual's own spirituality.

References

American Bible Society (1992). *Good News Bible: With Deuterocanonicals and Apocrypha*. New York.

Bandura, A. (1997). *Self-efficacy: The exercise of control*. New York: W. H. Freeman.

Baumeister, R. F. (1991a). *Escaping the self: Alcoholism, spirituality, masochism, and other flights from the burden of selfhood*. New York: Basic Books.

Baumeister, R. F. (1991b). *Meanings of life*. New York: Guilford Press.

Baumeister, R. F. (Ed.), (1993). *Self-esteem: The puzzle of low self-regard*. New York: Plenum.

Baumeister, R. F., Heatherton, T. F., & Tice, D. M. (Eds.), (1994). *Losing control: How and why people fail at self-regulation*. San Diego: Academic Press.

Baumeister, R. F. (1997). Esteem threat, self-regulatory breakdown, and emotional distress as factors in self-defeating behavior. *Review of General Psychology, 1*, 145–174.

Baumeister, R. F., Smart, L., & Boden, J. M. (1996). Relation of threatened egotism to violence and aggression: The dark side of high self-esteem. *Psychological Review, 103*, 5–53.

Benziger Publishing Company, (1988). *The new American Bible*. Mission Hills, California.

Ciarrocchi, J. W. (1992). Pathological gambling and pastoral counseling. In R. J. Wicks, R. D. Parsons, & D. E. Capps (Eds.), *Clinical handbook of pastoral counseling*, Vol. 2, (pp. 593-617). New York: Paulist Press.

Ciarrocchi, J. W. (1993). *A minister's handbook of mental disorders*. New York: Paulist Press.

Ciarrocchi, J.W., & Hohman, A. (1989). The family environment of married male pathological gamblers, alcoholics, and dually addicted gamblers. *Journal of Gambling Behavior, 5*, pp. 283–291.

Ciarrocchi, J. W., & Reinert, D. (1993). Family environment and length of recovery for married members of Gamblers Anonymous. *Journal of Gambling Studies, 9,* pp. 341–352.

Custer, R., & Milt, H. (1985). *When luck runs out: Help for compulsive gamblers and their families*. New York: Facts on File Publications.

Dulles, A. (1994). *The assurances of things hoped for: A theology of Christian faith*. New York: Oxford University Press.

Heatherton, T. F., & Ambady, N. (1993). Self-esteem, self-prediction, and living up to commitments. In R.F. Baumeister (Ed.), *Self-esteem: The puzzle of low self-regard* (pp.131–146). New York: Plenum.

Karris, R. J. (1990). The Gospel according to Luke. In R. E. Brown, J. A. Fitzmyer, & R. E. Murphy (Eds.), *The new Jerome biblical commentary*. Englewood Cliffs, N. J. : Prentice-Hall.

Lesieur, H.R. (1984). *The chase: Career of the compulsive gambler*. Cambridge, Mass.: Schenkman.

Marlatt, A. (1985). Situational determinants of relapse and skill training intervention. In A. Marlatt & J. Gordon (Eds.), *Relapse prevention*. New York: Guilford Press.

Nolen-Hoeksema, S. (1987). Sex differences in unipolar depression: Evidence and theory. *Psychological Bulletin, 101,* 259–282.

Oglesby, W. (1980). *Biblical themes for pastoral care*. Nashville: Abingdon Press.

Politzer, R. M., Morrow, J. S., & Leavey, S. D. (1985). Report on the cost-benefit/effectiveness of treatment at the Johns Hopkins Center for Pathological Gambling. *Journal of Gambling Behavior, 1,* 131–142.

Propst, L. R. (1988). *Psychotherapy in a religious framework: Spirituality in the emotional healing process.* New York: Human Sciences Press.

Volberg, R. A., & Steadman, H. J. (1989). Prevalence estimates of pathological gambling in New Jersey and Maryland. *American Journal of Psychiatry, 146,* 1618–1619.

Wolski Conn, J. (1993). Spirituality and personal maturity. In R. J. Wicks, R. D. Parsons, & D. Capps (Eds.), *Clinical handbook of pastoral counseling*, vol. 1, Expanded Edition. New York: Paulist Press.

Part Four

Pastors and Spiritual Directors

CHAPTER 10

By Love Possessed

Lyn G. Brakeman

A Biblical Theology of Addiction

> And no one could restrain him any more, even with a chain; for he had often been restrained with shackles and chains, but the chains he wrenched apart and the shackles he broke in pieces; and no one had the strength to subdue him. (Mark 5:3b–4, NRSV)

Whenever I think of addiction; whenever I am in the company of someone caught in the bondage of addiction; whenever I experience my own addictions, I recall the biblical story of the Gerasene demoniac. Shivers run up and down my spine. Written in the New Testament book of Mark, this is a hair-raising story of the torment of possession and the healing of exorcism, a radical and catastrophic transformation of body, mind, and spirit.

This poor man in the story is described as a person "controlled by an unclean spirit"; one who "made his home in the tombs"; one who "howls and keeps bruising himself"; one who cannot be "restrained" or "subdued." This is a painful picture. This is clearly a person in chronic torment. This is a person out of control. This man is starring in the drama of addiction.

Does this seem like too harsh a description? Is this language too severe? Too ancient? The Bible is an ancient document. They had different understandings then, different "stuff." What did they know about addiction? "Demoniac," the titular word used to identify this story, is not a word of much relevance these days. Demons, in Old Testament parlance, were "that which were not God" (Deut. 32:17). Demons in this story are against

God's will and made this man "unclean," a social outcast and untouchable, impure. But that was way back then.

We don't talk about demons and possession nowadays. We're more comfortable talking about human sociopathy, or cult madness, or insanity. Surely, this is a description of severe mental illness at the very least, psychosis, no doubt. This cannot be the portrait of a plain old "alkie" or a "druggie." This is a description of someone *possessed*, that is, someone possessed, apparently by an evil, external force not within the person's control. This must be an exaggeration.

Perhaps the Bible knows more about the addictive experience than we think. The portrait of the Gerasene demoniac is, I think, quite an accurate picture of the soul of an addict in the throes of possession. The spirituality of addiction *is* the spirituality of possession. An addict's total being is possessed, owned, not by the divine spirit of peace and wholeness, but rather by a spirit of violence and violation. Our modern phrase "under the influence" correlates well with the ancient term "possession." A person possessed or addicted has no sense of being, no identity. It is the spirituality of a lost soul.

In the demoniac we see reflected the pattern of chaos that characterizes the addictive experience. Spiritually, addicts are possessed subtly and incrementally over time until they are dominated, mind, body, and spirit, by something outside their control: their addiction not their substance, which after all is only perched innocently on a shelf or in a bottle. When responsible use of substances becomes addiction and is categorized as disease, the issue is control not substance. What makes an addict an addict, is the fact that he or she has no consistent control over the use of substances or over engaging in destructive compulsions. The definition of an addict that makes the most sense to me is that s/he is consistently unable to make changes in her or his behavior despite increasingly negative consequences in all or some areas of life: medical, legal, relational, economic, vocational, emotional, and spiritual.

Spiritually, this is being *in* sin: being deeply disconnected from God, self, and others in a profoundly emotional way. One's heart may be beating, but it is not taking in, or giving out, much love, either to oneself or to others. This kind of sin is not a moral category, characterized by unethical behaviors, although plenty of these result from the addiction. This is a "not-God" state. By "not-God" I mean the state of being out of touch with the holy, that mysterious font of grace that translates experientially into the feeling of being fully known and fully loved at the same time, both inside and outside oneself. This grace is what addicts often glimpse, perhaps for the first time, when they take a drink. It is an artificial high. It is the powerful feeling of having a self, but it is not a self rooted in their flesh. "I'm okay. I'm beloved. I belong"—these are the words that are felt. It's enough to make them drunk with joy. It is a like-God experience, but actually is a not-God experience. It's addictive: irresistible and total.

Addicts try with all their might to control the substance, thinking it to be the problem, the culprit. They have excellent willpower and at times actually deceive themselves into thinking they are in control, when in fact the pattern of their relationship with their substance is controlling them completely. By "pattern of relationship" I mean the ongoing attraction/repulsion, love/hate affair that repeats and repeats itself, no matter what the specific content or details. The pattern unfolds with maddening perpetuity regardless of the details: wine or martinis, weekends or all week, before dinner or late at night, functional or nonfunctional. The whole pattern is entirely present in every small episode of intoxication, and even in the pre-intoxicant mental deliberations, as the battle for control rages on.

Addicts get addicted to the narcotic properties of chemicals. They also get addicted to an experience: the experience of being free, free of pain, inhibition, anxiety, rage, isolation, social phobia, shame, self-hatred, relational fear, and many other "demons." In a word, addicts, unaware, choose sin to get relief from sin. They exchange one bondage for another. Neither substance nor the other "demons" are of God. They are not-God, just like the scriptural "demons."

And this is an irresistible experience. If you've never really felt whole and beloved, and you have a parched soul, how could you resist the waters? The initial experience of freedom is so spiritually intoxicating that it cannot be refused. It also appears as if it cannot be had by any other means than alcohol and other drugs. Other drugs include many things: Food, money or the high of gambling, and even people, for example, the intoxication of infatuation and dependency often mistaken for love. When you believe someone loves you, and you've never believed it before, you lap it up like a lost-and-found "sheep," crazed with starvation. Then, out of fear of returning to the former state of starvation, you cling tenaciously to the new "food," the new relationship, even tolerating, or not noticing, that it may not be as nourishing as you thought. And the more you take in, the more you need, thus escalating the addictive/possessive pattern. There is nothing wrong with the need for the emotional "food" of relationship, but for the deprived, skills must be learned about proper nutrition.

Addicts often present a semblance of order and functionality in their lives. But inside it's hell. Ask anyone who has been there. The biblical story of the demoniac need not be taken literally for it to be an accurate soul-picture of addiction. Addicts beat themselves against the "rocks" of their inability to control what they cannot resist. They deny, but deep down recognize, that they live among the "tombs," as spiritually, mentally, and emotionally dead people playing at life. They robotically perform the minimal habits of life with little consciousness, awareness, or grace, needing more and more of what their substance provides in order to abate the pain their substances induce.

Whether we see the story of the exorcism of the demoniac as an actual historical event;[1] whether we believe in exorcism and possession, or whether we see the story as a descriptive experiential metaphor for the spirituality of possession, the meaning is still the same: People possessed have no control; they cannot help themselves, and they need intervention by whatever means from a power greater than themselves.

Twelve Step wisdom

The wisdom of the Twelve Step recovery programs is congruent with the theological wisdom of the biblical story. The Twelve Steps begin with a confession of powerlessness and the need for help from a "Higher Power," whose will is to restore the addict to health and sanity, a power into whose care and compassion the addict agrees to surrender her-or himself in hopes of a better way to meet the appropriate need for love and acceptance.

Looking more closely at the story now, we notice that it begins chapter 5 of Mark's Gospel and immediately follows Jesus' teaching the disciples to understand the reign of God as being like a mustard seed. After this, Jesus stills the stormy seas and saves their boat from disaster, to say nothing of their endangered lives. We get the idea that that which is of-God has certain characteristics: a community of welcome and belovedness that doesn't take much to start (a simple mustard seed) and yet provides shelter for, and is inhabited by, all sorts and conditions of "birds"; a community in which belovedness begets belovedness; a community that grows by divine grace and not by human effort or awareness, in the same way things grow in the earth; a community whose God uses power and will to save people who cannot save themselves; and, a community whose ruling spirit is one of faith and serenity that prevail over chaos.

Does this not sound like the spirituality of the Twelve Step meetings? These meetings are communities of belonging and belovedness. They are structured to minimize judgment and encourage listening without interruption. Their ministry serves to de-pattern and re-pattern addictive styles of thinking, feeling, and behaving. They are free and open to all who desire to break the pattern. (Further elaboration of these themes can be found in Jampolsky, chapter 3 and Larsen, chapter 8, as well as Albers, chapter 7.) They are centered around the Twelve Steps, which in turn are centered on the healing power of God, as God is understood by each participant. The principle of anonymity provides shelter from shame until it grows into the grace of acceptance. And, despite the more popular slogan—"God helps those who help themselves"—recovering addicts experience the truth that God also helps those who cannot help themselves, just as Jesus, in God's name, is portrayed as stilling the wildness of the sea. The Twelve Step programs are intended to be mediators of grace and serenity, stilling the internal

[1] The story in Mark's Gospel bears the marks of reminiscences of an eyewitness, according to C. S. Mann in *Mark, Anchor Bible.* (New York: Doubleday, 1986, p. 277). According to this author, bits and pieces of oral tradition are thrown together in disarray, creating a lively if spotty dramatic account. The author contends that v. 8 ("because Jesus had been saying to it: 'Come out of that fellow, you filthy spirit!'") is inserted in an attempt to "relieve the confusion of detail."

storms of addiction and guiding members in a process of liberation from the bondage of spiritual sin.

The placing of the mustard seed and storm stilling stories just before the violence of the demoniac story provides a context of hope that foreshadows the peaceful reign of God. Just as the followers of Jesus are beginning to appreciate God's healing powers and are in awe, they are suddenly thrown into the turmoil of the scenario at Gerasa. Here is another "storm." The man possessed "accosts" the group, coming out from the tombs in ambush. They must have felt terrified again and maybe a little offended at this disturbance of their peace.

Sound familiar? Addicts, even if they are passive and passed out, disturb the peace of everyone around them, of everyone who might desire to connect with them and have a sane relationship. They, like the demoniac, cannot be bound. There is nothing predictable about the force of an addict in full sway! As with the man possessed by evil spirits and gone mad, so it is with an active addict: The utilization of force, or attempts to control, prove futile. Ask anyone who has lived with an active addict and tried by an array of very clever means to control the addiction. Control measures may even exacerbate the situation by providing openings for self-justifying defensiveness. At the level of social control, even today, the legalistic "fetters and chains" approach of crackdown and punitive measures does little to prevent or arrest addictive disease and its consequences, and even less to create health and well-being.

The man is pictured as kneeling before Jesus and "shouting at the top of his voice,... 'What do you want with me, Jesus, you son of the Most High God? For God's sake, don't torment me!'" This is a standard question in the demonology of the time. Demons don't like the smell of exorcists and often are heard to shriek out in fear. Understood in an addictive context, this question is one that I have heard addicts, both newly recovering and active, ask in one way or another. They say things like: "What is this Higher Power thing?" "I don't like all this God talk in AA." "What has God got to do with me and my problems?" There is often in these questions a combination of attraction and avoidance, a mixture of reverence, skepticism, and anger masking fear.

Then comes the little explanation (v. 8) about Jesus' having already ordered the rotten spirits to come out of the man. The explanation doesn't help much really. When would Jesus have had a chance to confront the demons, and why would this invoke an apparent act of worship? Who is shouting, the man or the demons? What does kneeling mean: worship, humble obedience, or recognition of the presence of divinity? Or, is it just plain fear of being punished for an illness he cannot control, as would certainly be characteristic of an addict? Who calls Jesus "son of the Most High God," an identity about which the followers are clueless? Is the calling out a demonic response to Jesus' command? Or, could it be the human initiative at work here: the man, in spite of himself, recognizing his powerlessness and reaching out?

The phrase, "For God's sake don't torment me!" is extraordinary. It is stock demonology, and at the same time it is intriguing because of the unclear referent. Who is really talking here? Is it the man talking to his demons, as an addict would to his or her substances? Does the tormented one realize that it is for God's sake, because of God's power, that his wellness looms large in the figure of Jesus? Is it the evil spirits themselves talking to Jesus and realizing that he could be dangerous to their health? Is this not the true paradox of addiction—panic at being without the familiar "demons" of the disease, at losing the only known solace, and yet at the same time knowledge at a deep spiritual level: It is only for God's sake that freedom can come?

Now Jesus begins to question the man. A dialogue occurs. The confusion of pronouns becomes more intense and, to me, fascinating at this point. It is no less confusing in Greek than it is in English. And, it continues throughout the dialogue with Jesus addressing "he," the man, and "they," the demons, answering. Jesus begins by asking the man his name, and "they" answer, saying "they" are many and their name is "Legion."

The switching from the singular to the plural accomplishes much. It vividly underscores the plurality of impulses and compulsions by which the one single person is tortured. This is accurately descriptive of an addict's inner state. He or she is double-bound and triple-bound by numerous conflicting thoughts and feelings, scarcely able to move at all. At the same time, s/he is chaotically whipped about and pulled rapidly in many different emotional directions. It is like being both immobilized and at the same time in a constant state of flux and directionless motion. To move and move, and not to move anywhere, is the painful condition of an addict in the throes of possession.

The pronoun confusion vividly highlights the man's perilous condition, not grasped by ordinary diagnostic means. It also creates the impression that the man's personality is all but obscured by the demons whose voices speak for the man. His diseased condition takes over his entire identity as well as his physical, emotional, mental, and spiritual health. The close identification of disease with personal identity is something recovering addicts perpetuate. The intent of this is to promote humility and awareness and to serve as a reminder that they can fall into disease again the moment they forget the lethal possessive powers of addiction, the moment they forget that it is not their substance that empowers them but their God. However, the identification also has the potential to inhibit the spiritual progression toward wholeness—the movement from "I am my illness" to "I am a person with an illness."

As Jesus talks with the man and the demons, it seems as if the power of the demons, the "Legion" as they name themselves, transcends the man altogether. At the climax of the scene, the spirits beg Jesus for mercy, asking him to allow them to exist in a herd of swine. An impression is created that there are two nonhuman powers in confrontation, two spirits: good and evil. It feels to me as if the man's humanity is transcended, and Jesus' humanity is transcended as well. I envision the healing scene as two spiritual powers battling it out for territorial rights, the end result of which will determine the man's return to sanity and Jesus' connection to God.

Jesus asks for the man's name. He gets the name of the evil spirits and not the man's. It is a twist. In biblical thought, to name someone, or to know a person's name, would give someone access to and a certain authority over that person. This, of course, could work for good or ill. But it is significant that Jesus now has the demons' name, "Legion." He does not have the man's name. This is all that appears necessary: that Jesus have authority over the illness and not the man. By implication, there is nothing intrinsically wrong with the man; nothing from his nature needs to be exorcised. His human freedom and character remain intact. This alone is good news for a demoniac or an addict, ashamed and fearing total moral and spiritual condemnation. Jesus apparently neither knows nor needs the man's name for purposes of healing.

But doesn't the man's name matter? Perhaps it doesn't. I see a parallel here with the Twelve Step programs' principle of anonymity. Anonymity, of course, protects recovering people from the social stigma of their addiction. It provides also a way to focus on principles and not personalities. The Twelfth Tradition of Alcoholics Anonymous reads: "Anonymity is the spiritual foundation of all our Traditions, ever reminding us to place principles before personalities." This is an excellent counter to our culture's compulsive individualism. The common good and the common goal of recovery are at the center. It is not one's name, identity, social status, or reputation that matter in the recovery ethos. It is the disease, the addiction, and a person's desire to be free, sober, and well, "clothed and in his right mind," as the biblical story describes the former demoniac. This is also, it would seem, what matters to Jesus.

Free of "drunkenness" by whatever means, this question of possession is now a choice as well as an accountability. The second of the Twelve Traditions reads: "For our group purpose there is but one ultimate authority—a loving God as *He* may express *Himself* in our group conscience. Our leaders are but trusted servants; they do not govern" (italics mine). *By whom possessed* is a question and a daily choice.

About Jesus' giving the evil spirits permission to enter the herd of swine and the swine's rushing frantically to their collective death over a nearby cliff, not much can be said. Personally, I think it adds color and drama and also some humor to the story. The story originated with the oral transmission process. What would make a good story better but a few egregious and colorful details. Many have expressed concern about Jesus' lack of compassion for animals or their owners and their livelihood. Some have even suggested that Jesus has compassion even for demons. A stretch. Maybe, as some commentators suggest, the herd of swine simply engaged in typical animal panic behavior, reacting themselves to the traumatic exorcism. In relation to addiction, one thing this suggests to me, metaphorically, is that the effects of addiction are far reaching, and "demons" can continue to possess family, friends, and larger spheres of influence, sometimes long after an addict has become "clothed and in his right mind" (RSV). This is why recovery of whole families is encouraged and sought.

Which brings us to the startling conclusion of the story: The people who witnessed and heard about the healing of the demoniac are scared! They are so alarmed that they actually "beg" Jesus to leave their region. Isn't this a painful irony? Imagine their fearing sanity more than insanity! Imagine their fearing drunkenness less than sobriety! How could this be?

This is, sadly, a familiar story. Besides the struggle to keep peace with the lingering internal mental "ghosts" of the legion of addictive temptations, and the hard work of staying abstinent, addicts also often have to cope with the fear of others. These are family, friends, colleagues who don't know how to relate to their sober friend. The "demon" they knew, in a word, is safer than the person they do not know. They may also miss the positive social graces the addict exhibits before moving into inebriation. The sober person is now a threat, a force to be encountered, a relationship to be had. He or she is now one who will want some accountability from those around her or him, some professional, personal, relational accountability. A man "in his right mind" now exposes the self-righteousness and the controlling behaviors of those who have built their lives around "handling" the addict and being victim to his or her craziness. They have not taken care of their own spiritual development. In short, sobriety makes others aware of their own addictive behaviors and codependencies.

"Sitting at the feet of Jesus" presents a further threat. The demoniac, the addict, now has a new alliance. Those who were close to him are no longer his "higher power," no longer his judge and jury, no longer his enablers and caretakers. And whatever the substance was that kept him drunk and "living in the tombs," it is no longer his lord and master. No, this man now has a new "lord" and is under a new influence. This "higher power," represented in Jesus, is a healer and a liberator; it wants the man to be whole and well. And, a surprise to some perhaps, this power desires this man to take full responsibility for his own well-being from now on, giving full allegiance and love to his own life and to his relationship with the God who has freed him.

The denouement of the little story is far from anticlimactic. One would think the healing miracle at the story's climax would be the most important focus, and for most of us it probably is. For the onlookers in the story it is so overwhelming that they refuse to appreciate the momentous change that has occurred. They cast Jesus out, and we can imagine that they are about to do the same to the man now sober and in his right mind. How tragic! How allergic we are to change!

The final movement in the story is Jesus' leaving town. He is getting into his boat and is about to sail away. As in the beginning of the story, he is again accosted by the (now) ex-demoniac, who begs Jesus not to leave him alone but rather to take him along with him. Quite a switch! A glass-half-empty perspective will see this as the man's fear of the hostile and scared crowd. A glass-half-full perspective will see this as the man's new-found love relationship. At last he has a relationship that is safe, nourishing, and attentive, one in which he feels completely known and loved, healed, and forgiven. This is a brand new and intoxicating reality for this demoniac/addict.

But Jesus says, "No!" We at first feel startled. This seems almost mean and rejecting. However, in Jesus' final words is the greatest theological and spiritual wisdom of the story. He answers the man's plea: "Go home to your people and tell them what your patron has done for you—how he has shown mercy to you" (5:19). In other translations, "Lord" is used instead of patron. The translation I am using, however, is significant in this regard (Funk and Hoover). In Jesus' time, the social structures were based on patronage and brokerage. Every privilege and resource had to be earned and mediated by a patron or lord to a lesser subject. Someone higher on the socioeconomic scale controlled access to all the basic resources for living. Everyone except the very upper classes had a "higher power!"

Jesus here is referring to his God, the only legitimate higher power who, through his ministry, restored the man to sanity and health. There is only one higher power. Jesus identifies the spiritual power of divine healing that not only restores the diseased person to full health but also restores that person to the social mainstream. Healing comes from divine grace and not from any human source. This is a radical message both then and now. Jesus offers an unbrokered, unmediated source of spiritual power to which all are eligible, a "kingdom" in which everyone is welcome and all can belong without fear of judgment. The reign of God ushers in the beloved community.

The reason Jesus tells the healed man he cannot come with him is not articulated. It is an unusual thing, in fact, for Jesus to say. Some suggest that Jesus sends the man off to be a gospeler in the Gerasene territory because it will be more hospitable, unlike Galilee. This is a possibility that seems pale to me. I think Jesus sends the man out to witness because it is crucial for them and us to understand the necessity of the divine role in cases of possession and addiction. As is the wont of biblical narrative, there is no explanation or elaboration of this apparent rejection of the man's heartfelt request and obvious need: He "begged" Jesus to be with him. He saw in Jesus the source of his life and health. The Bible is maddeningly skeletal in its presentation of events. The gift of this is that it leaves much room for our own spiritual experience and feelings to flesh out the story and bring it to life in ourselves.

An addict, unwilling or unable to cooperate with divine grace, might read this rejection as abandonment and use it as a cause to resume addictive behavior, to "drink" again. The demoniac could reinvite possession, allowing self-pity to return him to the tombs to recreate his former isolation, not believing himself worthy of wholeness.

A close reading with spiritual understanding reveals that in Jesus's rejection there is a vocation. He gives the healed man a mission, a calling, a purpose in his new life. He tells him to go home and tell people what God has done for him. Jesus does not point the man to himself, but rather to God, Jesus' own Higher Power who works through him. He gives the man an awesome task, not easy at all. He asks him to go back home where he has been known for erratic and socially unacceptable behavior and where people would still be in the habit of fearing, shunning, or distrusting him; and where he will probably have to make a few amends for having hurt people. He will have to prove to them his wholeness, and he will have to take no credit for it himself. How humbling!

This is the true test of any spiritual awakening and healing: that it bear fruit in devotion and witness to God, gratitude in life, and humble service to others. The emotional high of the spiritual renewal must come down from the mountain and be channeled into the humdrum routine of daily life, becoming a source of renewal to others. Jesus' injunction is designed, in part, to prevent the temptation of a prideful ego to boast of its newfound spirituality and healing. The commission also helps one resist the temptation to become attached to the spiritual high (metaphorically, to become dependent on Jesus), becoming "drunk" on it, or addicted to it, so that it is never free to mature and be shared. God is all too often betrayed by human pride that takes all the credit for new life, and by human fear that refuses to take any responsibility for new life.

The end of the story parallels the Twelfth Step: "Having had a spiritual awakening as a result of these steps, we tried to carry this message to others, and to practice these principles in all our affairs." This is the mission and the task. It is what Jesus is telling the man he must do to stay well. He must tell people what God has done for him. *For him!* Yes, this is a gift for him, the one they excoriated and labeled as unfit for life in the community. It is a gift for this one, and it is a gift for the whole community. It is a gift that must be passed on to grow. A gift unshared is a gift without worth, a gift without life-giving capacity.

The central grace in this story, I believe, is the relationship of Jesus with the demons. I am looking through a Christian lens, seeing in Jesus a revelation of the human face of God. Christians believe that Jesus is fully divine and fully human, having both natures, neither one compromising the other. It seems to me that the power of healing in Jesus' divine nature cooperates with the human nature of Jesus to enter into a relationship with the demons for the sake of the man's wellness. It is this cooperative effort within the one person of Jesus that saves the man and restores him to sanity. The man's true nature, created in the image of God, is temporarily overpowered by demons/disease. Demons may be understood as anything that is an "enemy of our human nature," anything that works against God's desire for human wholeness and goodness. God in Jesus acts to assert another greater power. Step 2 of the Twelve Steps of recovery says: "Came to believe that a power greater than ourselves could restore us to sanity." Both addict and demoniac come to believe, both in God and in their own sanity.

For God to establish a relationship with demons for our salvation is remarkable. It is trivializing the love of God to say that God has all the power anyway, so why does God have to worry about demons. Demons are as free as humans, and only great love and great faith can embrace and subdue them. What is portrayed in Jesus is not only a higher power for healing; but, even more importantly, a serene confidence with which he trusts the cooperating grace and confronts the demons, knowing them well and respecting their power, but calmly declaring that it is God who is in charge. It is God who will reign here in this man's soul, and it is God whose great love will henceforth possess this man, and not demons of any kind.

Jesus represents divine "tough love" in action. The kind of power represented here is the power of love in relationship. It is not the power of control or conquering, but the power of a relationship of knowing and loving. Much more than powerful, God is mediated as loving: as loving the man enough to risk an encounter with Legion; as loving the man enough to expose the human Jesus of Nazareth to possible harm; as loving the man enough not to be afraid of his illness; as loving the man enough to see his true character through his madness; as loving the man enough to desire him to be free of torment; as loving the man enough to trust him with a ministry of reconciliation and humble witness to the higher power of Love.

This is the understanding of God—a theology—portrayed in this story. The Twelve Step process requires recovering addicts to do theology, that is, to come to their own understanding of God. They have then to wrestle with their images of God, perhaps work mentally and emotionally to transform unfriendly images they may have learned. They are then asked to turn their will and life over to the care of the God of their understanding.

This possession story helps the discernment of a new understanding of God. Here is a God who embraces all our life experience, even the most ugly and ferocious. Here is a God who, unlike us, does not shrink from, or punish, that which is powerful, violent, out of control, and desperate. Here is a God whose arms enfold the excommunicated. Here is a God who recommunicates those who are relegated to the tombs, those who have been pushed further and further out of the community. Here is a God who actually chooses the most loathed and feared member of the community to be a messenger of God, an angel to tell and to live the truth about the way of God. And how much courage it will take for this chosen one to return to those who had banished him and assert a new and radical theological and spiritual truth. Recovery, being and staying well, is an arduous lifework with much spiritual reward. It is also a risky business. Many will be threatened by envy, disbelief, or cynicism. Many will be closed or hostile to the message of spiritual recovery.

Practical Application

> "Go home to your people and tell them what the Lord has done for you—how he has shown mercy to you." And he went away and started spreading the news...about what Jesus had done for him, and everybody would marvel. (Mark 5:19–20)

Go home to your community and tell everyone what has happened and how your God has acted in your life!

Do addicts/demoniacs and their loved ones return to your community, to your religious community? Do they proclaim? Do people listen? Marvel? Do you who sit in the pews even know who they are and what their God has done for them? Do they know who you are and what your faith story is? Is there a life-giving relationship, one of knowing and loving, formed between people in recovery from addictions and people who worship in churches or other sanctified spaces?

These are questions a faith community would do well to ponder and pray about. It is said that people *marvel*. But how can people marvel if they do not know the witness? In addition, marveling may not always be a friendly activity, even if it does occur. Being liberated from a state of disease is indeed a marvel, but addiction is not a friendly disease. Most people have mixed feelings about addiction. Some don't even think it a disease. It does not attract the same unbridled joy at its healing as do other diseases.

In addition, addiction has demoniacal behaviors. It scares everyone! That fear does not subside easily at a healing, neither for addicts nor for their neighbors. Liberation astonishes and repels. People fear what they cannot control and understand. They fear the power of witness to a great and transforming love. They fear what they themselves have not caused or initiated. They fear the loss of their "crutches," that is, strategies, often unconscious, by which they disconnect from the fear itself, creating disconnection as well from other people. People fear grace. People fear God.

Addiction, besides being fearful, is a shame-bound disease. It is anonymous. It hides. I believe the recovery community and the religious community collude in this secrecy. Anonymity is designed to keep ashamed people safe until they are ready to come out into the light to claim their own names and their own wholeness. Anonymity is also designed to prevent rampant individualism and personal ego from occupying positions of dominance, overshadowing the spiritual principles of Twelve Step recovery. Some recovery stories can take on the character of arrogance thinly cloaked in humility! There is, however, a hairline tightrope between anonymity and secrecy. Secrecy feeds shame, and shame separates.

It is the vocation of Christians, both as individuals and communities, to be reconciling agents in the world, following the example of Jesus. We are not called to keep the gospel of love a secret. We are called to let it shine. Jesus, in the face of the man possessed, was neither afraid nor ashamed, and even the demons did not get to keep their powers secret. It is my belief that spiritual healing happens, for addicts or anyone else, through a new kind of possession, stronger than the former.

In his introduction to the classic work on contemplative spirituality, *The cloud of unknowing*, William Johnston (1973) writes of such possession:

> As the contemplative enters more deeply into the cloud, love comes to guide him, teaching him to choose God, who cannot be thought or understood or found by any rational activity. As it grows stronger, it comes to take possession of him in such a way that it dominates every action. It *orders* him to choose God…the blind stirring of love…impels him to do God's will…He seems to be in the grip of something more powerful than himself that he must obey at the risk of losing interior peace when it smites upon his heart…No longer fidelity to law but submission to the guidance of love. (pp. 22–23)

The author of *The cloud* writes to individual contemplatives. Is such a spiritual goal and state possible for a community? Wise people from time to time admit that we are all in recovery from something. And God knows we all have our demons, some louder than others, to be sure. Therefore we all need to be re-possessed by love. Re-possessing by love is God's work. How can we partner with the Spirit to do God's work? More particularly, how can Christian communities partner with recovering communities in the ministry of re-possessing love that has already begun in the tombs?

In the demoniac story, Jesus sends the now sane and sober man back into the community, not only for proclamation but also for relationships. There is no way that the divine goal of spiritual recovery can be accomplished without the incarnation in Jesus and the incarnation in the Christian community. We, like Jesus, must be the human face of God, acting boldly and with courage and commitment to appropriate the gift of love for ourselves and to offer it to others. This can only happen within the context of relationships, connections.

Addicts seek to maintain their experience of grace through relationships within the context of their Twelve Step communities. There they find a community of love to listen, encourage, and comfort. There they talk about grace and the wonders of healing and new life. There they talk about the experience of possession, its horrors and its wonders. There they tell a great paradox: I am possessed and I am free! There they find acceptance and nonjudging love by which they are repossessed. The power of a community constituted by love has, by itself and of its nature, the capacity to facilitate ongoing healing. Is not the Christian community, by its own definition, a community so constituted? What's wrong with this picture?

The Christian community is to image what Jesus called the "kingdom." Martin Luther King called it "the beloved community," a more accurate verbal image of what Jesus told and lived. The beloved community is not a place we have to get to by using a map or a set of directions. It is not a hierarchy with a ruler on a throne and some loyal subjects. It's not even simply a subjective experience of one's own belovedness, reigning in the individual heart. It is more like a way of relating as a group, so that everything we say and do contributes to our common belovedness. When we live into our common belovedness and that of all creation, we begin, like the contemplative, not just to see God in and through all creatures, but to see all creatures in and through God. That's quite a lens! We will fall short always, but we can return to the simple, though not easy, recipe: Belovedness begets belovedness begets belovedness.

Returning demoniacs/addicts find their beloved communities in the Twelve Step groups, not in the church. Someone once said to me that she found nothing in the church but a divine power trip and judgment. "I want a healthy Bible study," she said. She meant one that communicates a loving image of God, a God who does not demand a pound of flesh in return for the grace of salvation. She didn't want to have to live timidly, wondering when the next bomb would go off, as she had growing up with her alcoholic father. She did not want to lose herself to the stress and anxiety of wondering when, where, how, and to whom God meted out *his* favors. She did not want to become a cosmic codependent!

What is the church doing to help addicts return to community?

I remember once attempting to organize an education program for religious communities in my area. My goal was to educate these communities about addictions and to teach them how to be healing agents in the process of recovery. Part of my process was to survey local communities to see what kind of awareness was already present and what programs, if any, local churches and synagogues were offering. Most of my phone calls left me both depressed and irritated. My contacts, more often than not, responded to my inquiries with assurances like, "Oh yes, we're already taking care of that problem. We have a ministry to them; we let their groups meet in our basement."

Their groups? There was a not-so-subtle separation being made between *their* groups and *our* groups. I wondered if the upstairs group and the downstairs group ever got together or had anything in common. The basement strategy of ministry is a charitable use of space to be sure. It also allows communities to feel satisfied with ministry, while simultaneously staying out of relationship. Spiritually, the strategy disconnects people from the "other" and also from their own fears and shame.

So could the addict/demoniac return to the worshiping community, the upstairs? Would someone from the worshiping community, for that matter, feel welcome and safe in the downstairs community? I sometimes envision all the people wearing jeans and sneakers who gather regularly in the smoke-filled, coffee-redolent lower rooms of church buildings to laugh, tell jokes, weep, share *hell* stories and embrace with full-bodied hugs suddenly flooding the upper rooms on Sunday morning. Up there, people wearing suits and Talbot frocks gather regularly in the quiet sanctuary to kneel and pray, look somber, listen to *heaven* stories, consume little white wafers or bread cubes, sing music we don't hear much on our local radio stations, and do A-frame hugs or shake hands. And what if the reverse were to happen: all the upper room people flooding the lower room? Both communities would probably be traumatized, shock waves of anxiety and spiritual paralysis rolling through *both* upper and lower rooms.

And yet, with some modification of the excesses of this vision, this is precisely what I think needs to happen to fulfill the goal of "spiritual recovery by love possession" in both upper and lower rooms. When Jesus sent the healed man back into his community, he was not only giving the man a mission; he was giving the community a mission, namely, to establish its own belovedness and to integrate those who have been "living in the tombs." Such a mission is the vocation of religious communities and should not be relegated to individual counselors or to the Twelve Step communities alone. There is already a commonly held and powerful core conviction in both religious groups and Twelve Step groups: We need God or Higher Power to redeem and restore us to sanity, wholeness, and sobriety of mind and spirit. Both upper and lower rooms live by the faith that divine grace is a crucial ingredient in the spiritual recovery journey from possession by addiction (or any other sinful attachment) to "possession by love." The two God-based communities have much to offer and learn to and from each other.

If I were such a person in a parish, I would begin by sharing the vision with the leader. I would simply start a conversation. It doesn't take much intelligence to realize that addiction is at the center of most problems that plague our society and separate us from God, self, and neighbor. It doesn't take much intelligence to realize that addiction is intimately bound up in poverty, domestic and street violence, mental illness, crime, and death.

A parish could develop a small group willing to be in relational conversation about a mission focus on the partnership of upper and lower rooms. The group would be constituted of people committed to enacting the beloved community, for the purpose of providing a context of healing of the fear and shame that possess both addicts and nonaddicts alike, and keep us all in denial and isolation. The group ideally would include one or two faithful, but not zealous, people from both upper and lower rooms. If there are "bridge people" who find spiritual sustenance in both rooms and who are interested in making positive connections between the two, they would be welcome additions. A consultant skilled in process facilitation and addictions work could be a helpful but not necessary addition.

The main point of such a group is to do nothing more and nothing less than talk. It is a getting-to-know-you group. This is the entire work of love: to establish open, communicating, and understanding relationships to replace the shame and fearbound ones that currently exist between upper and lower rooms. The means, caring relationships, are also the end. I believe what French philosopher/theologian, Jacques Maritain (Miller, 129), has said: "The means are…the end in process of becoming." No big outcome or program may result from the conversations. No big conversions may take place. The interconnective spiritual energy of the process itself may be its own reward, so it is important for this group to agree from the outset to be free of task orientations, problem-solving, church growth motives, or any other hidden power agendas. A plan or mission strategy by which to expand the circle of love-in-relationship may emerge from the process, but if it does not, the process will not have failed. Seeds will have been planted, later to be reaped.

Now that we have let go of the often compulsive need for immediate and satisfying outcomes, and now that we realize that all of this depends on the nature of the small group process and how it evolves, I will offer some suggestions or possible routes for expanding the vision for ministry.

A parish, or a group of parishes, could develop a three-pronged mission focus: teaching, prayer/worship, and pastoral.

1. *The teaching mission*

The teaching mission might be implemented through education forums, church school curricula, and the use of the pulpit. A preaching series might be inaugurated on the topic of addictions and their role in our personal and communal lives. Guest speakers might be invited to share in this, by telling their own stories of addiction and codependency and to share the amazing graces of the Twelve Step recovery process. Safe learning is the beginning of breaking down denial. Sermon discussion groups could be offered to bring more people into the process.

Besides teaching about addictions and addictive/compulsive strategies in general, religious communities would benefit from learning about the amazing graces of their own tradition of both Word and Sacrament. How do we root ourselves in belovedness through the Word in scripture? We have a model in Luke's Gospel: the story of the prodigal son and the embracing, forgiving father. This story is really the only word we need to remember for ministry with addicts. It is about God's way of relating to the ones who leave home, to the ones who stay home, to the ones who return home, to the ones with no home.

The grace of this story could be the focus of an extended program of spiritual awareness and training in humility and forgiveness. One way to implement such a process could be to start a recovery group for Christians in the parish, a group modeled after the Twelve Step groups in the lower rooms. There, people could pray with, rather than analyze, the prodigal story. They could be encouraged to share and listen without judgment or feedback, as they get in touch with their own stories of addictions or addictive patterns in their relationships.

A group like this goes a long way to create an energy field of both safety and hospitality, to develop the discipline of listening, and to enable attitudes of humble forgiveness for excommunicant "addicts," both inside and outside the individual self. A group such as this goes a long way in promoting honesty and getting fears into the light in order to disempower them. A group such as this goes a long way toward healing the arrogant temptation to mark off in one's mind the beloveds and the non-beloveds, behaving as if Christians have a corner on the market of grace by dint of their tradition and gospel. A group like this goes a long way in reminding people that belovedness is not theirs by possession, but comes from God. It belongs to us by virtue of divine prodigality, not by our own efforts. A group such as this goes a long way in helping Christians become as prodigal and profligate with belovedness as any addict/demoniac was in the throes of possession, wasting the gift of life itself. A group such as this goes a long way in creating a communal base of belonging, safety, and hospitality, like the Twelve Step groups. Re-possessing by love over and over and over again, while, at the same time setting boundaries on behavior so as not to grant wholesale permission for the abuse of love, is a job best done by a community. It requires the strength and courage of numbers. It calls for many to love not just a few, and for many to love in shifts so resources can be replenished as human limits are recognized and respected.

The Christian community is a sacramental community. Education for living sacramental lives and understanding the body language of the eucharist/holy communion could be another focus of the teaching mission through preaching as well as forum groups.

We have seen in the possession story how rejecting the community is possible, not only for the possessed person but for the well and dispossessed person also. Jesus built the beloved community using his body. He literally moved his flesh and blood into and through all the conventional boundaries of socioeconomic compartmentalization, the boundaries that keep the sick sick and the well fearful. Jesus did not respect conventional divisions. He conversed with demons face to face. He ate with outcasts. He exchanged spittal with a blind person. He touched leprous bodies. He allowed a woman to anoint him lavishly with the oil of burial, pouring it onto his head and rubbing it into his flesh. He put his body on the cross for the sake of his faith and hope in the prodigal love of God, the love of repossession.

Do we have the courage to follow Jesus' example? Can we begin to appreciate that everyone's body and blood is a sacrament, an outer, visible sign of an inner and invisible grace: the Christ within? It is no accident that the language of our central ritual, the eucharist, is about body and blood! It is the body language of belovedness in community. We place our bodies in receptivity. We stand, kneel, and sit shoulder to shoulder gathered in body. We eat at a table to which, in many traditions, all bodies come. All bodies are welcomed and fed. All bodies have enough, not too much or too little.

The food is evenly distributed, and all flesh and blood is graced. This is God's feast we enact with our bodies. It is also a protest meal: Every time we bring our individual bodies and our communal body to this banquet, we re-member Jesus' body and protest against everything in our world that keeps our bodies at fearful distances. We protest against all the places in our world where, by policy and purpose, resources are unevenly distributed, so some bodies get whole loaves and some bodies get crumbs. What we do with our bodies Sunday after Sunday is nearly seditious, if only we knew.

For a community to understand its "sacramentality" is a first step to being able to know that all human embodied experience is sacred, touched by God. When we allow demoniacs and addicts to become untouchable, we violate the spirit of the eucharist and desecrate the body of Christ. We excommunicate both them and ourselves, failing to discern the body. What we do is as important to the integration of addicts into belovedness as what we say. I know a recovering addict who attends church and regularly invites people from her meetings to come with her. It's a good example to follow. Most Twelve Step meetings are open to whoever wishes to attend. So is the church.

2. *The worship mission*

Besides teaching, a way to embrace the excommunicants in upper and lower rooms is to recognize the presence of addictions and addicts, and those who love them, in our praying. A petition for the healing of those in bondage to addictions could be included weekly. A Sunday could be set aside each year, or even twice yearly, to recognize and celebrate not only disease by possession but "recovery by possession." Speakers might be invited to preach on different topics and various curriculum resources used in forums and with children.

Another way to bridge the gap between upper and lower rooms is for some people from both rooms to get together and plan a Recovery Service or Mass. This could be open to the public and offered regularly as a special worship opportunity for any Twelve Step recovering people and their friends. It could include some Christian ritual of Word and Sacrament, including holy communion and the "laying on of hands" for healing, as well as some Twelve Step readings, prayers, and talks. It would be a time for worship not a meeting, but the focus would be on the themes of addiction and recovery. I have been part of such an endeavor and talked to others who have started services in their churches. It can be a reconciling, God-centered celebration. As part of this ministry, I used to offer as well a yearly worship service with holy communion for those who were survivors of abuse.

3. *The pastoral mission*

The pastoral mission may be the most important in a ministry to create a beloved community inclusive of all exiles. This might start with a core group composed of church people and Twelve Step people. The idea would be for each group to get to know the other in their natural settings. By prearrangement, and after a base of relational understanding had been built, recovering people would come to church, and church people would come to a meeting. This would probably have to happen several times, so upper room and lower room people could get a real taste of the other community.

If such a mission were undertaken, it would be important to arrange for debriefing times for each group to talk about what the "foreign" experience had been like. I can think of no better way to reduce fear and shame, share resources, and grow spiritually. I can think of no better way for each group to experience directly what it feels like to be perceived as an outsider, and what it feels like to be gradually known and loved just as you are.

Church people have many false, if not distorted, ideas about what goes on at recovery meetings, and recovering people often have church teaching and ritual frozen in time and personal bad memories. We could give each other a chance. There is no better way to live than the Twelve Step model provides. There is no better way to get to know and share yourself and the God of your understanding than to listen uncritically and with compassion, and to feel the immanence of the divine, life-giving spirit. There is no better way to praise, give thanks, pray, learn about the Bible, commune, and raise voices in song, than to attend a church service where the entire focus of the whole community is on Higher Power.

I can think of no better way for communities of denial and false assumptions to become communities of forgiveness and love. The Twelve Step process relates to church tradition in its focus on spiritual conversion and ensuing growth from idolatry into a life of faith in God. Intimacy with God, self, and neighbor through the re-presentation of the divine immanence is the gift of a recovery meeting. The church offers the gift of worship and the re-presentation of divine transcendence. In this wholeness the beloved community is embodied, and the shared mission of both upper and lower rooms "to live by love possessed" can be realized.

References

Funk, R. and Hoover, R. (1993). *The five Gospels*. New York:Macmillan Polebridge Press.

Johnston, W. (Trans.) (1973). *The cloud of unknowing*. New York: Bantam, Doubleday, Dell.

Miller, R. (1996). *Cloudhand clenched fist*. San Diego: Luramedia.

CHAPTER 11

Beyond Abstinence and Toward Spiritual Integration

Howard J. Gray, S.J.

Spiritual direction, spiritual guidance, spiritual companionship, and soul friendship are terms for the privileged relationship between one who seeks help in the life of the spirit and one who offers that help.[1]

An intentional relationship of Christian spiritual direction is not so much a matter of one person having authority to direct another; rather, both parties in the relationship are expected to become attentive listeners to the Holy Spirit, who continually provides providential direction in the life of each man and woman, whether they are aware of it or not. Gradually individual blocks will be uncovered and brought to consciousness. With increasing depth, the desires of the true and core self are revealed when compulsive reactions of the false self give way to positive, truly free responses to divine initiatives.[2] Carolyn Gratton's succinct description of the process within that intentional relationship correctly emphasizes the mutuality of both "director" and "companion" listening to what the Spirit of God has to say. The focus in spiritual direction is on the narrative that one Christian presents to another; the aim is to discern what in that narrative leads to life and to love and what in that narrative leads to death and enmity. Gratton also underscores the time that such a relationship takes place *gradually*. In a culture of instantaneous communication, God seems

[1] On terminology, see Gerald May, M.D., *Will and spirit, a contemplative psychology* (New York: HarperCollins, 1982), pp. 291–193.

[2] Carolyn Gratton, "Spiritual direction," in Michael Downey, editor, *The new dictionary of Catholic spirituality* (Collegeville: : Liturgical Press, 1993), p. 913.

to be notoriously slow-moving; or, perhaps, we are slow-moving and only over time come to appreciate the leadership God has been exercising, the patient adaptation to minds and hearts dulled to the silent humility that is God's way, souls that are pervasively self-conscious but not always self-aware, and energies constantly demanding fulfillment but rarely guided by any commanding purpose. The task of the spiritual director and that of the psychiatrist or clinical psychologist touch, but they do not blend into one another. What is the distinction, then?[3]

Spiritual direction focuses on the mystery of oneself and one's relationship before God. The therapist focuses on the problems that intrude within oneself and between oneself and others. There are times when the problems of a man or woman are so persistent and so defeating, that the person cannot move until these problems are confronted and resolved. Frequently, these problems are rooted in the early years of a person's narrative and have been ignored or suppressed. To uproot these problems, to look at them with integrity and wisdom, and to help structure ways of coping with these problems—this process requires skills beyond those even of a good spiritual director. One of the most persistent of such problems is that of addiction—be it chemical, alcoholic, sexual, gambling, overeating, or work-excess. This essay is about addiction and spiritual direction, about that moment when a spiritual director discovers a pattern of behavior that is both destructive and controlling within the narrative of someone who comes to him or her. My reflections fall under three subheads: (1) the parameters of spiritual direction, (2) the stages of relationship between a spiritual director and therapist, and (3) the future cooperation between spiritual directors and therapists.

Parameters in Spiritual Direction

One of the finest descriptions of spiritual direction is the narrative of the two disciples on the road to Emmaus (Luke 24:13–35).

> Now on that same day two of them were going to a village called Emmaus, about seven miles from Jerusalem, and talking with each other about all these things that had happened. While they were talking and discussing, Jesus himself came near and went with them, but their eyes were kept from recognizing him. And he said to them, "What are you discussing with each other while you walk along?" They stood still, looking sad. Then one of them, whose name was Cleopas, answered him, "Are you the only stranger in Jerusalem who does not know the things that have taken place there in these days?" He asked them, "What things?" They replied, "The things about Jesus of Nazareth, who was a prophet mighty in deed and word before God and all the people, and how our

[3] For a succinct discussion, see H. John McDargh, "Psychology, relationship and contribution to spirituality," in *The New Dictionary*, pp. 792–800; Gerald G. May, M.D., *Care of mind/care of soul, a psychiatrist explores spiritual direction* (New York: Harper, 1982).

chief priests and leaders handed him over to be condemned to death and crucified him. But we had hoped that he was the one to redeem Israel. Yes, and besides all this, it is now the third day since these things took place. Moreover, some women of our group astounded us. They were at the tomb early this morning, and when they did not find his body there, they came back and told us that they had indeed seen a vision of angels who said that he was alive. Some of us those who were with us went to the tomb and found it just as the women had said; but they did not see him." Then he said to them, "Oh, how foolish you are, and how slow of heart to believe all that the prophets have declared! Was it not necessary that the Messiah should suffer these things and then enter into his glory?" Then beginning with Moses and all the prophets, he interpreted for them the things about himself in all the scriptures.

As they came near the village to which they were going, he walked ahead as if he were going on. But they urged him strongly, saying, "Stay with us, because it is almost evening and the day is now nearly over." So he went in to stay with them. When he was at the table with them, he took bread, blessed and broke it, and gave it to them. Then their eyes were opened, and they recognized him; and he vanished from their sight. They said to each other, "Were not our hearts burning within us while he was talking to us on the road, while he was opening the scriptures to us?" That same hour they got up and returned to Jerusalem; and they found the eleven and their companions gathered together. They were saying, "The Lord has risen indeed, and has appeared to Simon!" Then they told what had happened on the road, and how he had been made known to them in the breaking of the bread.

This beautiful incident is also a deeply theological statement, centering in large part on the way the early Christian community interpreted its life and scriptures.[4] For our purposes the Emmaus episode illustrates the frame for spiritual direction within the Christian tradition. Note that the Lucan narrative emphasizes that the two dejected disciples did not at first recognize Jesus. To them he was simply a "stranger," and an amazingly uninformed one at that. The narrative deftly dramatizes the transformation in relationship as the stranger becomes a companion, a trusted interpreter, and finally, the Risen Jesus. The story is in part about relationships. It is also about process, the way in which Jesus brings the disciples *out of* sadness and the decision to separate themselves from the community and *into* new insight, an integration of their experience of suffering and death

[4] In this and in subsequent treatments of Luke's Gospel, I have relied on two commentaries: Joseph A. Fitzmyer, S.J., *The gospel according to Luke, introduction, translation, and notes,* vol. 1 (1–9) and vol. 2 (10–24) New York: Doubleday, 1981 and 1985); Luke Timothy Johnson, *The Gospel of Luke*, Sacra Pagina Series #3 (Collegeville: Liturgical Press, 1991).

and humiliation with the revelation that had grounded their faith but now needed to be reinterpreted in the light of these painful events. This basic structure is the process of spiritual direction, a relationship that helps another to interpret his or her experiences in the light of religious faith. Spiritual direction is a process that moves from what is called desolation, an estrangement from the peace and harmony that should be the result of faith, and into consolation, a state of peace and harmony with oneself, one's community, and God. Within this frame of movement, what is the role of the spiritual director (or guide, companion, or soul-friend)?

Jesus offers a paradigm of what a good spiritual director "does" in direction. Jesus keeps pace with the two disciples, joining them where they are, not only physically but psychologically, entering their world, moving into their conversation, listening attentively to their narrative and the emotional coloring that surrounds all they relate. He *accompanies* them; and in that accompaniment they come to trust him enough to let him question them, to help them touch their present anguish, their past hopes, and the sources of their discouragement and estrangement. Only when the trust is assured—indicated by the intimacy that they offer in describing their hurt—does Jesus intervene. He is honest but not destructive, identifying their problems—slow to believe, too superficial in reading their own tradition, narrow in their expectations of redemption—but never separating himself from their companionship. Jesus stays with them as one who has genuinely become part of their narrative. His role evolves into that of the teacher, not so much bringing new data but rather refocusing the way the disciples interpret both their lives and their religious tradition. Jesus does not deny their pain or disappointment. But he does recontextualize them. The two disciples move from self-absorption to concern about this stranger on the road, expressing concern about his safety and even inviting him to join them for a meal. It is at the meal that the narrative reaches its climax, in recognition that God in Jesus had been walking with them. Finally, the disciples move from this encounter into a renewed sense of themselves as part of the community they had abandoned. They return with swiftness and surety to share their story and to strengthen the community because they had learned to understand their faith, their sorrow, and their purpose in life.

The process of spiritual direction is not as compact as the Emmaus narrative. Listening takes time and patience; trust can move slowly, not because of ill will, but simply because disclosures represent a surrender of the self. If that sense of self has been betrayed or ignored or trivialized or ridiculed, then people need time to be healed. A wise director is a patient director, giving those who come to him or her the freedom to open themselves as they are comfortable. At the same time, the wise director looks for progress in self-revelation, a gradual but real movement toward the truth. The "truth" of spiritual direction centers on two areas: It is about the life of the man and woman who come for direction, and it is about their religious experience, the ways that God meets them within life.[5]

When the ability to trust has been so seriously enfeebled that real communication is impossible, or when the narrative reveals a pattern of severe problems that inhibit the basic freedom to live a normal, adult life, then the spiritual director ought to advise another professional intervention. The reason is that the director is now moving into therapy, not spiritual direction. Even if the director has some skill in counseling, I would advise him or her to help the troubled directee to get someone else, trained and competent, to treat recurring, serious psychological problems. While the spiritual direction relationship can be sustained, it will be a relationship recontextualized by the therapeutic process. One of the major instances that necessitates such recontextualization within a spiritual direction relationship is the discovery that a directee is suffering an untreated addiction.

Confronting addictions in spiritual direction

There are three distinct, but related, moments when a spiritual director deals with a man or woman suffering addictions: the moment of discovery, the moment of support when the addict is in therapy, and the moment of integration as the former addict lives with a wisdom and freedom born out of struggle.

Before considering these three moments of encounter between spiritual direction and addictions, let me say something about how a religious person might look at addictive behavior. First of all, I agree with Terrence Real that "In theory an addictive relationship can be established with just about anything, so long as the substance, person, or activity relieves the threat of overt depression."[6] I also agree with him that covert depression has to become overt depression before a person can be genuinely helped, even when the addiction is being treated.[7] Whatever the addiction, it involves a bondage that dehumanizes a man or woman. While the Christian gospels are rich with instances of Jesus' compassion, there is a strange, yet powerful episode narrated in all three of the Synoptic Gospels (i.e., Matthew, Mark, and Luke) that symbolizes the pain and alienation of addictive behavior. This episode is the story of the Gerasene demoniac. (The reader may refer to Brakeman's chapter 10 for a more extended reflection on this gospel story.)

> Then they arrived at the country of the Gerasenes, which is opposite Galilee. As Jesus stepped out on land, a man of the city who

---

[5] While there are several excellent treatments of this topic, I suggest Janet Ruffing, S.M., *Uncovering stories of faith, spiritual direction and narrative* (New York/Mahwah: Paulist Press, 1989).

[6] Terrence Real, *I don't want to talk about it, overcoming the secret legacy of male depression* (New York: Scribner, 1997), p. 63.

[7] Ibid.

> had demons met him. For a long time he had worn no clothes, and he did not live in a house but in the tombs. When he saw Jesus, he fell down before him and shouted at the top of his voice, "What have you to do with me, Jesus, Son of the Most High God? I beg you, do not torment me"—For Jesus had commanded the unclean spirit to come out of the man. (For many times it had seized him; he was kept under guard and bound with chains and shackles, but he would break the bonds and be driven by the demon into the wilds.) Jesus then asked him, "What is your name?" He said, "Legion"; for many demons had entered him. They begged him not to order them to go back into the abyss.
>
> Now there on the hillside a large herd of swine was feeding; and the demons begged Jesus to let them enter these. So he gave the permission. Then the demons came out of the man and entered the swine, and the herd rushed down the steep bank into the lake and was drowned.
>
> When the swineherds saw what had happened, they ran off and told it in the city and in the country. Then people came out to see what had happened, and when they came to Jesus, they found the man from whom the demons had gone sitting at the feet of Jesus, clothed and in his right mind. And they were afraid. Those who had seen it told them how the one who had been possessed by demons had been healed. Then all the people of the surrounding country of the Gerasenes asked Jesus to leave them; for they were seized with great fear. So he got into the boat and returned. The man from whom the demons had gone begged that he might be with him; but Jesus sent him away, saying, "Return to your home, and declare how much God has done for you." So he went away, proclaiming throughout the city how much Jesus had done for him.(Luke 8:26–39)

Immediately before this scene of the Gerasene demoniac, Luke has narrated the story of Jesus' calming of the storm on the Lake of Gennesaret. A noted scripture scholar says of this parallelism, "Evil threatening human beings in the form of natural cataclysms (Luke 8:22–25) now has a counterpart in evil afflicting the psychic being of a mortal man…The story depicts Jesus using his power to heal an unfortunate demented human being, an outcast of society, thus restoring him to soundness of mind and wholeness of life." (Fitzmeyer, 1985).[8] The religious person, especially one who claims the gospel as normative for his or her belief and conduct, reads in this episode the Christian reaction to all that dehumanizes and enslaves men and women. That reaction is to confront, to expel, to cure, and to restore to dignity and freedom.

[8] Fitzmyer, Luke, p. 733.

This attitude is enhanced when the spiritual director meets someone caught in the cycle of any addictive behavior. The addiction drives a man or woman to the fringes of human life, frequently estranging the victims from family, friends, and neighbors. The addiction strips away self-respect and self-worth. Addiction is often the choice to live with the dead rather than with the living, seeking companionship with those whose shared addictions offer a grotesque community of support and denial. The Gerasene demoniac is a symbol of the destruction that addiction brings to the human person; the healing of the Gerasene demoniac, clothed, quiet, in the posture of discipleship is a sign of the human integration God intended. The confusion and fear of the townspeople can represent the awkwardness and confusion that good people feel when an addiction has been confronted and treated. Too often those who have been close to the addict in family, religious community, or work place have also been, willingly and unwillingly, partners in the addiction, covering up the drunkenness or gambling or over-eating or drug abuse with excuses, lies, or quiet indifference. Too often living with the disease of addiction can become a way of life; learning to live with wellness can be a threat and a challenge.[9]

The narrative of the Gerasene demoniac can be read as a fable about addiction; and, like every good fable, it can be read on many levels and be applied to a variety of situations. A good spiritual director will see addictive behavior for what it is, an enslavement and a dishonor to the human spirit, a demon whose name is Legion and who deserves to be expelled. Whoever helps in that healing process is in partnership with Jesus, regardless of whether or not he or she claims an explicit religious orientation. This partnership is the reason why spiritual directors should work in cooperation with the therapist who is treating a directee's addiction. It is a commitment beyond professional courtesy.

Moment of discovery

Miriam was a moderately attractive, highly intelligent graduate student in political science.[10] She was a convert to Roman Catholicism from a strict fundamentalist church, having made that transition in her undergraduate years. I had been seeing her for monthly spiritual direction for about six or seven months. She was in her second year of graduate work and inaugurated spiritual direction because she wanted help in deepening her prayer and assessing her future. While she was dutiful in coming to the spiritual direction sessions and articulate in talking about her studies, her relationships with peers, and the rubrics of Catholicism (e.g., her attendance at Sunday liturgy), I found she had little to say about her prayer, her deeper relationship with God, or her life either as a child or as a young adult or during undergraduate studies. After about seven sessions, I found

[9] Very helpful to me has been Patrick Carnes, *Out of the shadows, understanding sexual addiction* (Minneapolis: CompCare, 1983).

[10] Miriam is a composite of many cases, composed to protect people's rights to confidentiality and privacy.

Miriam superficial and vague, despite my efforts to specify a couple areas that I thought it might be good for us to discuss. I confronted her on this, suggesting that it could be that she did not feel comfortable with me and that she might want to choose another director. At this suggestion Miriam broke into tears. "I have no self to share," she protested.

We sat in silence for a minute or two. I handed her a face tissue to dry her tears. Finally, she told me that her studies were a constant preoccupation, not merely something she enjoyed, but a kind of tyranny. She lived only to study and to get good grades. For many years she found her self-worth in academic success, but that was no longer true. Now she felt only that she was trapped by what she had allowed studies to become—her whole life. I asked her to describe a typical day for me. What she described was a day of unrelenting work. I asked, gently, if there was anything else that bothered her. Now Miriam began to sob. Gradually, she was able to tell me that she was masturbating twelve to fifteen times a day, caught in an endless cycle of study and self-stimulation. Even more complicated was the fact that she had not been to the sacrament of reconciliation for over a year, receiving communion, she felt, in the state of mortal sin.

We talked in ways we had not been able to talk before, about Miriam's desire for a normal social life, for friends and not academic competitors, for someone who would love her and want to spend his life with her. It also came out that Miriam had avoided any medical examination for a number of years, afraid that this would reveal her masturbation. The masturbation had begun when she was sixteen; and now, at twenty-six it was totally out of hand. I told her that she was loved by God exactly where she was and as she was, that I was honored that she could share her pain with me, that I also thought the time had come for her to talk this through with a fine clinical psychologist whom I knew and trusted. When I told Miriam that this clinician was also a woman, she expressed relief and a willingness to schedule an interview. Miriam also asked whether I would be willing to continue to talk with her. I assured her that I was happy to see her, that we had crossed over into sensitive areas of her life that touched her self-image, her affections, her sense of God's judgment and forgiveness, her need to be free from the tyrannies of secrecy and shame. I told her that we can be redeemed only if we need a Redeemer. She had discovered why Jesus had come among us—to bring us peace and to free us. "Let's work on finding that more permanent peace and deeper freedom God wants you to have."

Miriam's therapy moved quickly for two reasons, I think: (1) Once Miriam had disclosed her addictions, she wanted to be free from them, and (2) she had an excellent therapist who inspired trust and disclosure. My role was to support the disclosures in therapy, neither expecting Miriam to report these to me nor avoiding integrating these, if they came, into our work. But I told Miriam the major asceticism, or discipline, was fidelity to the therapy, that within the total process she would begin to find God's direction.

Miriam's case is not atypical. There are many serious professionals, many pastoral ministers, many in the helping professions for whom excessive work and sexual compulsion prove to be unhealthy combinations. Frequently, the shame of sexual disorder drives a person to self-punishing excess in work or in studies. The excess in studies or in work, in turn, drives the person to look for some sort of release in pleasure. Sex is one form of release, but so, too, is alcohol, food, TV, gambling. What triggered Miriam's self-disclosure and her willingness to seek therapy was that, without my realizing it, my seven sessions of growing frustration with her lack of depth were giving her a privileged time of communication that was neither study nor sexual stimulation. What I did not know until later on, was that she had stayed at the surface because she had never given herself permission to talk, just to talk. What was important for Miriam was to have someone she could waste time with. When I challenged the direction of these sessions, she felt the threat of loss, but also the deeper desire she had to talk about her pain, even if that caused her shame.

I wish that I could claim a mastery of such situations, that I knew there were things deeply troubling to Miriam, and that my intervention was needed if these were to surface. In truth, I had no plan and no prior direction. Within the context of spiritual direction, I simply felt we needed to be talking about more significant areas of Miriam's life, and we were not doing that. For me it was a question of being patient but also of being authentic. I had practiced patience for seven sessions and felt it was now the time to move to explicit and centered authenticity. If, after seven sessions, we were still negotiating the interpersonal territory, it was time to say this. I would underscore the virtues of patience and authenticity, giving people time and space to tell their truth, as crucial in the initial stages of spiritual direction. What Miriam finally shared was her painful authenticity, so my patience had worked. But it could have been otherwise. Miriam could have buried her pain and said that she wanted to change spiritual directors. Miriam could also have taken this intervention as one more intellectual challenge and begun to talk around and above her real spiritual problem and create a false spirituality. Had Miriam acted in this way, I think and hope I would have recognized what was happening, but she could have tried.

Moment of support

I have already indicated that in Miriam's case my work as a spiritual director was to support the process of therapy and to relate it to the healing honesty that seems to be God's way of working within people. Miriam and her therapist decided at some point that it would be helpful for the three of us to have a joint session. I neither asked for that nor did I refuse it. When I was asked to participate in a joint session, I was peaceful with this because I could see how Miriam was becoming less and less addictive and more confident of God's love, forgiveness, and blessing on her gifts and her efforts to liberate those gifts. Gradually, Miriam's prayer moved from petition for health and the acceptance of the asceticism of her therapy to more contemplative prayer.

In the session with Miriam and her therapist, Miriam took the initiative. She disclosed that as a young child of about three or four years of age she had been playing in her back yard as her mother spoke to a neighbor. The neighbor mentioned that another neighbor, a woman in her forties, was pregnant again.

> "You'd think that they would be more careful at her age. They don't need more children," said the neighbor.
> "Well, you just never know," replied Miriam's mother. "We never wanted this one. She was an accident."

As she recounted this incident, long buried in her memory and her heart, Miriam sobbed. The feeling of not being wanted, of needing to prove her worth, of feeling unlovable were all at the core of the academic success this young woman seemed to be having. She was performing for the mother who called her "an accident." The recovery of this memory was brutal for Miriam but absolutely essential for her psychic health, for her ability to see the source of her addictions and, thereby, gain some control over them. Similarly, it was important in that freedom for Miriam to forgive her mother, to see the need to bring to light the sinfulness of a life situation that could have tyrannized her for the rest of her life. (The chapters in this book by Doweiko, Jampolsky, Kasl, Albers, and Larsen speak to these dynamics underneath addiction.)

It was also important for Miriam to put the masturbatory addiction into a context other than sex. To be denied love—or, at least, *to feel* that love has been denied—can lead to all kinds of substitutions. She could see the difference between looking for comfort and being an uncontrolled sex addict. In Miriam's case "seeing" was the key to recovery. What Miriam also had to learn was a whole set of new social skills to create a more balanced emotional and affective life. From the asceticism of clinical therapy, Miriam was ready to move to the asceticism of hospitality, of learning how to welcome peers into her life as friends. Miriam had to learn how to transform the stranger into the neighbor. In our spiritual direction sessions we began to use more sections from the gospel of Luke. Without making it a project (substituting one addiction for a religious one), I helped Miriam to pray over the human relationships of Jesus in that gospel, his capacity for friendship, his ability to let people be who they were with him. Correctly, Miriam noted and was consoled by the special relationship Luke dramatizes between Jesus and women. Her increasing responsiveness to contemplative prayer helped Miriam to enter into the gospel scene.

The addictive drive in studies gradually gave way to a rhythm of work, prayer, and play. Miriam knew that she would never be someone who liked big parties. But she also came to appreciate the time that could be spent with small groups of like-minded people. Miriam met people from outside her department. She began to go to concerts, to hike. There were some failures, of course; but Miriam was able to integrate these into her growing awareness that God teaches wisdom and compassion by helping us to learn from our failures and to forgive ourselves as well as other people. It is a cliché, but Miriam was learning how to be her own friend, to tell herself that she was her friend too, that she was happy that she had been born, that God rejoiced in what God had created in Miriam.

Throughout this interplay of clinical therapy and spiritual direction, both the therapist and I were turning over to Miriam the responsibility for her recovery. Her confidence grew as she structured her life around a mix of adult responsibilities, not proving anything to anyone but simply responding to the relative importance she freely gave to the various parts of her life. A crucial time was Christmas, when she was to return to her family home to celebrate the holiday. Miriam wanted to talk to her mother, to tell her mother what she had remembered about not being wanted, "an accident," to share her efforts to regain a sense of balanced self-worth, to forgive her mother. But Miriam realized that what was so prominent in her mind and heart could well be lost in her mother's memory. She knew that her mother was proud of her success as a student, but Miriam was not confident that she possessed her mother's love. Then there was the Christmas holiday itself. Was this really the occasion for confrontation about something that had happened so long ago? Miriam was at an important juncture in her therapy. Her recovery had been good, but there was still a fragility in her sense of self and a tentativeness in her self-assertions outside the academic.

I have called this period a moment of support. The support centers on the freedom to choose what leads to life and to love. It is not a sentimental substitute for experiencing the pain of personal decisions and their consequences. In this the spiritual director and the therapist are one, I believe. Certainly, Miriam's therapist and I agreed that how Miriam handled the Christmas holidays was her decision not ours. We both encouraged Miriam to look at the situation, what she wished to accomplish and why, to foresee the results, and to be willing to live with these. As Miriam's spiritual director, I suggested only one other element, her personal prayer about what to do. This was a rich time for Miriam's spiritual development. For what she began to do was to discern, to weigh the alternatives, to try to understand what God was asking through her freedom and her compassion both for her mother and for herself, to assess the various movements.

The Christmas holiday went well for Miriam. She renewed a friendship with a former high school classmate who had become a teacher and coach at the high school he and Miriam had attended. There was some tension about Christmas worship. The family planned to attend the fundamentalist church for the midnight service. Miriam said that she would be going to the nearby Catholic church instead. To Miriam's surprise, her mother said that she would like to join her. So while the rest of the family went to the church of their youth, Miriam and her mother attended mass. Miriam asked her mother why she had decided to come, while expressing delight that she would do so. Her mother said simply, "I owe you companionship."

Miriam returned to school, not having confronted her mother because she felt that she had her answer in those simple words, "I owe you companionship." Miriam returned feeling that she had deeply forgiven her mother and herself. Something as simple and humble as "I owe you companionship," had loosed from Miriam's heart the last burden. It was nothing I did as a spiritual director and nothing that therapy could claim as its final technique. It was Miriam and, I believe, God who did it together. God had become Miriam's support, and she found that support was love.

Moment of integration

As the recovering addict attains more and more internal freedom and healthy control over his or her life, the direction within the relationship between him or her and the director also changes. It is difficult to specify a set of "signs" for this transition because people and specific addictions are different. However, some of the indications would be an impatience to move along with one's life, to use the experience of personal recovery to help other people, to begin to talk about intimacy and/or generative issues rather than identity ones. It is important that this interest in moving on not be an impatience with the tedium of recovery or an easy dismissal of the need for ongoing support (like AA). This transition is also a moment of integration.

What is being integrated? The affective and spiritual history, the narrative, of accepting one's illness and the efforts to regain physical, psychological, and spiritual health. Whatever the pain and embarrassment of the past, this was a powerful and important part of the total story of someone in direction. People can be tempted to bury the past, to put the painful and the shameful behind them. Certainly, it is good to move beyond therapy and into more autonomous living, but it is also good to integrate the realities of past suffering into the rhythm of the new life. Wisdom and compassion as abilities to see more deeply and to feel more profoundly do not just happen in life. These gifts emerge out of the reflection we bring to the struggles that mark every human life. Consequently, an alert spiritual director will be ready to help the recovered addict revisit the experiences of the past in order to enrich the reflections and sensitivities of the present. There is a process in this, a way of helping people to use the past in order to respond more humanely to the present. Again, within Christian spiritual direction there is a power in using the gospels to illustrate this transition, this moment of integration.

> Just then a lawyer stood up to test Jesus. "Teacher," he said, "what must I do to inherit eternal life?" He said to him, "What is written in the law? What do you read there?" He answered, "You shall love the Lord your God with all your heart and with all your soul, and with all your strength, and with all your mind; and your neighbor as yourself." And he said to him, "You have given the right answer; do this, and you will live."
>
> But wanting to justify himself, he asked Jesus, "And who is my neighbor?" Jesus replied, "A man was going down from Jerusalem to Jericho, and fell into the hands of robbers, who stripped him, beat him, and went away, leaving him half dead. Now by chance a priest was going down that road; and when he saw him, he passed by on the other side. So likewise a Levite, when he came to the place and saw him, passed by on the other side. But a Samaritan while traveling came near him; and when he saw him, he was moved with pity. He went to him and bandaged his wounds, having poured oil and wine on them. Then he put him on his own animal, brought him to an inn, and took care of him. The next day he took out two denarii, gave then to the innkeeper, and said, 'Take care of him; and when I come back, I will repay whatever more you spend.' Which of these three, do you think, was a neighbor to the man who fell into the hands of the robbers?" He said, "The one who showed him mercy." Jesus said to him, "Go and do likewise."(Luke 10:25–37)

The encounter between Jesus and the lawyer is the occasion for this marvelous story that risks being weakened by a hermeneutics of sentimentality.[11] It is, in fact, a tough narrative that centers on an act of human violence that leaves another human being totally vulnerable, unconscious, unclothed, bloody. Within the culture of Jesus this rendered a Jew unclean, for whoever touched this victim would become contaminated by the blood that had been spilled. Consequently, to become involved was to put oneself at risk. That risk was compounded by the circumstances of the lonely road and the singular set of travelers, hurrying along lest they encounter the same band of robbers. Jesus underscores the dilemma by introducing two representatives of the religious class—a priest and a Levite—who see one of their own desperately in need and move as far away as possible and hasten on their journeys. The incident and the reactions were designed to shock Jesus' listeners on several levels. But the most startling of all is the introduction of the Samaritan, a representative of a people hostile to the Jews. This outsider and potential enemy not only sees the victim at the side of the road but draws near to him and becomes his neighbor, his brother,

[11] Luke Timothy Johnson is excellent in explicating this aspect of the Lucan account, see pp. 172–176.

his savior. The despised Samaritan has become the ethical and religious hero of the narrative. His actions become normative for how one is to treat the neighbor.

The final words of Jesus to the lawyer, "Go and do likewise," invite us to examine exactly what the Samaritan had done. What distinguishes the Samaritan from the priest and the Levite, what made him "neighbor" to the victim at the side of the road? Four sets of actions characterize the response of the Samaritan: He really saw, he felt for the victim, he did the practical good he was able to do, and he established a sustaining presence even in his absence. The "doing" of the Samaritan was a process, and in that process one finds the essentials to moral and religious life within the Christian tradition. [12]

To see means to take more than a quick glance. Clearly, the priest and the Levite "saw," but their "seeing" was uninvolved. The "seeing" of the Samaritan was the kind of contemplative attentiveness that prayer should develop in people, the ability to let the total reality of another engage our soul. It demands a willingness to take the time to let life enter into us, to reverence the differences in creation, and to lose oneself in order to find oneself enlarged and challenged by the mystery of the other. We cannot live this intensely all the time. But there are moments when the contemplative surrender is demanded. Clearly, the victim at the side of the road was one of those times, the test of how religious people have learned to look, to see, and to let reality sink in.

The Samaritan "was moved to pity," an emotion attributed to Jesus earlier in Luke 7:13, when Jesus encounters the widow of Nain and feels her grief. The compassion that the Samaritan feels is the result of his willingness to see all that is before him—the victim, the context, the loneliness, the total vulnerability. Seeing all, the Samaritan is moved, his interior is drawn to care about the man on the road. Out of that contemplative compassion comes the series of concrete actions—healing, transporting, detouring his own journey, spending his time and his money— which return humanity to the stranger found at the side of the road.

Finally, the Samaritan enlists the aid of one of the least likely allies, the innkeeper. While the Samaritan must move on, his contemplative compassion and involved concern will continue. The Samaritan has established a network of sustained good. This kind of process, Jesus says, makes neighbors, makes the gospel come to life.

When someone asks what is the purpose of spiritual direction within the Christian tradition, he or she ought to be directed to this section from Luke's gospel. The integration that we aim for in spiritual direction is not simply mental health or psychosomatic harmony. Christian integration, the aim of spiritual direction, is contemplative and practical, personal and social, liberating and responsible. It is a balance that frees a man or a woman

[12] For an alternate application see Howard J. Gray, S. J., "Integrating human needs in religious formation," *Review for Religious* 53 (1994), pp. 107–119.

to be the "neighbor,"to be someone who leads others to life and to love. If spiritual direction does not do this, then it risks lapsing into an asceticism that abuses religion or a private moralism that risks self-righteousness. For these reasons it is imperative that those who direct a recovering addict also help that man or woman move beyond recovery and into donation, into living the call to "go and do likewise," the command that concludes and explains the parable of the good Samaritan.[13]

All four elements are important—contemplative attention to the life around you, a development of one's heart and the ability to respond to others, especially those in need, a willingness not only to help but to be a skilled and competent helper, and the maturity to relinquish any possessiveness over a project or an enterprise so that the entire community or generations yet to come can also find the opportunity to give contemplative and compassionate service.

Of course, this process of Christian integration cannot be imposed. It is a process of grace, of God's invitation and support. Moreover, not every good has to be done by every person. Not every good a person could do must be done by him or her, or done immediately. Sound discernment includes the ability to adapt the demands of the gospel to the abilities and graces a person possesses. A generous willingness to form one's life within the gospel imperatives must be accompanied by discretion, also a gift from the Spirit. Helping a recovering addict to learn how to choose generously and appropriately is especially important for the spiritual director.

Miriam's Christmas experience focused her energies and her emotions. She seemed to find peace and an ordered direction in her life. Her choice not to confront her mother came not out of fear or a reluctance to face conflict. Rather it seemed to her that the peace which she had sought now was hers. She had forgiven her mother; and, more importantly, her mother had reached out to her in a gesture of mutuality that moved their relationship into one of adults. In time Miriam shared some of her struggles and the effects of her therapy with her family. Gradually, in our spiritual direction sessions Miriam expressed a desire to get on with other issues. What kind of scholar and teacher would she be? How would her Christian convictions inform her professional life? Should she pursue the relationship with her high school friend? Miriam's sessions with the therapist lessened.

As Miriam's autonomy developed, her prayer took a strongly apostolic turn. She looked at the figure of Jesus less for support and more as a model of service, as one who brought the care of God into the human condition. She began to use the Examen of Consciousness, a prayer that looks at the day's events and evaluates the directions that bring her closer to or farther from God. Through this prayer Miriam began to appreciate that her life was not so much a set of departments, each claiming a loyalty all its

[13] Helpful on this point is Kenneth Leech, *The eye of the storm, living spirituality in the real world* (New York: Harper, 1992) and William Reiser, S.J., *To hear God's word, listen to the world, A Liberation of Spirituality* (New York/Mahwah: Paulist Press, 1997).

own, but rather a continuum of opportunities to help people and to be helped by them. The healthy realization that relationship was central to organizing her life liberated Miriam to make other choices. Soon she was spending an afternoon a week tutoring inner-city high school students in math and English. The high school coach invited her to a championship game and she accepted. She found new and creative avenues in her graduate work. What I found heartening was that Miriam could see and communicate that her suffering and isolation had made her sympathetic towards the suffering and struggles of others, especially those graduate students who were not as sharp as she.

It was not an uninterrupted victory march, of course. Years of self-doubt and patterns of inappropriate defense strategies had conditioned Miriam to be both socially protective and professionally aggressive. But now she understood why these were part of her personality and how they could damage her peace of soul and her ability to be available to other people. Her asceticism was shaped by her desire to be relational and to be productive. Her affective realization of God became more tender and familiar. Miriam realized the importance of maintaining a healthy rhythm in her life—including hard intellectual work but also time for friends, prayer and worship, and physical exercise. The struggles that Miriam now talked about were oriented towards living more fully and loving more universally. She was on her way to becoming an important scholar who took the demands of faith and of social justice to heart.

Future Cooperation: Spiritual Directors and Therapists

The process of spiritual direction involves many of the same elements that one finds in therapy. Central to both is the narrative, the story that the client shares with the director or the therapist. Addictive behavior causes pain and suffering, could involve legal action, and seriously impairs the ability a man or woman has to live freely and productively. Miriam's addiction was painful and potentially dangerous. But it could have been much worse. Moreover, Miriam had resources—intelligence, a professional future, and a religious faith that, ultimately, sustained her. Not all addicts are so fortunate. Both spiritual directors and therapists see the importance of breaking the addiction, of helping the client understand what is going on in his or her life and, if this is possible, to trace its origin in his or her life. In this process of uncovering the addiction and its causes, therapists have skills that most spiritual directors do not possess. Spiritual directors have much to learn from psychotherapy. At the very least, spiritual directors ought to be sensitive to signs of addiction and to be quick to help the addict receive professional help in confronting the illness.

During the initial stages of therapy spiritual directors should take the lead from the therapists. While it involves a sensitive area of professional confidentiality, it is helpful for the spiritual director to have some understanding of the progress of the treatment so he or she can support this. In the case of Miriam, I had an opportunity to talk with Miriam and her therapist. Not every therapist is peaceful with such mutual consultation; but it is important that therapists realize that spiritual direction is an increasingly important area of reflection, healing, and integration for believing patients.

Spiritual direction can be invaluable in a patient's movement from therapy to reintegration into a life without addictive behavior. The Christian spiritual director has the resources of the gospel narrative and if these are used with reverence both for the tradition of faith and the findings of biblical scholars, then they provide a powerful companion narrative for the recovering patient. The therapist should understand and appreciate the significance of the Christian addict finding in the traditions of faith guidance for his or her life. On the other hand, Christian spiritual directors have to appreciate that recovery within the Christian tradition means an appropriate participation in the mission Jesus gave to his community: to promote peace, justice, and love. People do not just get well; they get well to give something back to others.

While I have restricted my reflections to what I know best—the Christian tradition of spiritual direction—I am confident that those of other traditions have similar wisdom to contribute to this conversation. (The chapters in this book, particularly those in this section, provide ample evidence). Moreover, my experience has been that if ever there was an area of ecumenical cooperation, then care for those who suffer addictions is a privileged instance of such. [14]

In a wider, "ecumenical" context, the exchange between therapists and spiritual guides is a potentially rich and rewarding one. Granted that religion has frequently contributed to an addict's disease through abuses like the imposition of excessive guilt, misplaced moralisms, the intrusive use of authority, and the inappropriate disclosure of personal defects, nonetheless, for many addicts religion constitutes an important abiding influence, one that can become liberating, creative, and empowering. Granted, too, that some therapists exhibit hostility toward religious influences in a client's narrative, still many other therapists reverence the religious reality that helped to shape their client's interior life and recognize the emotional and spiritual health that religion has fostered. There is a need to further the partnership between religious and therapeutic professionals.

I have been profoundly aided by the insights and guidance that have come from clinical psychologists and psychiatrists, both those given to me in personal consultations and conversations and those derived from professional journals and books. On the other hand, I have been warmly welcomed as an active contributor to workshops, seminars, and courses

[14] An excellent example of what I mean is found in Ernest Kurtz and Katherine Ketchem, *The spirituality of imperfection, storytelling and the journey to wholeness* (New York: Bantam Books, 1992).

conducted by professional clinicians and/or therapists. In other words, there is no substitute for interaction among professionals.

At the heart of such interaction is the mutual concern religious professionals and therapists have for the men and women whom they attempt to serve. The focus on case studies strikes me as a valuable means towards fostering this interaction between religious professionals and therapists. If such forums, centering on case studies and with each participant bringing her or his expertise, experience, and compassion to the discussion, were encouraged, then the practical result would be a community of helpers bonding for the good of the wider community and for deeper competency within their own profession.

Spiritual guidance transcends religious denominations and invites cooperation and mutual learning. Similarly, psychological health transcends schools of psychology or psychiatry. Both professions are committed to help men and women to integrate their lives for their own happiness and for that of their families and communities. That they should find ways to bond in order to effect this integration is both an invitation and a challenge.

References

Carnes, P. (1983). *Out of the shadows: Understanding sexual addiction.* Minneapolis: CompCare.

Fitzmeyer, J. A. (1981, 1985). *The Gospel according to Luke: Introduction, translation and notes.* New York: Doubleday.

Gratton, C. (1993). *Spiritual direction. The new dictionary of Catholic spirituality.* Collegeville: Liturgical Press.

Gray, H. J. (1994). *Integrating human needs in religious formation. Review for Religious*, 53, 107-119.

Johnson, L.T. (1991). The Gospel of Luke, *Sacra Pagina Series #3*. Collegeville: Liturgical Press.

Ketchen, K. and Kurtz, E. (1992). *The spirituality of imperfection: Storytelling and the journey to wholeness.* New York: Bantam Books.

Leech, K. (1992). *The eye of the storm: Living spirituality in the real world.* New York: Harper.

May, G. (1982). *Will and spirit: A contemplative psychology.* New York: HarperCollins.

May, G. (1982). *Care of mind/Care of soul: A psychiatrist explores spiritual direction.* New York: Harper.

McDargh, H. J. (1982). *Psychology, relationship and contribution to spirituality, The new dictionary of Catholic spirituality.* Collegeville: Liturgical Press.

Real, T. (1997). *I don't want to talk about it: Overcoming the secret legacy of male depression.* New York: Scribner.

Reiser, W. (1997). *To hear God's Word, listen to the world: A liberation of spirituality.* New York/Mahwah: Paulist Press.

Ruffing, J. (1989). *Uncovering stories of faith: Spiritual direction and narrative.* New York/Mahwah: Paulist Press.

CHAPTER 12

Addiction and Recovery through Jewish Eyes

Carol Glass

> Rabbi Moshe Leib of Sassov once said: How to love people is something I learned from a peasant. He was sitting in an inn along with other peasants, drinking. For a long time he was silent like the rest, but soon he asked the one sitting next to him: "Tell me, do you love me or don't you love me?" The other replied: "I love you very much." But the first replied: "You say that you love me, but you do not know what I need. If you really loved me you would know." The other had not a word to say to this, and the peasant who had posed the question fell silent again. But I understood. To know the needs of people, and to bear the burden of their struggle—that is the true love of humanity. (adapted from Martin Buber *Tales of the Hasidim—Later Masters)*

It is a great irony that this profound Jewish lesson about loving and understanding others is learned from people who are (over)drinking at a tavern. For it is only within recent times that the Jewish community has even been willing to admit that there *are* Jewish alcoholics, and it has been an equally slow process for the community to reach out and try to love and understand the burdens of Jews affected by addiction to alcohol and other chemical substances. Over the years, this long legacy of denial among Jews has resulted in unnecessary pain, heartache, and a great deal of alienation from Judaism by those suffering from addiction. It has also served to prevent some suffering Jews from seeking or accepting appropriate help for themselves or their loved ones. Finally, it has presented a stumbling block for Jewish alcoholics and addicts who have wanted to embrace their spiritual heritage as a step in their recovery process.[1]

A Shikkur Is a Goy

The myth of Jewish immunity from addiction is typified by the well-known Yiddish adage "A Shikkur is a Goy"—one who is a drunk is a non-Jew. From this we learn that alcoholism is seen as a problem that lies outside the Jewish community. This kind of thinking, which was common "wisdom" among Jews until only a decade or two ago, is not only incorrect and *un*wise, it is actually quite damaging to individuals who have needed understanding and help, rather than anger and rejection. Imagine the intense shame that has been felt by Jews who have gotten the message from this "wisdom" and the thinking it represents, that they are considered less than full Jews because of their addiction. Imagine their identity confusion over this issue, when they have understood a Yiddish proverb to declare that one could not be both a Jew and an alcoholic; and imagine their guilt and anger over not being able to find acknowledgement and help from within their own culture. Many recovering Jews now report with great pain how, in the past, they hid their addiction from their families and friends because they feared being run out of the community if they openly admitted to their "other" identity. A number of these same Jews, in fact, have true stories to tell about being chastised and chased out of counseling sessions—and even all the way down the street—by an ignorant or threatened rabbi, who refused to accept what was being said when the subject of alcohol or other drug dependency came up. Others sadly report that when they turned to the organized Jewish community for help with their addiction, their pleas fell on deaf or immobilized ears.

The following true story, told in 1986 by Rabbi Abraham J. Twerski, poignantly demonstrates the unfortunate consequences of this disbelief and ignorance:

> At a weekend retreat for Jewish alcoholics, chemically dependent people, and their family members, a mother declared: "For whatever I did or failed to do which contributed to my daughter's alcoholism problem, I will always bear the responsibility and perhaps the guilt. But the fact that my daughter is now a devout Catholic and has left the faith of her family, for that I hold the rabbinate responsible. It is not as though she was primarily attracted to another religion, but rather by default of the Jewish resources." The mother went on to explain, "My daughter was an excellent student, and, when her grades began to drop, we knew something had to be wrong. We eventually discovered she was drinking too

[1] It would not surprise this author if Jews reading this story over the years have assumed that the "peasants" must have been non-Jews. While that interpretation sends an important message that Jews learn from those outside the fold, it simultaneously reinforces a false stereotype that has resulted in Jewish suffering and even death over the years.

> much. When she failed her courses, she sought help for her problem in an alcoholism clinic. She told her counselor that she felt spiritually empty, and he advised her to see a rabbi. The rabbi she consulted admonished her to control her drinking, and told her that it was a disgrace for a Jew to drink excessively. The rabbi offered no response to her feelings of spiritual bankruptcy.
>
> "Her counselor then told her of a priest who was knowledgeable in alcohol problems. She began to see this priest, and progressed well in her recovery. She is now happily married, eight years sober, and a devout Catholic." This is a serious indictment, but one which I believe has great validity. Nowhere in the years of my training to become a rabbi was I taught anything about alcoholism, nor do I recall any attention given to the problem either in rabbinic journals or at conventions.

This persistent inattention and denial reflects a wish among Jews to be a people without flaws, without the "problems" of other nations. As Rabbi Susan Berman (1988) has written, this wish

> arose for practical reasons. Our ancestors, as well as our own parents, often lived in fear of the more virulent [*sic*] forms of antisemitism. They were people (and some of us have had the same experience ourselves) who knew what it meant to see Jews suffer for the simple reason that they were Jews. Any negative characteristic that might be used against the Jews was greatly feared. In this manner our "self-protective" myths [such as the Jewish immunity from addiction] arose. It was as if it were safer to deny problems than to risk retribution. We [also] believed that Jewish men did not beat their wives, that there was no such thing as a Jewish homosexual or lesbian, etc. Our community assumptions taught us that to be a Jew seemingly granted a person immunity.

Unfortunately, it is only in retrospect that we see how this need to see Jews as unblemished from the outside, and therefore less vulnerable, has worked against Jewish efforts to strengthen the community on the inside.

Important Changes

Things began to change in the 1970s. In 1975, concerned Jewish professionals in the New York City area were awakened to the reality that Jewish alcoholics *do* exist when Rabbi Sheldon Zimmerman, then the spiritual leader of Central Synagogue in Manhattan, broke the news that the Alcoholics Anonymous groups in his synagogue consisted of 60 percent Jews. Armed with this evidence, which affirmed their informal observations that addiction *was* a Jewish issue, Rabbi Isaac Trainin, then the Director of the Department on Religious Affairs of the Federation of Jewish Philanthropies of New York, along with Rabbi Zimmerman and others, established the first Task Force on Alcoholism in the Jewish Community. Looking back on the Task Force's early efforts to educate the organized Jewish community, Rabbi Trainin has reflected:

> A questionnaire was sent to the entire New York rabbinate (close to 1,000) and to our Federation agencies. It was understandable that practically no rabbi knew of the problem, since an alcoholic would seldom go to a rabbi. [Yet] at that time, it was puzzling to us that our family agencies were [also] unaware of the problem. However, we should not have been surprised. In the late '50's it was made known to me by several Catholic priests that Jewish teenagers and young adults were seriously engaged in drug addiction. Then, too, a questionnaire to the rabbinate revealed nothing. Not one of our Federation agencies knew a thing about drug addiction among Jews...[In both cases] there was simply a total disbelief that this problem affected the Jewish community. The first conference held on the subject (of alcoholism in the Jewish community) aimed primarily at rabbis, attracted exactly nine rabbis. (quoted in Levy, 1986)

Rabbi Trainin continued his reflection adding that: "the denial syndrome among our Orthodox Jews is even stronger than among the rest of the Jewish community...I still recall the young Hassidic lady [*sic*] who attended a meeting of our Task Force in 1982, asking for help in obtaining space in a Brooklyn synagogue for an AA group. She and other alcoholics (all Hassidic) had visited close to fifty Orthodox synagogues in Brooklyn, not one of which would make space available. They were ashamed, the young lady pointed out, that it would be a reflection on the synagogue to admit that there were not only Jewish alcoholics, but alcoholics among Traditional Jews." (Levy, 1986)

In the two-plus decades since the Task Force on Alcoholism was established, there has been slow but steady progress across the denominational spectrum. For the most part, the organized Jewish community has acknowledged the incidence of alcoholism and addiction within our ranks. This has enabled affected Jews and their significant others to speak out, thereby breaking the denial syndrome. In 1982, in recognition of the complex nature of addiction and the frequency of dual dependency, the task forces on alcoholism and on drug addiction were fused into a single entity, called the Task Force on Addictions in the Jewish Community. Its mission was to deal with the reality of all chemical dependency in the Jewish community.

In terms of community awareness, Jewish professionals from clergy to youth workers are pursuing various levels of education and training related to addiction recognition, referral, and treatment. Some have become specialists in addiction counseling. Others have offered workshops and discussion groups in synagogues, Jewish schools, and at Jewish youth gatherings. In addition, regional and national conferences relating to addiction and healing have become popular sources of continuing education for Jewish professionals.

Within the last several years, there has been a marked increase in the quantity of published resources about addiction and Jews. Books, school curricula, Jewish spiritual guides, Jewish versions of "*One Day At a Time*" (a popular daily meditation book of readings and prayers), and other materials are available from a variety of publishers. Most Judaica stores or general bookstores with a well-stocked spirituality section are good places to begin browsing. In a number of communities, there are informal study groups and support groups for Jewish addicts and those in recovery, as well as for Jewish professionals who may be interested. Twelve Step meetings are being held in synagogues and other institutions across the country. Meetings held in communities with significant Jewish populations now vary portions of the Twelve Step ritual so that it is more inclusive of Jewish experience. For example, the Serenity Prayer or the *Shema* (a Jewish prayer excerpted from parts of the Pentateuch) is sometimes recited in place of the Lord's Prayer.

JACS

The most important development, however, in breaking the denial syndrome among Jews, and in creating support for Jews in recovery, was the 1980 establishment of the JACS Foundation. JACS stands for Jewish Alcoholics, Chemically dependent persons, and Significant others. Born of a concern among Jewish leaders and committed recovering Jews, JACS is an organization dedicated to the needs of chemically dependent Jews and their loved ones. While there is a national JACS office with a small salaried staff, the heart of the work is done by JACS volunteers on the local and regional level.

In 1985 a network of JACS groups from around the country developed a mission statement to express commonality of purpose, even as individual groups varied in how they carried out the mission. The statement declared:

> A JACS group is an autonomous, nonprofit, volunteer membership organization with the threefold purpose of:
>
> 1. providing spiritual and communal support for addicted Jews and their families;
> 2. serving as a resource center and information exchange;
> 3. conducting community outreach and education.
>
> A local JACS group supports existing Twelve-Step programs, but is not a substitute for them. Rather, JACS supplements and complements existing self-help programs and attempts to assist Jews and their families in integrating Jewish traditions and heritage with the recovery process.

Perhaps the most engaging work of JACS, at least in the initial years, was its sponsorship, along with the Task Force on Alcoholism in the Jewish Community, of weekend retreats for recovering Jewish alcoholics, drug-dependent persons, and family members. These semiannual gatherings, which continue today, have grown in size and impact over the years. They bring together the entire spectrum of suffering and recovering Jews to share common concerns including isolation from the spiritual nature of their Jewish heritage, and ignorance and denial of their disease by religious and other leaders. The retreats offer the possibility of Jewish study, Jewish worship, and contact with supportive Jewish leaders who often are recovering persons themselves. For many, these retreats are the first step back into a Jewish setting after years of avoidance and anger. They can be important turning points for Jewish addicts and their family members.

Spiritual Issues

Despite the significant progress in community attitudes and awareness, organizational change, and institutional support described above, a troubling degree of shame, and its accompanying anger and identity confusion, persisted among Jewish addicts well into the 1980s. This shame led those of us working to help Jews affected by addiction to speculate about the existence of an additional factor in the Jewish experience of addiction and recovery.

Ironically, as it became more acceptable to talk about Twelve Step meetings, AA, and recovery, and as better-informed Jewish leaders encouraged Jews to make use of Twelve Step programs, the Jews who attended those very programs began to reveal strong feelings of discomfort connected to their involvement. Their discomfort stemmed from concern that the beliefs and principles of the Twelve Steps were Christian in orientation and therefore in conflict with the tenets of Judaism and Jewish spiritual practice. These Jews worried that the Steps might be "forbidden" to Jews. Some asked if they were "bad" Jews for participating in AA and related programs. Others claimed that they felt compelled to choose between their religion and their desire to survive. Understandably, many of those concerned chose survival and went to Twelve Step meetings while hiding their Jewishness. And in some cases, they abandoned their Judaism altogether.

Several factors contributed to the Jewish impression that Twelve Step programs are "Christian." First of all, most meetings took place in churches; few were held on Jewish premises. Secondly, meetings frequently ended with The Lord's Prayer, and often participants were encouraged to kneel in prayer and to offer personal, spontaneous prayers at home. Finally, the actual wording of the Steps, and the ideology it implied, troubled many Jews. It read to them as Christian theology. It was necessary then, as it still is today, to clarify for all recovering Jews and those who would offer them counsel that Jews can feel comfortable participating in Twelve Step programs.

Rabbi Susan Berman (1988) has written an excellent article on this topic entitled, *"Judaism, Jewishness and recovery: Bridging the gap."* I will summarize the main points here.

First of all, the text of The Lord's Prayer has so many parallels in Jewish sacred literature that many claim this prayer was Jewish in its original inception. Certainly, there is nothing in the wording of the prayer that is forbidden for a Jew to say. What *is* problematic for Jews is that The Lord's Prayer has come to be associated with Christianity and it is known today as part of the Christian liturgy. While there are other prayers that might be more palatable to Jews to recite at meetings, there really is nothing in Judaism prohibiting its recitation. As Rabbi Berman has stated: "The need for meetings and fellowship should override any squeamishness. The purpose of AA is to save lives…"[2]

Second, with regard to the issue of personal or spontaneous prayer, it is true that Jews as a community have most often prayed from a fixed liturgical text. It is also true, however, that Jewish law considers prayers of the heart, offered honestly and with sincere *Kavanah* or intention, to be valid and worthy. The language of the prayers, their form, and their length are of far less importance than the *Kavanah.*

The other concern regarding the form of prayer is the question of the permissibility for Jews to kneel in prayer. First of all, this is not a requirement of the Twelve Step fellowships. Today, Jews do not kneel when praying (the exception being specific moments when the cantor kneels during Jewish High Holy Day Services). In contrast, there have been historic periods when Jews did kneel during prayer. Jews ceased praying on their knees, however, as a way to differentiate themselves from Christians, the result being that this Twelve Step tradition may have more than the usual awkwardness for Jews to whom it is recommended.

Finally, we come to the issue of the seeming Christian content of the Steps themselves. This is an important issue to explore in some detail. As we shall see, Twelve Step ideology clearly echoes established beliefs found in mainstream Jewish liturgy and thought. Its step-by-step process for altering addictive behavior, thereby bringing about a return to sobriety and right living, bears a striking resemblance to the Jewish step-by-step method for changing so-called "sinful" behavior and initiating a return to Jewish ethical living.

Theology of sin and repentance

We begin by looking at the Jewish concept of sin. The Hebrew word for sin is *chet*, a word derived from a term in archery meaning "to miss the mark." *Chet* refers to behavior which is off-center or off-target. Judaism teaches that each of us is born with a pure soul and that when we transgress, we deviate from this basic core; that is, we behave in a way that is missing the mark. In broader terms, Judaism regards each person as essentially

[2] For more on this subject see Cohen, 1956.

good, while acknowledging that sometimes individuals behave in ways that distance them from that goodness. At those times it is the misguided behavior (or sin) that is judged as in need of change, not the essential worth of the human being involved. The Jewish method for letting go of this unwanted behavior and returning to ethical living is a step-by-step process known as *Teshuvah* , or "repentance." Literally, *Teshuvah* means "the process of return," and Jewish tradition teaches that it involves a return to a complete relationship with God as well as a return to the whole self. It is accomplished by a return to centered, ethical living. In traditional Jewish terms, this means a return to faith and the observance of the *Mitzvot,* or "commandments," as they are spelled out in the Hebrew Bible and Jewish interpretive literature.

The American Medical Association, of course, has long defined alcoholism as a disease. Interestingly, Judaism recognizes sin as a disease, a disease of the spirit. Employing the technique of Biblical textual parallelism, Rabbi Joseph B. Soloveitchik, a leading Jewish scholar of the twentieth century, has cited the verse "God forgives all your iniquity, heals all your diseases" (Psalm 103:3) as a proof text for the idea that Judaism regards sin as an illness and repentance as the healing cure. "The idea is clear: sin is an abnormal phenomenon," writes Rabbi Soloveitchik. "The healthy person living a normal life, does not fall into the ways of sin. Sin constitutes a sort of spiritual pathology, just as many diseases of the flesh constitute a physical pathology." Along the same lines, Maimonides, a twelfth-century Jewish philosopher, referred to those who stray from the "good path" as *cholei n'fashot,* that is, "people of sick spirit."

Clearly then, there are strong similarities between the phenomenon of addiction and the Jewish view of improper conduct. They are both considered diseases, and their respective "cures" are achieved by a step-by-step process which incorporates personal responsibility and faith in a Higher Power. Since the stated goal of both systems is to discard unhealthy behavior, it appears that the discomfort some Jews have had with the Twelve Steps is based on something else.

In 1984, I conducted some research which led me to the conclusion that the problem lay in the differences of language and style between the two systems, Judaism and the Twelve Steps. To eliminate these variables, I constructed a "translation grammar," a method used by scholars to restate cultural disparities in neutral language. To see how this relates to our discussion, first consider the lists that follow:

Maimonides

The Laws of Repentance

A. Confession before God which includes:
  (1) Naming the specific sin.
  (2) Statement of regret at having sinned.
  (3) Expression of shame felt at having sinned.
  (4) Pledge not to repeat the same sin.

B. Abandonment of sin.
C. Change of thought.
D. Change of name.
E. Supplication to God.
F. Public confession (is praiseworthy).
G. Acknowledgement of your sins on this and the following *Yom Kippur*.
H. Reparations (compensation) for sins against other people.
I. Apology to victims of the sin.
J. Self-restraint from repeating the sin when the opportunity to do so presents itself.

Rabbenu Yonah of Gerona

The Gates of Repentance

I. Regret for having committed the sin.
II. Forsaking the sin.
III. Experience sorrow over the transgression.
IV. Bodily suffering in relation to the sin.
V. Worry over the punishment for the transgression.
VI. Feel shame at having transgressed before God.
VII. Behave with humility (speak in a low voice…).
VIII. Have a humble attitude.
IX. Break the physical desire to commit the sin.
X. Compensation (in actions) to prevent recurrence of sin.
XI. Moral inventory.
XII. Consider the punishment from God and the consequences of sin.
XIII. Minor transgressions as equivalent to major ones.
XIV. Confession.
XV. Pray for forgiveness.
XVI. Reparations (monetary, apology, request forgiveness, confession).
XVII. Pursue acts of loving-kindness and truth.
XVIII. Keep your sin before you always.
XIX. Fight off your evil inclination. Don't give in to sin when the desire is strong.
XX. Turn others away from transgression.

These are two versions of the prescribed way for a Jew to do *Teshuvah* (repentance), that is, the method for Jews to change and redress unethical behavior, thereby achieving a return to acceptable conduct and spiritual wholeness.

Though the sages who composed the above lists wrote them centuries ago, their work suggests a guided spiritual journey that is nearly identical to the spiritual journey suggested by the Twelve Steps. Employing the translation grammar method, the similarities between *Teshuvah* and AA's Steps become apparent, as seen when the next two lists are put side by side (refer to the previous lists for a full understanding):

The Twelve Steps of Alcoholics Anonymous

1. We admitted we were powerless over alcohol—that our lives had become unmanageable.
2. Came to believe that a Power greater than ourselves could restore us to sanity.
3. Made a decision to turn our will and our lives over to the care of God as we understood Him.
4. Made a searching and fearless moral inventory of ourselves.
5. Admitted to God, to ourselves, and to another human being the exact nature of our wrongs.
6. Were entirely ready to have God remove all these defects of character.
7. Humbly asked Him to remove all our shortcomings.
8. Made a list of all persons we had harmed and became willing to make amends to them all.
9. Made direct amends to such people wherever possible, except when to do so would injure them or others.
10. Continued to take personal inventory and when we were wrong promptly admitted it.
11. Sought through prayer and meditation to improve our conscious contact with God as we understood Him, praying only for knowledge of His will for us and the power to carry that out.
12. Having had a spiritual awakening as the result of these steps, we tried to carry this message to alcoholics and to practice these principles in all our affairs.

Generic steps for change

The three categories following each generic step represent the number or letter of the corresponding steps of AA (Arabic numerals), the steps of *Teshuvah* according to Maimonides (capital letters), or the steps of *Teshuvah* by Rabbenu Yonah (Roman numerals). See preceding lists for specifics.

It is evident that the Twelve Steps and the concept of *Teshuvah* are spiritually as well as tactically compatible. Both offer directives for behavioral improvement. Both include reliance on God (or a Higher Power), the taking of a moral inventory, confession to others and to God, appropriate reparations, and evidence of changed behavior. Both systems also imply that unacceptable behavior is the result of spiritual emptiness.

Steps 3, 6, 7 are those most likely to give Jews some difficulty. Taken literally, they seem to advocate the relinquishing of free will and the abdication of personal responsibility for directing one's life. These are concepts which Jews associate with Christianity, while passionately denying a place for them within the tenets of Judaism.(Similar misgivings arise among women and minorties, that is, other groups with an awareness of oppression. See Smith and Seymour, chapter 5, and Kasl's chapter 6.) From this point of view, it is easy to see how one might conclude that the Steps are

GENERIC STEPS	AA STEPS	MAIMONIDES	RABBENU YONAH
THE GREAT AWAKENING	1	A	III, V, VI, XII
BECOME A BELIEVER	2	Rabbinic Judaism assumes this step to be a given.	Rabbinic Judaism assumes this step to be a given.
TURNING TO A HIGHER POWER	3	F	VII
MORAL INVENTORY	4	A, H	XI
ADMITTING OUR WRONGS TO GOD AND OTHERS	5	A, G	XIV
PRAYING FOR GOD'S FORGIVENESS	7	A, F	VIII, XV
ACKNOWLEDGING THOSE WE HAVE HARMED AND PREPARING TO FACE THEM	8	I	XVI
REPARATIONS	9	J	X, XVI
CONTINUING THE MORAL INVENTORY	10	H, K	IV, XV, XVIII, XIX
MAINTAINING THE SPIRITUAL PATH	11	E, H, K	IV, XV, XVIII, XIX
SPREADING THE WORD	12		XX

not consistent with Jewish values. This reasoning could lead to the assumption that the Twelve Steps are not appropriate for Jews. Such language, however, is not to be taken at face value. It is simply one way of stating the more generalized idea that faith in a Power beyond the self can lead to behavioral transformation.

Biblical reflections

Concepts in the Twelve Steps *are* found throughout Jewish tradition, though the phrasing may be quite different. Take, for example, the following excerpt from traditional Jewish High Holy Day liturgy: "May it be Your will, my God and God of my ancestors, that I sin no more. In Your abundant mercy cleanse the sins I have committed against You." Another example, from Psalm 51, can be found in both liberal and traditional prayer books: "Hide Your face from my sins; blot out all my iniquities. Create in me a clean heart, O God; and put a new and right spirit in me...Do not cast me out away from Your presence, or take Your holy spirit away from me." Or, more dramatically, this selection from Psalm 116: "I suffered distress and anguish. Then I called on the Name of the LORD: 'O LORD, I pray, save my life!'"

In these passages the speaker first implores God to help change undesirable behavior. The speaker then asks that God take control and assert his divine will to alter the situation. What I have understood is that the authors of the Twelve Steps no more intended such phrases as "turning our will over to the care of God" and "ask God to remove our shortcomings" to be taken literally, than Jews take their requests for God to "blot out sins" or "refrain from taking the holy spirit away." What we have in the Twelve Steps and in Teshuvah are two different systems of symbolic language used to express the common idea that *improvement of behavior comes about by the inclusion of a God in one's life*. A moving section in the book of Leviticus (see below) teaches the same lesson in another way. In so doing, it expresses the fundamentals of Jewish spirituality, and at the same time provides a message that echoes the lesson of the Twelve Steps.

The essence of Jewish Biblical spirituality proclaims that a loving God exists, who awaits the Israelites' willingness to acknowledge that human beings are ultimately not in control. This God is anxious to be a partner with people in creating a society where individuals forgo the drive to be overly independent, choosing instead to live interdependently with each other, and consciously dependent on God. This dependency is made manifest through the commitment to live by the Mitzvot (Commandments). The Mitzvot, in turn, symbolize acceptance of living with moral and ritual limitations.

As Leviticus 26 focuses on the process of human change, it gives us insight into how some people can move from a state of personal chaos and utter despair to a state of life that is meaningful and grounded in a covenantal relationship with God. According to the text, that change begins with an awareness of a living God in one's life.

With the implicit acknowledgment that people are stubborn and reluctant to surrender control or independence, God first predicts (Leviticus 26:14ff) that an obstinate Israelite nation will stray further and further from the covenant, that is, they will fail to take the Mitzvot seriously and will neglect their observance. As they fail to keep the Mitzvot, they will, according to the text, fall deeper and deeper into a morass and into spiritual despair. Ultimately, they will hit rock bottom, becoming "fainthearted," powerless, and homeless. But, the purpose of this prediction was not to frighten or intimidate people, but rather, to give them hope for the future; and so there is more.

"If then their uncircumised heart is humbled and they make amends for their iniquity, then will I remember my covenant with Jacob." (Lev. 26:41). This humbling or opening of the heart shall lead to a restored life, one in covenant with God once again. The text is teaching us that when a people reaches the lowest point possible, ascent can only begin with a change of heart. *K'niat HaLev,* the humbling of the heart, is a process of opening oneself to God. For biblical Israel, this meant coming to the realization that life without Mitzvot was difficult and lonely, that it had no purpose and led to self-destruction as it drew the nation further and further from a peaceful life in the promised land. What Israel did in humbling her heart was to confront the meaninglessness of life without God, a life symbolized by the absence of the observance of Mitzvot. Israel came to *K'niat HaLev* by looking hard at her own limitations, her human failings, and by admitting that she couldn't "go it alone" forever. Israel acknowledged that she needed God's guidance. Israel also realized that she needed healing. She found it in making a commitment to the Mitzvot, as a way of welcoming God back into her life.

Note how the text continues by indicating the rewards of being open to God's presence: "Yet, even when they are still in the land of their enemies, I will not reject or spurn them so as to destroy them…I am Adonai their God, who freed them from the land of Egypt" (v. 44). When Israel will open her heart to hear God's voice, she will not be alone anymore. When she reclaims the Mitzvot as her own, even if only "one step at a time," her life will start to have new meaning.

Conclusion

When a person struggling with addiction and the attendant issues of control and dependency can reach the point of beginning to 'work the Steps'—when s/he can let in the notion that a Higher Power can offer the strength needed to overcome—this is *K'niat HaLev,* the humbling of the hardened heart. This is the essence of Jewish spirituality, and the beginning of recovery for the addict. In this is confirmation that The Holy One who took the Israelites out of Egypt, the Higher Power who can bring alcoholics and addicts from despair to sobriety, is available to anyone, Jew or non-Jew, searching for the means to a life of serenity and direction.

References

Berman, S. (1988). Judaism, Jewishness and recovery: Bridging the gap. *JACS Journal*, 5(1), 3ff. [426 West 58th St., New York, N.Y.].

Buber, M. (1948). *Tales of the Hasidim: The later masters.* New York: Schocken Books.

Cohen, B. D. (1956). *Jacob's well: Some Jewish sources and parallels to the Sermon on the Mount.* New York: Bookman Associates.

Levy, S. J. (1986). *Addictions in the Jewish community.* New York: Federation of Jewish Philanthropies of New York, Inc. [130 East 59th St., New York, NY 10022].

Twerski, Abraham J. (1986). *The truth about chemical dependency and Jews.* Gateway Rehabilitation Center, pamphlet no. 8, 1–2.

Part Five

Conclusion and Reflection

CHAPTER 13

Addiction and Spirituality: a Clinical-Theological Reflection

Oliver J. Morgan

and Merle R. Jordan

And oftentimes,
To win us to our harm,
The instruments of darkness tell us truths,
win us with honest trifles...
To betray us in deepest consequences.
—Shakespeare, *Macbeth*

In this concluding chapter, our task is to reflect theologically on some issues involved in studying addiction and spirituality as well as to reflect on the ideas and suggestions offered by the authors in this volume. Both of us are ordained pastors, trained theologically to examine human experience with an eye toward the deeper issues it reveals. Both of us are also clinical counselors, trained to work in partnership with human persons as they struggle with personal difficulties, relationships, and issues of meaning in their lives.

Don Browning (1987, 1975), one of the important voices in pastoral care and practical theology today, has alerted us all to the fact that underneath every theory of human behavior is a theological anthropology, that is, a theology about God and God's interactions with human beings, as well as a theology about who (and whose) human beings are. Addiction and recovery are all about human behavior.

As we have seen throughout this book, there are many ways to address these two issues; biological, psychological, systemic, sociocultural, and narrative theories are all valuable in this task. We have seen authors from different theoretical perspectives and points of view try to address the notion of spirituality and its relation to addiction and recovery, using the scientific, clinical, and religious resources at their command.

However, a book like this must also try to address the phenomena of addiction and recovery, as well as spirituality and its relation to these two phenomena, from an *explicitly theological* point of view (Mercadante, 1996). As "clinical theologians" we will try to address this task.[1]

Key Themes

Using the insights of the contributors in this book as well as other sources, we will sketch below some key themes for developing a pastoral theology of addiction and recovery. The ideas developed below do not comprise a fully developed practical theological statement. However, we believe that any theology of addiction and recovery must addres: (a) notions of grace, creation, finitude, and selfhood that are part of the human situation; (b) a basic spiritual and theological understanding of addiction; (c) recovery and the transformation of self; and (d) the role of God in the recovery process.

1. The human condition

We suggest that human existence is characterized by (at least) five overarching domains.

A. All of us swim in an ocean of *grace*. The great Catholic theologian, Karl Rahner, describes the essence of humanity in this way: "The capacity for the God of self-bestowing personal Love is the central and abiding existential of man [*sic*] as he really is" (1974, p. 312). This is an astounding statement. What is *most basic* to human beings, Rahner says, is the capacity for God's gift of self as Love.

> Everything else exists so that this one thing might be: the eternal miracle of infinite Love. And so God makes a creature whom he can love: He creates man [*sic*]. He creates him in such a way that he can receive this Love, which is God himself, that he can and must

[1] The term "clinical theologian" has been used by a number of pastoral psychologists and practical theologians, including Jordan (1986) and Lake (1987); it is similar to the term "theologian of care" used by Schlauch (1995). Clinical theologians orient and interpret their work and ministry primarily through theological reflection, as the fundamental ground for their identity, commitments, authorization and worldview. They work and think clinically; they interpret theologically. They "live on the bridge" of care, bringing to bear on complex human problems multiple disciplines and languages, multiple foundation texts and lived experiences, what some have called "multiple citizenships" (Schlauch, 1995). Their contribution is to lift up the explicitly theological roots and meanings of clinical and ministerial work, so that these can be in true dialogue, a "collaborative conversation" with clinical and other contemporary sciences.

at the same time accept it for what it is: the ever astounding wonder, the unexpected, unexacted gift. (Rahner, 1974, p. 310)

Rahner's theology then goes on to explain that God wishes to give the gift of God's own life and love, and so creates humans capable of receiving Love and to be "partners" in experiencing and accepting (or rejecting!) it. And, because of God's desire, humans are "always addressed and claimed by this Love" (Rahner, 1974, p. 311); nothing can change this fact of human life.

Christian theology begins with such an astounding statement about God, that is, it begins with a theology of grace. It is, from a theological point of view, what is most basic about us. And yet the *experience* of it can be hidden and obscured. Addiction has the power to do that. Yet many recovering people also insist that it is the God of grace who restores them to health and wholeness, that is the catalyst for renewed loving.

Many of the chapters in this book understand love, or blessedness, or quality relationships, or connectedness as essential to recovery, understood as a return to our true humanity. Implicitly (and sometimes explicitly), they are presuming such a theology of grace.

B. All of us are created in the *image of God*. This brings us to the essential dignity of human beings made "in the image of God" (Genesis 1: 26–27 and 9:6). The Judeo-Christian tradition affirms that persons have inherent worth and dignity before God, that persons are called into fullness of life and deepening relationship with God, with one another, and with all creation. The *imago Dei*, that divine image that is basic to each human person as created by God, is not a substance or entity, but rather a *relation* that specifies the peculiarly human vocation of responsible caring for one another and for all of creation (Patton, 1993), or alternatively a *call to full communion* with God and all creation (Kopas, 1994).

Where previous classical Western models of Christian theology emphasized human rationality as the seat of the image of God in humans (we will see in the next section that this position is still important to maintain), more contemporary models are reclaiming a complementary Eastern Christian anthropology that sees the capacity for relationality, communion, and solidarity among persons and with all creation as the essence of the *imago Dei*.[2]

This central fact of human created existence must be accounted for in any theological anthropology. It is also crucial in understanding the dynamics of addiction and recovery. One of the hallmark traits of addiction is its assault, not only on the ability of an individual to reason and discern

[2] As "ecological theology" is guided by themes of communion and solidarity, themes that are underexplored yet (potentially) seminal for a modern theology of addiction and recovery. Within this newer framework questions of stewardship, the "right relations" regarding creatures (a notion that arises in several important AA publications), and human creation as imago Dei need not rely on an older anthropology that is characterized by sovereignty, intellect, and hierarchy. Rather, themes of collaboration, relationality, and sustaining fellowship may be brought to the fore.

right attitudes and behavior, but also its powerful negative impact on all of the addict's important relationships, including the relationship with God.[3] As a number of the chapters in this book suggest, and as a number of studies of recovery clearly indicate, it is the return of the capacity for full human relatedness that is one of the hallmarks of quality recovery over time.[4]

C. All of us are embedded in a world of *creatures*. Created ourselves, we are born deeply connected to the world of created things. Here the viewpoints of feminist and ecological theologies, emphasizing connectedness, relationship, and solidarity, are also important.[5]

In biblical terms the ultimate context for human living is the essential goodness of all created things, of creation as a whole (Genesis 1 and Psalm 104). God intends that all humans live in harmonious relationship with creation (Kopas, 1994; Patton, 1993). The biblical-theological term for this harmony in creation is *Shalom* (Morgan, *in press a*).

Humanity is entrusted with the care of creation, and persons are to act as "responsible stewards" of this gift of God (Patton, 1993). Humans are to exercise caring relationship toward the whole of creation. The cooperation of human and divine care, that is "responsible stewardship," maintains creation's *Shalom*.

Thus, all created things are ready-to-hand for our use and potential misuse. Failure of stewardship consists of a "denial of responsible relationship." it is to become, like Adam and Eve, "estranged from a proper relationship to their Creator and the creation" (Patton, 1993, 162). Humans are understood as capable of such abuse; *Shalom* can be injured or destroyed by misuse of God's creation. Whenever there is harm to God's creatures, to one's neighbors, injury to the community, or activities that block communication with the Creator, creation's *Shalom* is tarnished.[6]

Part of good stewardship is understanding that each creature has its own nature. When used as God intends, the creature brings beneficial results; however, when used incorrectly, as in chemical abuse or addiction,

---

Moltmann (1993, pp. 215–243). points out that the biblical notion of *imago Dei*, while viewed in terms of *rationality* among the Western fathers (Augustine and Aquinas, for example), could also be viewed as pointing more toward *relationality* on the model of the inner fellowship of the Trinity, as Orthodox theologians (for example, Gregory of Nazianzus) often did. In view of chemical use and misuse, this difference of approach may help to provide a new theological language and approach to issues of Christian lifestyle and prevention based on sustaining and rightly-ordered relations. This relational view may help to complement the theology of *imago Dei* based on the rational nature of human persons, and will be more consonant with modern sensibilities.

[3] For more extensive discussion of these issues from a Catholic and biblical theological point of view, see Morgan (*in press a & b*).

[4] Chapters 3 (Jampolsky), 6 (Kasl), 7 (Albers), and 8 (Larsen) in particular address this theme. For a brief survey of qualitative studies of recovery and their attention to themes of relationship and connectedness, see chapter 1 (Morgan).

[5] A number of important publications are appearing in these two areas of theology, too many to cite fully. The interested reader may wish to consult the following authors and works as a way to begin studying these areas: Boff, 1995; Johnson, 1993; Moltman, 1997; Ruether, 1992.

[6] For an extended discussion of these themes, see Morgan *(in press a)*.

creatures can be disruptive. Wise stewards understand the nature of the substances they use and their impact on self, others, and the rest of the created order. Thus, human beings, intended by God to be responsible stewards, were given intelligence, freedom, and the capacity for loving care in order to understand the nature and uses of created things, and to choose the path of wise stewardship.

These essential elements of human existence—grace, *imago Dei* ,and creaturehood—are part of a fundamental unity in theological anthropology. In addiction, we "forget" or deny this unity; in recovery, there is a reclaiming of the sense of connectedness and gracious existence that is our birthright.

D. All of us live in a context of *finitude*. Ernest Becker's *Denial of death* (1973) and Friedman's *To deny our nothingness* (1967) describe this context well in contemporary terms. Philosophers and theologians like Heidegger (1962), Kierkegaard (1944), Tillich (1952), and Moore (1977) have also described this phenomenon.

Early in human development, we experience the limits of our situation. We experience "impaired control" vis-a-vis our bodily functions and, in later development, learn more deeply about it in our relationships. We face the ultimate limit in the serious illness or death of those we love, and experience the rumblings of finitude in our own aging and confrontation with mortality. The addict whose physician confronts him with "keep drinking and you'll be dead in six months" also faces the finite limits of existence.

This is all part of what Doweiko (chapter 2) describes as the "pain of living" that we experience from early caretaking and in later living, but which is rooted in our created nature as finite beings. Charlotte Kasl's story (chapter 6) eloquently describes her own brushes with finitude as part of her life journey.

Another experience of finitude comes in the seldom-discussed sense of personal restlessness. Saint Augustine was correct: Created for God, our hearts are restless until they rest in God. Yet this restlessness creates an anxiety at the core of existence. Doweiko, in chapter 2, utilizes a similar notion in speaking of a "divine discontent" as part of the human situation. He relates it to our "self-awareness" and experience of existential isolation. Other chapters (Jampolsky, chapter 3; Albers, chapter 7; Larsen, Chapter 8) speak of the alienation and estrangement that we all experience at times.

A sense of limits, restlessness, and estrangement are all part of the human situation.

E. All of us struggle with *self*. Both psychologically and spiritually, the core human struggle for growth and integrity might be described as grounding and expanding the self; this has to do with overcoming narcissism and grace-fully wrestling with sin (Moore, 1977; see also Albers, chapter 7; Brakeman, chapter 10; and Glass, chapter 12).

In the lives of addicts, this struggle—at least in part—takes chemical or process form. Addicts struggle with self in similar, yet different, ways from the struggle that is inherent to us all. This is one of the reasons why a stance of "moralism" in dealing with addiction so much misses the mark. Moralism is a way of trying to distance ourselves from addicts, creating a "them" over against "us." Yet, the truth is that we *ALL* struggle with self.[7]

These last characteristics of human existence—finitude, restlessness, and the struggle with self—are "vulnerabilities" rooted in the human condition. They create anxiety and can easily become sources of depression.[8] They form the background for all of human living; they also form the canvas on which the drama of addiction and recovery is painted.

A basic question posed by human living is: *How shall we cope with the restlessness, finitude, and struggle with self?* Each of these elements of the human condition bring anxiety with them.[9] How each human person copes with this anxiety will significantly affect his or her existence. Human beings are sensitive to these issues in different ways. We suggest that addicts attempt to cope by traveling a common pathway that leads to deep, existential trouble.

2. *The addictive path: A way to cope*

In confronting the sources of anxiety and depression described above, addicted persons attempt to cope by reaching out and clinging dependently to creatures, which are misused as "crutches."

Underneath the addict's struggle is a dark and commanding perspective on life. The addict "forgets" (or because of crippling experiences during the course of development, has never known, or has rejected in the face of life's troubles) the pervasiveness of loving grace and the sense of connectedness with living as part of creation. Rather, the addict experiences a sense of alienation, estrangement, loneliness, unloveability, and hopelessness, often felt as a sense of being "different from" or "less than" others. In the face of this "pain of living" (Doweiko, chapter 2), the addict accepts a host of false and negative beliefs about the self, about the world, and about God (Jampolsky, chapter 3, and Ciarrocchi, chapter 9, both elaborate in some detail this negative "Addictive Thought System").

[7] Howard Clinebell, Jr., one of the earliest and enduring advocates for a pastoral theological understanding of alcoholism, puts the matter this way: "The important thing to remember is this—the factors which separate alcoholic-sinners from other sinners (that is , the factors which make alcoholics alcoholics) are factors over which there is little self-determination...This is not sentimentalism, but the essence of psychological insight and the basis for real Christian charity. When one reaches this point in his [*sic*] feeling toward alcoholics—a point which involves considerable self-understanding—he is no longer interested in trying to pin sin on the alcoholic" (1961, p.163).

[8] Jordan (1986) speaks of depression in a theological frame as "unhope" that is "based on faulty perceptions of ultimate reality and one's own identity, and on an implicit belief system holding that crucifixion has overcome resurrection, that death has overcome life, that evil has overcome good, that the demonic has overcome God" (p. 89).

[9] Some writers speak of angst (Heidegger) or dread (Kierkegaard) to refer to the core existential anxiety that accompanies this basic question of human living. Tillich thought of the response to this question as "the courage to be" (1952). H. Richard Niebuhr addressed these issues and an adequate response in his model of the "responsible self" (1963).

The addictive person has an implicitly negative theological script or drama, that is, a personal narrative based on erroneous beliefs, a distorted worldview, and a story of the self and its perceived ultimate reality (or "higher power") that is doomed to self-destruction.[10] For example, the alcoholic believes that alcohol will soothe, comfort, narcotize the pain of living, liberate from troubles, and overcome the suffering and loneliness in one's life. Likewise, persons with other addictions use their substance, object, relationship or high to deceive themselves that they can overcome life's problems and unhappiness by false messianic means. The objects of their addictions function as "false saviors" or "pseudo-messiahs" to deliver people from the struggles, conflicts, pressures, and problems of living—all of which are perceived as ultimate reality (Jordan, 1986). What is perceived as *really real* are the anxieties and pain of living; what is forgotten are the grace, love, interconectedness and *Shalom* of authentic human life.

Doweiko (chapter 2) describes the addict's turn to "chemical solutions" in the face of this all-too-human situation as a way to "narcotize the pain of living." In his view this constitutes a kind of "spiritual narcissism" (see also Moore, 1977). In much the same way Larsen (chapter 8) speaks of "chemicals medicating pain." Jampolsky (chapter 3) develops these ideas more extensively, describing addiction as a metaphor for the human condition in that persons who experience a deep loneliness and a "spiritual thirst" for something more "pursue happiness outside the self" in things that are external. Faced with the anxiety that is the common lot of humanity, addicts seek for solace by misusing God's creation.

All created things are given to us, in the Christian view, to be used as they help toward our final goal, namely our destiny to live with God, and they are to be avoided or used carefully to the extent that they deter us from this goal.[11] Addicts, however, misuse creatures (e.g., alcohol and other drugs, sex, money) as ways to cope with the anxiety of living, as ways to fill a "hole in the gut" (Albers, Chapter 7), as ways to comfort or medicate themselves in the face of restlessness, finitude, and self-struggle (Larsen, chapter 8; see also Ford, 1949, 1959, 1986). The pleasure, respite, conviviality, or a false sense of connectedness or achievement that this misuse brings allows the addict to "settle for less" than she or he is destined for. Here is a root notion of *sin* as it relates to addiction.[12]

---

[10]For an extended discussion of these dynamics from a theological and clinical point of view see Jordan (1986).

[11] *Spiritual Exercises of St. Ignatius*...For a modern treatment of the principles in the *Spiritual Exercises* and their application to the experience of addiction, see John C. Ford's *What about your drinking?* (1961). It should be noted that Ford's view was widely accepted both ecumenically and collaboratively through his teaching at the Yale Summer School of Alcohol Studies and his work with the North Conway Institute. For a more complete discussion of these issues see Morgan (*in press a & b*).

[12] Mercadante (1996) insists that the notion of sin must be dealt with if the implicit theology of AA and the recovery movement is to be reconciled with the Judaeo-Christian tradition. We agree. One route for this reconciliation is to remember that in Christian theology sin is *not*, first and foremost, related to behavior and concrete decisions/actions. In its most fundamental sense, sin is primarily a "state" or stance *and* an "active ingredient" that seeks actualization in human choices and actions.

Gradually, the addictive person discovers the sad truth of what John Rosen (1962) has referred to as alcohol being "poisoned milk." In other words, alcohol becomes the poisonous betrayer after it has been misperceived and misused as nurturing, comforting milk. Alcohol, or any other object of addiction, has been given the power, role, and place of being one's deliverer, messiah, and savior; and over time the falsity of the messianc claim is revealed and the illusion of booze is unmasked. The addictive substance or process becomes experienced as something other than the divine comforter and deliverer. As Shakespeare suggests in the quote that began this chapter, the object of addiction ultimately "betrays us in deepest consequence."

3. *Idolatry*

When creatures are misused in these ways, they become idols. Theologically, addiction may be conceptualized as a variation of *idolatry* (Daim, 1963; Jordan, 1986).

As we know from the Bible and other sources, idolatry leads to *degradation* of persons.

> The idols of the nations are silver and gold,
>   the handiwork of men [*sic*].
> They have mouths but speak not;
>   they have eyes but see not;
> They have ears but hear not,
>   nor is there breath in their mouths,
> Their makers shall be like them,
>   everyone who trusts in them (Ps. 135:15–18 NAB).

This process may be viewed as the (negative) spirituality of addiction; that is, the person becomes more and more degraded personally, more and more controlling and dishonest interpersonally, more and more manipulative, and more and more insensitive to the call of her spirit and the graciousness of his world. Looking back, recovering addicts describe themselves in their addiction in nonhuman terms, referring to themselves as living like animals or behaving like machines (Morgan, 1992). Many of our works of fiction and film, as well as the autobiographies published by persons in recovery, poignantly depict this growing degradation (see Morgan, chapter 1).

AA and other Twelve Step groups continue to describe addiction as a "triple illness," a disease of body, mind, and spirit. We have learned much about the biological, psychoemotional, and social elements of addiction. The spiritual illness, or "sickness of soul," that characterizes addiction may best be described by the degradation of spirit that follows from idolatry. Albers (chapter 7) and Brakeman (chapter 10) address this notion more explicitly.

Jordan (1986) speaks convincingly about a dual dynamic that underlies the phenomenon of idolatry. Applied to the experience of addiction, it is clear that, on the one hand, the addict perceives the tribulations of living and the power of human authorities (e.g., parents, employers, clergy) as having ultimate sway over one's life. The negative addictive script is a powerful force at the center of the addict's personality. The oppressive, abusive, rejecting, and terrorizing "authorities" of the world (including for many addicts not only their negative beliefs but also their early religious traditions and negative images of God) are misperceived as having ultimate authority over the person. This helps to account for the addict's notorious problems with authority and control. However, on the other hand, in order to survive in a world governed by such false absolutes, one has to find ways to rescue and save oneself. Attachments to drinking, gambling, drugs, sex, relationships, and achievements all promise a form of "rescue" (salvation), or at least comfort and surcease from anxiety and depression. One tries to overcome idolatrous mental representations of negative ultimate reality by the second idolatry of trying to save oneself by an attachment masquerading as a savior.

The addict is double-bound in idolatry, desperately attached to a negative view of self and world, and addicted to a misused creature (e.g., alcohol, sex) that is perceived as powerful and rescuing. The addict behaves as if one could, and needs to, save oneself by handing the self over in thrall to another.[13] For a whole host of interconnected reasons—biological, psychological, or emotional vulnerability; the formidable power of habit; the desperate need to hold on to a worldview, even if a negative and costly one, in the face of doubt or meaninglessness; the fear of confronting life's challenges and the results of one's addictive use—addicts find it quite difficult simply to give up their attachment. There is a tenacious attachment both to the idol as well as to the false hope that the addiction will save and rescue one from life's dilemmas and pains. There is a profound fantasy bond both with the negative image of ultimate reality and with the false messianic idol. As Larsen (chapter 8) reminds us, the "underlying living issues" and wounded personal core of love must be addressed if recovery is to be achieved.

4. *Recovery and transformation*

If the experience of addiction leads to a degraded spirit and a (negative) spirituality of increasingly dehumanized living, then the experience of recovery may be seen as a gradual *transformation of the self in context*.

Many of the chapters in this book portray the dynamics needed for successful recovery. First, it is surprising how often the description of recovery as a *journey* surfaces throughout the book. The authors are clear that the recovery process takes time and that there is work to be done along

[13] Here is the root dictionary meaning of the term addiction: "Devoted; consecrated. The handing over of oneself" into the care of, or in servitude to, another.

the way. David Berenson's chapter 4 suggests that addiction and recovery may be seen as patterned on the dynamic of a *fall and return*, that is, beginning in a blessed state of union with God and a sense of connectedness with all creation, human history and individual development may be seen as recapitulating a movement of "fall from grace" into a state of nihilism and a lessening of essential humanity, followed eventually by a "return" to blessedness in which there is an appropriate and positive set of relationships (the "between") among self, God and world. This "return" is accompanied by a transformation in the sense of self and of the world as a place in which humans live, and move and have their being.[14]

There are similarities in this pattern to the ancient theme of "adventure and return" in literature and the arts. The *Confessions* of Saint Augustine and Anton Boisen's *Out of the depths*, even J. R. R. Tolkien's *Lord of the rings* trilogy, echo this pattern. Some observers have noticed the similarity of this model to the narrative structure of stories told by alcoholics and addicted others (Cary, 1990). A number of contemporary films about addiction, including *The days of wine and roses* and *clean and sober*, use the same theme as a working convention.[15]

Particularly as it relates to the intervention of a "Power greater," this structure might be described as a narrative of "conversion"(Freccero, 1986) or as a story of the individual's journey from "degradation to transformation" (Morgan, 1992). The reader will notice that such a *journey* motif characterizes many of the chapters in this book.

Second, the importance of *relationships* and *connectedness* is emphasized throughout this book. Indeed for many of our authors, recovery is a process of "awakening to love" (Jampolsky, chapter 3; Kasl, chapter 6), of building an authentic sense of relationship (Smith and Seymour, chapter 5; Albers, chapter 7) and connectedness (Doweiko, chapter 2; Ciarrocchi, chapter 9), of returning to community (Brakeman, chapter 10; Gray, chapter 11), of repairing the damaged core of love (Larsen, chapter 8). As addiction strains the sense of family, community and relationships in living, so recovery may be seen as a return to fellowship and connectedness.

Third, the notion of fundamentally *altering negative scripts and beliefs* also runs throughout this book. Jampolsky's description (chapter 3) of the Addictive and Love-based Thought Systems, and his step-by-step way of identifying negative beliefs that underlie addictive attachments, is helpful in this regard. Ciarrocchi's catalogue of the false belief systems of "high and low rollers" (chapter 9) is likewise helpful. Kasl's (chapter 6) description

[14] Berenson's work owes its inspiration, in part, to the insights of Gregory Bateson (1971). Bateson discusses what he calls "AA's theology" and sees the outcome of recovery in a stance of "complementarity," that is, an awareness and lifestlye based on connectedness and interrelationship (Morgan, 1998).

[15] For a contemporary film that portrays the consequences of remaining in the "fall" and not pursuing a "return," see *The Boost*, starring James Woods. The final scenes vividly portray the cruel fate of too many addicts today who, for a variety of reasons, are unable to enter and maintain recovery.

of her own journey of epiphany and self-awareness and her presentation of the sixteen Steps of Empowerment provides another framework for altering negative cognitions and beliefs. Larsen's (chapter 8) description of the stages of self-discovery needed in order to maintain quality recovery shows another path that can facilitate the journey. These different tools and formats are already in use among clinicians and can be of enormous help in the recovery process.

Several of the explicitly "pastoral" chapters in this book provide another set of tools for the same process, tools that may be appropriate for use with believing and already recovering clients. Albers (chapter 7), Brakeman (chapter 10), Gray (chapter 11) and Glass (chapter 12) each use explicitly religious resources as catalysts for interpreting lived experience and thinking about addiction and recovery differently. The biblical narrative of the Gerasene demoniac (chapters 10 and 11) provides a rich resource for pastoral and theological reflection. Other biblical sources that are relevant include: the prodigal son (chapter 10), the good Samaritan (chapter 11), and the road to Emmaus (chapter 11).[16] The use of Jewish religious resources is addressed in chapter 12.

Chapter 1 reminds us that the testimony of recovering addicts often turns to a consideration of fundamental changes in beliefs, perspectives, and relationships—a radical *re-orientation of lifeworld and lifestyle*—as a consequence of the recovery journey (see also Morgan, 1992).

5. The "unhurried chase"

Finally, it is important to note that a crucial outcome of recovery, at least as conceived by Alcoholics Anonymous and other Twelve Step groups, is a "spiritual awakening." The "Big Book" of AA describes the "spiritual awakening" of the recovering person in these terms:

> He [*sic*] finally realizes that he has undergone a profound alteration in his reaction to life; that such a change could hardly have been brought about by himself alone…With few exceptions our members find that they have tapped an unsuspected inner resource which they presently identify with their own conception of a Power greater than themselves…This *awareness of a Power greater than ourselves is the essence of spiritual experience.* (pp. 569–570; *italics by the editors*)

Certainly, the altering of negative beliefs, the reengagement in positive relationships, and the positive reorientation of lifestyle often described by recovering addicts—all these are intrinsic to the spiritual awakening envisioned by the Twelve Steps and described by the authors of this volume.

Yet, for a full theological anthropology of addiction and recovery to be developed, another crucial theme must be developed.

[16] For another examination of the use of biblical resources in understanding addiction and recovery, see Morgan (*in press a*).

> We know that all things work for together for good for those who love God, who are called according to his purpose…
> What then shall we say about these things? If God is for us, who is against us? He who did not withhold his own Son, but gave him up for all of us, will he not with him also give us everything else?
> Who will separate us from the love of Christ? Will hardship, or distress, or persecution, or famine, or nakedness, or peril, or sword?…
> No, in all these things we are more than conquerors through him who loved us. For I am convinced that neither death, nor life, nor angels, nor rulers, nor things present, nor things to come, nor powers, nor height, nor depth, nor anything else in all creation, will be able to separate us from the love of God in Christ Jesus our Lord.(Romans 8:28, 31–32, 35, 37–39).

Many recovering persons and many trained observers of the recovery process (for example, Harry Tiebout, Gregory Bateson, Howard Clinebell, Jr., Stephanie Brown, Ernest Kurtz, and others) describe the entrance into recovery as a "conversion" or "surrender" (see Albers, chapter 7; see also Morgan's discussion of these dynamics in chapter 1). "Such a change," they say, "could hardly have been brought about by [the addict] alone." Yet surrender to what? To whom?

In our own work as clinical theologians, we have come to appreciate and respect the powerful grace of God who intervenes in the lives of troubled persons. We have also learned about the ways in which recovering persons speak about the active "intervention of a Higher Power" (Morgan, 1992). It seems that the God of grace takes an active hand in the lives of people, even addicted ones. God "saves" them, literally and actively.

In a study of long-term recovering alcoholics (Morgan, 1992), the founding moment of recovery—surrender, conversion—was understood as a moment of intervention and grace, pulling addicted persons out of the vicious cycle of addiction, degradation, and loss of self. Those who experienced this "saving moment" also spoke about a felt experience of being cared for, of being the recipient of providential care. Over time in recovery, these persons described a deepening attitude of trust, acceptance, and providence—attitudes not confined to past experience but involving deep beliefs about the present and future as well. They describe a strong sense that God ("power greater") continues to intervene and work in and through one's life. There is a sense of guidance and protection in living, a sense of "miracles" happening, which helps to explain the experience of "meaningful coincidences" or benevolent serendipity that these persons describe. These are not small changes in attitude or life stance. These changes make a difference in living!

The lives of many recovering people are grounded in confidence about the ongoing care and power of intervention of their Higher Power. They stake their recoveries, and their lives, on this confidence. Theologically, this profoundly altered view of the relationship between God and self lies at the core of recovery spirituality as expressed by many recovering persons (Morgan, 1992; see also chapter 1 in this book). This radically different (from addictive "unhope") perspective gives rise, not only to a transformed sense of self and self-in-world, but also to desires to join and foster community and to maintain contact with this Power, as well as to a desire to return the gift that was received. Prayer to a God who "listens," is "approachable," and can be "relied upon" in happy and difficult times becomes a simple, even childlike experience. Service to others, particularly to those still caught in the mire of addiction, becomes a vocation (Morgan, 1992).

From the double idolatry of enslavement to negative beliefs and addictive substances (or processes), recovering addicts experience a life of gracious miracles directed to them because they are loved and loveable, and a sense of commitment to service of others. This is profound change, indeed.

The lived and narrated experience of God's active intervention and continued care in the lives of recovering persons reminds us, as clinical theologians, of the testimony from another troubled person. In *The Hound of Heaven*, poet Francis Thompson speaks in a "voice" that resonates with the experience of many addicts and alcoholics over the years. At the end of a lifelong attempt to evade, divert, and escape the "unhurried chase" of Heaven's "Hound" (The "Power greater"), the author relays these words from the Seeker to the one sought:

"Whom wilt thou find to love ignoble thee
    Save Me, save only Me?
All which I took from thee I did but take,
    Not for thy harms,
But just that thou might'st seek it in My arms.
    All which thy child's mistake
Fancies as lost, I have stored for thee at home;
    Rise, clasp My hand, and come."
    Halts by me that footfall:
    Is my gloom, after all,
Shade of His hand, outstretched caressingly?
    "Ah, fondest, blindest, weakest,
    I am He whom thou seekest!"

The Future of Addiction Studies

At the conclusion of this volume exploring spirituality in relation to addiction and recovery, we would like to offer some final thoughts on future ventures that are needed in the field of addiction studies.

First, as the reader can readily see, we believe that there is value in developing a full practical theology of addiction and recovery. Such a theology can help to guide deeper understanding of the dynamics of addiction and recovery; it can also facilitate collaborative work between addiction scientists and pastoral caregivers, allowing for the utilization of church and religious resources in areas of prevention and treatment. Smith and Seymour (chapter 5), Brakeman (chapter 10) and Gray (chapter 11) each suggest creative and important ways in which such collaboration might be made practical. If part of the role of theology is to guide and enable spiritual experience, then any understanding and lived experience of spirituality in addiction and recovery will benefit from an adequate theology of these important issues.

Second, we believe that the ongoing development of such a theology will benefit from continued listening to and examination of stories of recovery. As told by persons in recovery, these stories of lived experience provide a wealth of narrative data that is invaluable. Indeed, it may only be through attention to narrative and personal story that the real experience of spirituality will reveal itself. The more personal and revealing tone struck by many of the chapter authors in this book came as something of a surprise to us. Yet on reflection we see how valuable and appropriate that stance has been when addressing such an important and challenging issue.

Third, having said this, we also believe in the value of continued development in areas more traditionally understood as "scientific." We applaud the work of scientists who are beginning to examine spirituality as a potential helpful resource to addicted and recovering persons (see Morgan, chapter 1). We welcome the interest from governmental and public-sector funding agencies in supporting these investigative efforts.[17] However, two cautions may be in order: (a) It will be important to remember that we are studying "persons with addiction" as well as addictive processes, and (b) real understanding, we believe, can come if we learn to complement quantitative and experimental results with humanistic, qualitative, and experiential/narrative data.

It continues to be important to develop appropriate hypotheses about spirituality, addiction, and recovery and to test the validity of results across many different and larger populations. Continued development of assessment and investigative instruments is also an important priority. In developing the investigative procedures and tools that are appropriate for these scientific studies, we believe it continues to be important to listen again to the stories of recovering persons and those who live with and care for them. It continues to be of benefit to conduct studies that are descriptive and narrative, if we want to learn about spirituality, and allow ourselves to be surprised and inquisitive about information that may be outside our usual paradigms and models (see chapter 1).

---

[17] As reported in chapter 1, both the National Institute on Alcoholism and Alcohol Abuse (NIAAA) and the National Institute on Healthcare Research (NIHR) are examining the possibilities for scientific exploration into many areas of spirituality, including its relationship to addiction and recovery.

Fourth, it seems to be time to reestablish the original interdisciplinary and collaborative efforts that characterized the field of addiction studies at its inception (see Morgan, chapter 1).

These four interrelated tasks—developing a full theology of addiction and recovery, pursuit of qualitative and narrative research into spirituality, new developments in empirical and "scientific" research, and reinstatement of collaborative research and model-building—comprise a new and exciting path for the field of addiction studies. We hope this volume has made some contribution in this direction.

References

Bateson, G. (1971). The cybernetics of self: A theory of alcoholism. *Psychiatry, 34*(1), 1–18. Reprinted in *Steps to an ecology of mind* (1972). San Francisco: Chandler.

Becker, E. (1973). *Denial of death.* New York: Free Press.

Boff, L. (1995). *Ecology and liberation: A new paradigm.* Maryknoll, N.Y.: Orbis.

Browning, D. S. (1987). *Religious thought and the modern psychologies: A critical conversation in the theology of culture.* Philadelphia: Fortress.

Browning, D. S. (1975). *Generative man: psychoanalytic perspectives.* New York: Delta.

Cary, S. (1990). *The alcoholic man: What you can learn from the heroic journeys of recovering alcoholics.* Los Angeles: Lowell House.

Clinebell, H. J., Jr. (1961). *Understanding and counseling the alcoholic: Through religion and psychology.* New York: Abingdon.

Daim, W. (1963). *Depth psychology and salvation* [K. F. Reinhart, trans.]. New York: Ungar.

Ford, J. C. (1986). The sickness of alcoholism: Still more clergy education? *Homiletic and Pastoral Review, 87,* 10–18.

Ford, J. C. (1961). *What about your drinking?* Glen Rock, N. J. : Paulist.

Ford, J. C. (1949). "Alcoholism." Talk given at John Carroll University lecture series on Medical Ethics [116, #2]. October 12, 1949. Cleveland, Ohio.

Ford, J. C. (1959). Chemical comfort and Christian virtue. *American Ecclesiastical Review, 141,* 361–379.

Freccero, J. (1986). Autobiography and narrative. In T. C. Heller, M. Sosna, and D. E. Wellbery (Eds.), *Reconstructing individualism: Autonomy, individuality, and the self in Western thought* (pp.16–29). Stanford, Calif: Stanford University Press.

Friedman, M. (1967). *To deny our nothingness: Contemporary images of man.* New York: Delacorte Press.

Heidegger, M. (1962). *Being and time*. [Trans. J. Macquarrie and E. S. Robinson]. New York: Harper.

Johnson, E. A. (1993). *Women, earth, and creator spirit*. New York: Paulist. [The 1993 Madeleva Lecture on Spirituality].

Jordan, M.R. (1986). *Taking on the gods: The task of the pastoral counselor*. Nashville: Abingdon.

Kierkegaard, S. (1944). *The concept of dread*. Princeton: Princeton University Press.

Kopas, J. (1994). *Sacred identity: Exploring a theology of the person*. Mahwah, N.J. : Paulist.

Lake, F. (1987). *Clinical theology: A theological and psychological basis to clinical pastoral care*. New York: Crossroad.

Mercadante, L. (1996). *Victims and sinners: Spiritual roots of addiction and recovery*. Louisville, Ky. : Westminster John Knox.

Moltmann, J. (1997). *The source of life: The Holy Spirit and the theology of life*. Minneapolis : Augsburg Fortress.

Moltmann, J. (1993). *God in creation: A new theology of creation and the spirit of God*. Minneapolis,: Fortress.

Moore, S. (1977). *The crucified Jesus is no stranger*. Minneapolis, Minn.: Seabury.

Morgan, O. J. (*in press a*). Practical theology, alcohol abuse and alcoholism: Methodological and biblical considerations. *Journal of Ministry in Addiction and Recovery*.

Morgan, O. J. (*in press b*). "Chemical comforting" and the theology of John C. Ford, S. J. : Classic answers to a contemporary problem. *Journal of Ministry in Addiction and Recovery.*

Morgan, O. J. (1998). Addiction, family treatment, and healing resources: An interview with David Berenson. *Journal of Addictions and Offender Counseling, 18*(2), pp. 54–62.

Morgan, O. J. (1992). In a sober voice: A psychological study of long-term alcoholic recovery with attention to spiritual dimensions. *Dissertation Abstracts International, 52*(11), 6069–B. [University Microfilms No. 9210480].

Niebuhr, H. R. (1963). *The responsible self: An essay in Christian moral philosophy*. San Francisco: Harper & Row.

Patton, J. (1993). *Pastoral care in context: An introduction to pastoral care*. Louisville, Ky. : Westminster John Knox.

Rahner, K. (1974). Concerning the relationship between nature and grace. *Theological Investigations, I*, pp. 297–317.

Rosen, J. (1962). *Direct psychoanalytic psychiatry*. New York: Grune & Strattons.

Ruether, R. R. (1992). *Gaia and God: An ecofeminist theology of earth healing.* New York: HarperCollins.

Scheibe, K. E. (1986). Self-narratives and adventure. In T. R. Sarbin (Ed.), *Narrative psychology: The storied nature of human conduct* (pp.129–151). New York: Praeger.

Schlauch, C. R. (1995). *Faithful companioning: How pastoral counseling heals.* Minneapolis: Fortress.

Tillich, P. (1952). *The courage to be*. New Haven: Yale University Press.